A
FIRE
IN
ZION

A FIRE IN ZION

The Israeli-Palestinian Search for Peace

MARK PERRY

WILLIAM MORROW AND COMPANY, INC., NEW YORK

It is the policy of William Morrow and Company, Inc., and its imprints and affiliates, recognizing the importance of preserving what has been written, to print the books we publish on acid-free paper, and we exert our best efforts to that end.

Library of Congress Cataloging-in-Publication Data

Perry, Mark, 1950–
    A fire in Zion : the Israeli-Palestinian search for peace /
Mark Perry.
        p.   cm.
    Includes bibliographical references and index.
    ISBN 0-688-12171-3
    1. Jewish-Arab relations—1973–   2. Israel-Arab conflicts.
3. Israel. Treaties, etc. Munaẓẓamat al-Tahrīr al-Filastīnīyah,
1993 Sept. 13.   4. Diplomatic negotiations in international
disputes.   I. Title.
DS119.7.P4556   1994
956.94′0049274—dc20   94-5908
                                                                CIP

Printed in the United States of America

First Edition

1 2 3 4 5 6 7 8 9 10

BOOK DESIGN BY SRS DESIGN

For Cal and Madeleine

ACKNOWLEDGMENTS

This book could not have been completed without the help of a number of my friends and colleagues here in Washington, and in the Middle East.

Several colleagues joined me in trips to the Middle East and spent hours talking with me on this topic. My thanks go to Tom Martin (who first introduced me to this subject) and to Dan Reynolds and Michael Keating who accompanied me on my trips to Israel, the West Bank, and Gaza. I wish to thank Palestinian journalist Jawdat Manna for his unselfish assistance in the occupied territories and the many other Palestinians and Israelis who cooperated with me, answered my interminable questions, and sat for hours discussing their own problems, perspectives, and solutions.

I express my appreciation to fellow researcher Daniel Shapiro, Paul Schemm and to journalist Cody Shearer. My thanks also to Jeff Goldberg for his continued inspiration. I worked for many months as managing editor of *Middle East Insight* magazine and, with their help, was provided access to Arab, Palestinian, and Israeli officials. I wish also to thank my agent, Gail Ross, who showed her usual patience and dedication, and

Adrian Zackheim and the people at William Morrow, who continued to express confidence in this book.

This work could not have been completed without the cooperation of officials of the Israeli government and leaders of the Palestine Liberation Organization. They showed unfailing cooperation. I am indebted to the work and thoughts of others, mostly journalists, who spent the last years walking this path with me. Finally, I have dedicated this book to my son, Cal, and my daughter, Madeleine, who were fatherless during the long hours of researching and writing. And I want to thank my wife, Nina, again, for giving me the time and support necessary to write yet another book.

CONTENTS

CHRONOLOGY

December 8, 1987
The Palestinian intifada, or uprising, begins in the Jebalya refugee camp in the Gaza Strip.

August 2, 1990
Iraq invades Kuwait.

January 16, 1991
The United States and its allies launch Operation Desert Storm.

March 1991
At the end of the Gulf War, U.S. Secretary of State James Baker begins a series of trips to the Middle East designed to win agreement of the Arab states and Israel to attend an international peace conference.

October 20, 1991
The Israeli cabinet votes to join an international conference on peace in the Middle East.

October 30, 1991
The Middle East peace conference convenes in Madrid, Spain. Delegations from Israel, Lebanon, and Syria, and a joint Jordanian-Palestinian one, attend the conference.

November 1991

A conference on the economics of Middle East peace is held at Harvard University. The organizers of the conference plan to organize a second conference on the need to detail the economics of peace among Israel, Jordan, and a Palestinian political entity.

November 3, 1991

Round one of the bilateral talks between the Israeli and Palestinian delegations opens in Madrid, Spain. The talks continue until November 9.

December 10, 1991

Round two of the bilateral talks between the Israeli and Arab delegations opens in Washington. The round ends on December 18.

January 1992

The issue of the $10 billion in loan guarantees is reopened in Washington.

January 13, 1992

Round three of the bilateral talks between the Israeli and Arab delegations opens in Washington. The round ends on January 16.

January 19, 1992

Yitzhak Shamir's governing coalition loses its majority in the Knesset and new elections are called for June.

February 24, 1992

Round four of the bilateral talks between the Israeli and Arab delegations opens in Washington. The round ends on March 4.

April 1992

Terje Roed Larsen visits Yossi Beilin in Jerusalem and proposes the beginning of back-channel negotiations with the PLO under the auspices of the Norwegian government.

April 7, 1992
Yasser Arafat's plane crashes in the Libyan desert, but the PLO leader survives the accident.

April 26, 1992
Round five of the bilateral talks between the Israeli and Arab delegations opens in Washington. The round ends on April 30.

June 23, 1992
Yitzhak Rabin wins election as prime minister of Israel.

July 1992
Terje Roed Larsen makes a second visit to Israel, to see Deputy Foreign Minister Yossi Beilin. Beilin expresses interest in beginning secret talks with the PLO and asks Larsen to contact Haifa University professor Yair Hirschfeld.

August 24, 1992
Round six of the bilateral talks between the Israeli and Arab delegations opens in Washington. The round ends on September 24.

September 1992
Johan Jorgen Holst contacts Yasser Arafat in Tunis and suggests that he send Abu Alaa to negotiate a secret agreement with Israel.

September 10, 1992
Larsen and a Norwegian official meet with Beilin in Tel Aviv to plan the details of back-channel negotiations.

October 21, 1992
Round seven of the bilateral talks between the Israeli and Arab delegations opens in Washington. The round ends on November 19.

November 3, 1992
Bill Clinton is elected President of the United States.

December 4, 1992
Yair Hirschfeld and Abu Alaa meet in London to begin secret negotiations between Israel and the PLO.

December 7, 1992
Round eight of the bilateral talks between the Israeli and Arab delegations opens in Washington. The round ends on December 17.

December 15, 1992
Nissim Toledano is found murdered near Jerusalem. Within hours, Yitzhak Rabin deports over four hundred activists of the Palestinian fundamentalist group Hamas.

January 1993
Secret negotiations between Israel and the PLO begin in Norway and are conducted over a period of the next eighteen months.

March 20, 1993
Yitzhak Rabin seals off the West Bank and the Gaza Strip from Israel and Jerusalem.

April 1993
The Harvard Group of economists from Jordan, Israel, and the occupied territories meets to discuss its conception of Israeli-Palestinian and Israeli-Palestinian-Jordanian economic cooperation.

Yossi Beilin informs Shimon Peres of the back-channel negotiations with the PLO.

April 27, 1993
Round nine of the bilateral talks between the Israeli and Arab delegations opens in Washington. The round ends on May 13.

June 1993
In Tunis, Yasser Arafat's leadership is questioned by PLO officials. Arafat survives the threat.

June 15, 1993
Round ten of the bilateral talks between the Israeli and Arab delegations opens in Washington. The round ends on June 30.

Mid-July 1993
The Harvard Group completes its study, "Securing Peace in the Middle East: Project on Economic Transition." The report is presented to officials in Israel and in Tunis.

Late July 1993
The peace talks in Norway nearly break down, but are salvaged by the intervention of Johan Jorgen Holst.

August 19, 1993
The "Declaration of Principles on Interim Self-government Arrangements" is initialed in Oslo, Norway.

August 25, 1993
Shimon Peres informs Secretary of State Warren Christopher of the success of the back-channel negotiations in Norway.

September 13, 1993
Abu Mazin and Shimon Peres initial the "Declaration of Principles on Interim Self-government Arrangements" in Washington, D.C., as Yitzhak Rabin and Yasser Arafat look on.

The Lord gave full vent to his wrath,
he poured out his hot anger;
and he kindled a fire in Zion,
which consumed its foundations.
—Lamentations 4:11

We don't have to love the Palestinians, we don't even have to
like them. But we do have to make peace with them.
—Amos Oz

A
FIRE
IN
ZION

PROLOGUE

On September 13, 1993, Israeli Prime Minister Yitzhak Rabin and Palestine Liberation Organization Chairman Yasser Arafat took a giant step toward ending one of the world's longest and most bitter conflicts. The declaration of principles that was negotiated by a small group of Palestinian and Israeli diplomats in Oslo, Norway—and then signed by their leaders on the White House lawn that mid-September morning—stunned the world. The handshake between Rabin and Arafat began to draw down the curtain on four decades of conflict between Israel and its most intransigent enemy. The signing of the Israel-PLO declaration of principles began the slow process of reconciliation that has as its goal the end of one hundred years of unremitting strife between Jews and Arabs over control of Palestine. During that struggle, thousands of Israelis, Palestinians, Egyptians, Lebanese, Jordanians, and Syrians died in battle; hundreds of thousands were displaced; and thousands of others were taken prisoner, maimed, widowed, orphaned, or confined in fetid refugee camps.

While the White House ceremony dominated the news in the weeks that followed, no one believed that all the years of enmity and bloodshed could be forgiven by the single stroke of a pen, or that decades of misunderstanding and bitterness could be forgotten by a simple handshake. So while the airwaves and newspaper columns trumpeted the fact that Rabin had actually shaken Arafat's hand, many knew that true understanding and cooperation would be much more difficult to achieve. It was one thing for national leaders to meet at a ceremony in Washington, and quite another for Palestinians and Israelis to learn to live with one another in peace.

One of the Palestinians who knew this best was Salah Ta'mari, an exile from the village of Za'tara near Bethlehem in the occupied West Bank, a senior PLO official, and a veteran of some of its most famous battles. Ta'mari, who has lived in the United States, was invited to the ceremony but decided to watch it on television. When Arafat left his suite at a downtown Washington hotel for the ride to the White House early on the morning of September 13, Ta'mari reached out his hand to the PLO chief and wished him luck. Arafat motioned him to come along, but Ta'mari shook his head; he was unimpressed by the trappings of power and had difficulty measuring the sacrifice of the hundreds of Palestinians he had led in battles in Jordan and Lebanon against the celebratory atmosphere that greeted the news of the accord. "There has been so much death," he said, "and we have so much work to do. The conflict remains, but the form of the engagement is different."

Itamar Rabinovich had similar feelings. As the Israeli ambassador to the United States, a leading expert on Arab affairs, the former rector of Tel Aviv University, and one of Israel's best-known intellectuals, Rabinovich harbored a view of the Israeli-Palestinian search for peace that was almost mystical. He understood how much of the past both sides had to put aside and how daunting the future remained. "In many ways, our negotiations with the Palestinians have gone beyond a simple discussion of differing political positions," he once said. "We are instead learning about each other's beliefs and fundamental principles. This is much more than a negotiation. We are now engaged in a crucial exchange of complex national narratives."

Rabinovich welcomed the PLO-Israeli accord, but like Ta'mari he found it difficult to get caught up in the atmosphere of triumph that greeted news of its signing. He was subdued when he left to attend the ceremony at the White House.

Ta'mari and Rabinovich's skepticism was by no means unique. While thousands of Palestinians celebrated the Israel-PLO agreement in the streets of Jericho in the West Bank, hundreds of thousands of others in the refugee camps of Lebanon, Syria, and Jordan looked on Arafat's agreement as an admission of defeat. And while a majority of Israelis applauded Rabin's new opening to the PLO, few of them believed the agreement guaranteed a future without threats or fear. On both sides, the declaration negotiated in secret in Oslo and then signed with great fanfare in Washington was viewed as an uneasy settlement to a nearly intractable problem: It was not a perfect solution, and perhaps not even a very good one, but it was the best that could be had under the circumstances.

Ta'mari and Rabinovich are fitting symbols of the Palestinian-Israeli struggle, for while they are starkly different personalities, their views of the conflict are almost identical. For Ta'mari, the agreement was neither an end nor a beginning. "We meet our enemy on many different levels," he said after the signing, "and even when we face the Israelis across a table, the exchange is as serious as it was when we fought them on the battlefields of Jordan twenty years ago." Ta'mari's words echoed Rabinovich's view—that the exchange of "complex national narratives" is part of a continuing process. The signing of the Israel-PLO declaration of principles was a significant political event and an integral part of a long and complex discussion between two very different peoples. But the transaction has yet to be concluded.

If the ceremony and the handshake that took place on the White House lawn were so difficult to carry through, and if the two sides still had so much work to do and so much remaining enmity and mistrust to overcome, then why come to Washington at all? What motivated their leaders to begin the serious search for peace? *A Fire in Zion* is an attempt to answer that question, or rather, an effort to allow the participants in the struggle to answer it for themselves. In Rabinovich's sense, this book is the presentation of two distinct and competing national visions, one Israeli and one Palestinian.

Until the late nineteenth century, a small but distinct Jewish community was all that remained in Palestine after the Romans destroyed the temple in Jerusalem and drove the Jews into exile in A.D. 70. The native Jews who remained were farmers who lived side by side with Arabs in small communities or in villages along the Mediterranean coast.

When Jews first began to return to Palestine in large numbers, they found a land of Arab farmers and few cities; Jerusalem was no more than a medium-sized trading town and Tel Aviv was a very small village. Many of the early Zionist settlers put down roots along the Mediterranean coast and built scattered agricultural settlements among the Arab towns. The movement of Jews out of Europe increased after 1897, when Theodor Herzl called for the establishment of a Jewish state in Palestine during the First Zionist Congress. After an intense lobbying campaign during the First World War, Zionist leaders convinced the British government to support their cause. In 1917, the idea of a Jewish national home was endorsed in a declaration issued by Lord Balfour, the British foreign secretary. While there were only fifty thousand Jews in Palestine at the time, Balfour's declaration, and a League of Nations mandate giving Britain control of the region, permanently transformed the political climate of Arab society.

The first organized political opposition to the British policy came in 1922, when Palestinian Arabs closed their shops and flew black flags of mourning to protest rising Jewish immigration. For Arab farmers and merchants living under the Mandate, the arrival of European Jews armed with the new political weaponry of Zionism spelled economic and social ruin. With the approval of the British government, more and more Jewish settlements began to intrude on Arab land. The breaking point came on a summer night in 1929, when a group of Zionists from the new Jewish city of Tel Aviv planted their flag on

Jerusalem's Wailing Wall, which sits at a holy site for both Jews and Muslims. The riots that followed claimed the lives of over 130 Jews. But the Arab threat to the growing Jewish community did not stem the tide of new immigrants: Pushed by growing anti-Semitism in Europe, many tens of thousands of Jews arrived in Palestine in the mid-1930s.

The growing conflict between Jews and Arabs reached a fever pitch in 1936, when hostilities broke out between the two communities. Led by Haj Amin al-Husseini, their chief religious figure, and Abd al-Qadir al-Husseini, the son of the former mayor of Jerusalem, the Arab inhabitants fought a series of brutal engagements against the British and Zionists. The Arab Revolt ravaged the Palestinian countryside for three years before the British government succeeded in imprisoning or expelling its leaders and suppressing its armed brigades. For five days, Jerusalem itself was under siege as British troops rooted out Arab guerrillas who had barricaded themselves inside the high stone houses of the Old City.

Zionist immigration sparked what Haj Amin and Abd al-Qadir could never have accomplished by themselves; it gave birth to the Palestinian national revolution. While it did not have the financial resources of Palestine's Jewish community or the modern tactics and weaponry adopted by the more adept Jewish political organizations, by the late 1930s Palestinian nationalism presented a formidable challenge to the Zionist community. The uprising of the 1930s also transformed British policies in the Mandate.

The Arab Revolt convinced British authorities that their pro-Zionist policy should be tempered to reflect Arab national aspirations. Britain retreated from the Balfour Declaration and, in 1939, issued a White Paper severely restricting Jewish immigration. Soon thereafter, various proposals began to circulate calling for the partition of the Mandate into Jewish and Arab states. The Arab leadership, however, consistently rejected these proposals, thereby setting an all-or-nothing precedent that was to be followed with disastrous consequences in the Palestinian community for the next six decades. The events that

followed are well known: The United Nations endorsed the
partition of Palestine in 1947, Israel was founded in 1948, and
its borders were established after a short war against the Arab
states.

The Jewish leaders of Israel erected a stable, economically
viable, democratic state with strong ties to the world's superpower—the United States. Israel's government stood the test of
time: It weathered the 1948 War of Independence, staggered
the world by defeating the combined armies of its adversaries
during the Six Day War in 1967, and reunited Jerusalem under
its rule. But just when the nation seemed at the very height of
its powers—when it was bathing in the afterglow of its most
astounding military triumph—things began to go wrong.

When Israel's armies conquered the West Bank and Gaza
Strip in 1967, they inherited responsibility for the lives of some
one and a half million Palestinians. The new conquests presented the young state with difficult problems: While Israel
claimed the lands of the West Bank as their ancestral home,
they could not just "transfer" the Palestinian population to Jordan; the word itself conjured memories of the Holocaust. Nor
could Israel assimilate the Palestinians, at least not if it wanted
to retain its essential character as a Jewish state. The only choice
left was to continue to occupy the West Bank and Gaza Strip
until a political settlement resolved the conflict, or until the
Palestinians of the territories left of their own accord.

Israel was founded by a group of idealists who believed they
could establish a Jewish state on their ancestral lands. But the
new nation was not conceived as merely a place of refuge;
Zionist leaders were dedicated to creating a new Jew and repu-
diating a past that marked their people as perpetual victims.
Freed from the ghettos of Eastern Europe, the early Zionists
believed that Jewish society and culture would flourish if they
were left unfettered by the destructive anti-Semitism that
haunted the Jewish diaspora. Zionism demanded strong,
proud, and nationalistic adherents. The early socialist agricultural settlements of Palestine were built with an eye toward

molding a cohesive, self-reliant community that could rebuild ancient Israel's claim to be a moral compass for the world.

The continued occupation of Arab lands after 1967 slowly undermined this view, and, inevitably perhaps, the foundations of Zionism's ideals—and its utopian exhortations—began to crumble. The very nature of military occupation and the necessities of national security pushed the Israeli government to adopt policies at variance with their movement's original ideals. Systematic economic expropriations, reliance on cheap Arab labor, and the everyday abrogation of individual rights subverted Israel's claim that it represented a new kind of society. Zionism had called the Jewish people to Palestine in order to build a new society and to repudiate the legacy of victimization. Now that dream was being undermined and, for some, Israel was becoming just another nation of victimizers.

Just as Israel's interaction with Arab society transformed Zionism, so the Arab engagement with Israel transformed the Palestinian community. The patriarchal social structure of the Mandate's Arab order was annihilated by the 1948 catastrophe and the Palestinian people were set adrift in the Arab world. For twenty years, from 1948 to 1968, Palestinian society was plunged into a state of political and social chaos. It was not until Yasser Arafat assumed the leadership of the PLO, in 1969, that Palestinians were able to begin rebuilding the national movement that had been sparked by the Arab Revolt three decades before.

Like all revolutions, the birth of Palestinian nationalism has been marked by bloody confrontations. At times, the Palestinian struggle has been more of a civil war than a single-minded national conflict against a recognized foe: In the forty-five years since the founding of Israel, more Palestinians have died at the hands of their conationalists than at the hands of the Israeli enemy. This inconvenient truth has been as difficult for Palestinians to admit as it has been for Israelis to acknowledge that their dream of a peaceful and prosperous Jewish state is still far from reality. By the end of 1987, both societies seemed locked in an endless and crippling battle.

Nevertheless, over the last seven years, key Israeli and Palestinian leaders have come to the realization that they could only reinvigorate their national movements by resolving their century-long battle. Ironically, the fears that permeated both their societies and moved their national leaders to the bargaining table were remarkably similar.

After years of hopeless struggle and sacrifice, the Palestinian leadership began to fear that by the time they had realized their dream of a national state, their movement would be drowned in a sea of hatred that would destroy their own society. The greatest anxiety among the intellectual and political elite of Israeli society, on the other hand, was *not* that they would be annihilated by their Arab enemies—Israel had never been stronger—but that they would be consumed by their own dread of those with whom they shared the land; that in their overwhelming fear for themselves, they would do unto others what had been done for over two thousand years to them, that they would lose the Zionist dream.

Individual Israelis and Palestinians have been trying to come to an understanding with each other since the founding of the Jewish state. But it has only been since 1987 that the contacts between the two sides have been matched by a serious commitment to resolve their differences. Even so, the first steps that were taken on the road to peace did not take place in the Knesset, or in the Israeli prime minister's office, or in the homes of upper-class Palestinian leaders in East Jerusalem, or at PLO headquarters in Tunis. Rather, the search for peace in the Middle East was first evident in places like Jebalya, a crowded Palestinian refugee camp in the Gaza Strip.

CHAPTER ONE
JEBALYA

You have to see Jebalya to believe it. The refugee camp is the largest of the Gaza Strip and houses just over seventy thousand human beings. Almost all of the camp's inhabitants live in appalling conditions. It is one of the most densely populated areas in the world—the people of the camp live literally on top of each other in two- and three-story hovels amid a gray mass of piled refuse, open sewers, human excrement, rotting pieces of food, and scavenging rodents who compete for the meager resources of the street. The garbage has not been collected in Jebalya in twenty-five years and the iron sameness of poverty is evident in the eyes of its inhabitants. Jebalya is a festering emotional boil.

Five months after the beginning of the Palestinian uprising, or intifada—which began in December 1987—Jebalya was held in awe by Palestinians and Israelis alike as a hotbed of radicalism, the flagship of the Palestinian revolution, and a symbol of resistance to Israeli occupation. Palestinian taxi drivers were suddenly enriched by the lucrative business of transporting Western journalists across southern Israel to Gaza to report on the intifada. But they skirted Jebalya, because it was simply too dangerous to enter. They glanced furtively at the high steel-mesh fences that surrounded the camp just off the main road through the Gaza Strip and shook their heads in awe. "That is Jebalya," one of these taxi drivers said on a hot afternoon in May 1988. "Jebalya is a very bad place; it is very difficult there. We are not going to go there today."

The taxi slows for a moment, moving around a rut in the road, and there is an Israeli checkpoint ahead. The young soldier reads the blue Palestinian license plate and seeing that the inhabitants are from Jerusalem, waves them through. "We are blessed," the driver says, "truly we are."

The fences that surround Jebalya are topped with barbed wire and glass and in some places have been replaced by huge walls of concrete. Some of the smaller homes on the edge of the camp have been bulldozed to provide clearer fields of fire for Israeli soldiers, and the open beach near the camp is continually patrolled by jeeps and armored personnel carriers. All of the main roads into the camp except for one are sealed by rows of stacked oil drums strapped together by huge links of rusting chains. These makeshift barriers are placed in strategic locations to keep the camp's inhabitants segregated from the rest of the Strip. The walls are high enough to keep the Palestinians from scaling them, but not so high that a well-aimed stone cannot be launched, often with great accuracy, at a passing Israeli patrol. The endless fences that surround Jebalya are punctuated by piles of concrete and brick.

Jebalya does not look like the Middle East, it looks like the no-man's-land that once separated East and West Berlin at the height of the cold war. The Palestinians, however, view the barriers with pride—they say that the walls were a form of punishment. "Jebalya," they say, "is under siege."

Young Israeli soldiers regularly direct Palestinian children away from the camp wall, except when there is work to do. A group of Palestinian children at the edge of the camp is being supervised by a patrol of Israeli soldiers; they have been given whitewash and brushes and are busily painting over a set of scrawled anti-Israeli slogans that have appeared on a store-

front. A group of Palestinians is watching this from afar, mut-
tering oaths under their breath. A soldier turns and brusquely
waves them on.

"That is Jebalya there, yes, just on the other side of the fence,"
the Palestinian taxi driver says warily. Some of the high Cyclone
wire has crumbled and been replaced by the Israelis with more
fences so that there are two sets of barriers separating the camp
from the main road to Gaza. Beyond one fence, women and
children shuffle along a nearly deserted street. The color of
Jebalya's streets is a shifting haze of gray-green that is tinged
with the brush of poverty and topped by dirt. A kind of indis-
tinct fog hovers over the camp, and the perimeter of the en-
closure seems endless. The driver nods his head and repeats his
warning. "It is not good in Jebalya today, we not go there," he
says.

"The camp has been under curfew for many weeks now," a
Palestinian in the front of the taxi explains. "It is possible to get
in, but maybe not to get out. It is very difficult. The people are
living in very bad conditions. There is very little to eat." He
pauses for a moment, looking at the camp walls, before continuing. "I have heard that there is some, well, not starvation . . ." He searches for the right word, then says it in Arabic,
the hard *ch* making a guttural sound in his mouth. Someone in
another part of the taxi gives the translation. "Malnutrition,
yes. There is some malnutrition," he says.

Jebalya is the third world's third world. While no part of the
Israeli occupied territories had escaped the harshness of military rule by mid-1988, the situation in Jebalya was beyond that.
Even in the depths of the most radical and violently anti-Israeli
parts of the West Bank, near Nablus and Jenin in the north,
there was always a way to make money. The black market in the
West Bank thrived in back alleys and on street corners and
there was a vibrant (though unofficial) international currency
market in the midst of Ramallah. Even the political life of the
West Bank—which had seen its share of violence and death—
was different from the reality of Jebalya. After a day of well-

planned confrontations with Israeli soldiers, the young men of the West Bank's mountain villages and small towns would meet for dinner in restaurants that were officially closed because of the strike—but which quietly reopened their doors to those who fought in the streets. Life went on.

But not in Jebalya. The strict discipline of rebellion had created a new world inside Jebalya's walls. If there was a black market there, it was in morsels of food and furtively arranged agreements on who would eat what and when. The camp leadership was young, radical, and single-minded. In any other part of the third world, in Bangkok for instance, hunger is a powerful aphrodisiac, but in Jebalya the young leaders of the uprising had enforced a mass moral discipline that was as much a part of their rebellion as any act against the Israelis. The green flags of Islam competed for space with the red, green, white, and black flag of Palestine, and the slogans of Islamic radicalism were more prominent than the tired and worn epigrams of the PLO.

"That is Jebalya, there and there," the taxi driver says. "And that is the end of the camp there, where the fence turns. It is very bad I think, to live in Jebalya."

Where Jebalya ends, the street into the Gaza Strip widens and skirts a small community of wooden hovels along a narrow beach. Ahead, Gaza City, with its rows of abandoned houses, barren street corners, and crumbling buildings, seems like a different world from the refugee camp. The streets are filled with rocks, and the heat of the spring day has made the Gazans listless, but there is a distant murmuring of crowds from the market in the center section of the city and soon stalls of fruits and vegetables and young men selling tea on card tables make their appearance.

The Palestinian driver pulls up before the entrance of Marna House, a hotel oasis and accepted meeting place of journalists and Gazans. A strict cease-fire is enforced at the hotel (no one is allowed to enter with any weapons—not even the Israelis), and its interior is filled with soft chairs. Cool drinks are served in the afternoon to journalists who spend their day tramping through Gaza's camps talking to Palestinians about their uprising.

Two young Palestinians wait at Marna House, sent as escorts for Western journalists by the hastily formed committee, the Unified Command, that has been put in charge of the intifada in the Gaza Strip. One of the journalists comments on the situation in Jebalya and talks at length on the rumor that women in the camp are beginning to cover their heads in accordance with Islamic custom. The new discipline is surprising, the reporter says, especially considering the relative sophistication of Palestinians and their reputation as the most westernized and modern people of the Arab world. The young Palestinian waves off the questioner.

"We do not have time for these philosophical questions," he says. "We are not asking for your acceptance of what we do. This is not simply a struggle against our occupiers; it is also an attempt to create a new national identity. Please keep in mind that we are not on display here for your benefit." He turns away from his questioner to face the other journalists. "You are our guests here and will be kept safe," he says. "But please understand, we do not care what you think."

The Gaza Strip is an ocean of misery. Stretching for sixteen miles along the Mediterranean coast southwest of the Israeli city of Ashkelon, it is the home of more than 750,000 impoverished Palestinians. The vast majority are packed into ten refugee camps—like Jebalya—which were built by the United Nations after the 1948 Arab-Israeli war. It took several years for the UN to accommodate the massive number of refugees, but eventually the temporary canvas tents were replaced by miles and miles of concrete boxes covered by corrugated tin. It is one of the poorest pieces of real estate in the world: Medical services are substandard, municipal utilities have collapsed, the population is mostly young and largely unemployed, and the infant mortality rate is approaching the levels reached in Bangladesh and Somalia.

That was not always true. For twenty years after the founding

of Israel in 1948, Gaza was administered by Egypt. In this forgotten backwater of the third world, Gazans followed the routine of most displaced Palestinians—their world revolved
around the family, market days, and the mosque. While everyday life held little prospect of enrichment, the burgeoning population, over 70 percent of whom were refugees from their
homes and farms in what is now Israel, began to build a work-
able society. The Egyptians rarely interfered: While officials of
the government security service were ever-present, the Cairo
government saw its primary task as making sure that Gaza was
not used as a base for attacks against Israel—unless, of course,
those attacks were approved by the Egyptian government.

To a large extent, the Gazans controlled their own lives. Administration of the major urban areas was overseen by Egyptian
officials, but Palestinians were charged with the everyday activities of governance. The traditional Palestinian hierarchy of the
Strip could do little to supplant Egyptian sovereignty, but social
order remained firmly in the hands of a group of selected
leading families—the "patricians" as they are called in Palestinian society—and their followers. The Egyptian government
controlled the courts, of course, but it was not unusual for
leading Palestinians to intervene with government officials to
plead leniency in special cases. (There were exceptions: Sedi-
tious acts—like suggesting that Egyptian President Gamal abd
al-Nasser be displaced—were met with swift, certain, and brutal
punishment.)

The Gazans themselves were put in charge of collecting cus-
toms duties and taxes, and most of the revenues were used to
maintain essential services. While a part of Gaza's income was
sent to Cairo, the tax structure rewarded work and provided a
safety net for the poorest part of the population. The refugee
camps, on the other hand, were under the control of the United
Nations Relief and Works Agency, which was established by the
UN in 1948 to deal with the Palestinian refugee problem. Clin-
ics, schools, small shops, and community centers were set up by
UNRWA officials in the camps, and the local Egyptian authorities were under strict orders not to interfere with their work.

While Gazans did not thrive in these circumstances, a number of businesses were established by a handful of enterprising Palestinian families. Oranges grown in the heavily irrigated fields bordering Israel's Negev Desert provided jobs for the young men of the camps, and citrus from the Strip provided badly needed export income. Palestinians are notoriously expert merchants, and this was true in Gaza. A lively small business community provided most of Gaza's essential needs and supported a stable middle class. Inhabitants of the refugee camps, on the other hand, were still in the most difficult economic circumstances, although most camp families discovered that they could supplement their meager income and modest diet by depending on the fresh shrimp, tuna, sardines, cod, and bass caught by the small fleet that put out every morning from the jetties just south of Gaza City. Life was bearable.

All of that changed in 1967. The Israeli Defense Forces—the IDF—entered Gaza after Egyptian military units south of the Strip were flanked and driven westward across the Sinai Desert. The independent Palestinian militias and a handful of Egyptian units left in the Gaza Strip had little help in waging an ongoing battle with the better-armed Israelis, but a series of sharp skirmishes near Khan Younis camp on the fourth day of the Six Day War—in the far western part of the Strip—bloodied several Israeli units and caused a temporary pullback (and one of the few outright Arab successes of the otherwise dismal conflict). The relatively well-armed population of the Strip kept the IDF at bay for nearly five days, and the IDF needed another four years to wipe out the last organized resistance to Israeli military rule.

The Israeli government imposed a harsh occupation on the people of Gaza. Palestinian leaders were immediately rounded up for prolonged detention and the rest of the population was required to carry identity cards and register with the civil administration. Every aspect of Palestinian life was monitored, controlled, and taxed. The high tax rates, far in excess of anything imposed by the Egyptians, drove Palestinian businesses into bankruptcy. Within years, the large source of fresh water provided by the aquifer under the Strip was rationed so that a great portion of it could be diverted for use in nearby Israeli farms. The Israelis patrolled Gaza's harbor, and Palestinian boats were prohibited from venturing into the deeper parts of the Mediterranean to fish. The price of food began to rise, and it eventually became scarce.

The Israelis believed they had little choice but to enforce a harsh occupation. The Israeli government was preoccupied with the threat against the lives of their citizens, who were now endangered by a population under their control. Palestinians once lived in a foreign nation, separated from Israel by a long, well-patrolled national border, and under the supervision of foreign governments. But that was no longer true—the Palestinians now moved among the Israeli population itself and the border between the two peoples was eliminated.

The tenor of everyday life in the Gaza Strip was transformed by the Israeli occupation. Over a period of two decades, thousands of Gazans who were driven off their land and out of their businesses became laborers in Israel. Each morning groups of men lined up at Israel's Erza checkpoint to board buses for jobs as janitors, construction workers, busboys, and garbage collectors in Ashkelon, Rehovot, Be'er Sheva, and Tel Aviv. Life was still bearable, but much less so. Slowly, inevitably, the social conditions of the crowded refugee camps began to deteriorate. Gaza became an Israeli colony.

The situation in Gaza proper was bad, but nowhere was it worse than in the Jebalya refugee camp. There, the harshness of military rule was more keenly felt and deeply resented than anywhere else in the Gaza Strip. One of the reasons for this was that Jebalya was Gaza's best-organized Palestinian community, with a strong and sophisticated network of Palestinian youth groups run, for the most part, out of the camp's mosques. Jebalya's mosques became a sanctuary for political dissidents—in large part because Palestinian political organizers discovered that Israeli soldiers (despite their officers' orders) were reluctant to enter the confines of Palestinian religious centers.

The ad hoc Palestinian political organizations of Jebalya enforced a loose discipline, and the camp's residents developed a heightened sense of political identity. In 1979, well before a rising wave of Islamic political movements began to shake the Arab world, the Islamic Jihad—or "Holy War"—resistance organization was founded right under the noses of the Israelis, who took two years to discover its existence. Most of Jihad's recruits and financial supporters came from Jebalya. Unlike in other refugee camps in the Gaza Strip, the Israelis had no clear idea what was going on in Jebalya and, despite their best efforts, information from Palestinians inside the camp remained nearly nonexistent. Jebalya was impenetrable.

Since 1979, Jebalya had been a center of opposition to the Israeli occupation, but the situation seemed to worsen during the summer of 1987. In August, there were a series of well-organized demonstrations in Jebalya that were only broken up after a strong show of Israeli military force. When the situation was reported up the line to Israeli military headquarters in Tel Aviv, the local commanders were simply told to be more vigilant. As a result, Israeli authorities increased foot patrols, identity checks, and random street searches of Jebalya residents. Monitoring of camp activities was increased. For a while this tactic seemed to work and incidents of anti-Israeli actions decreased. But the apparent return to normalcy inside the camp was short-lived.

By November, the political and religious slogans scrawled on the walls of Jebalya became more strident, and camp residents began an unofficial campaign of resistance against the Israeli military occupation: Patrols that had once been ignored were now openly confronted by jeering crowds, and otherwise docile Palestinians, who had once shown fear, openly hissed their anger. The Israelis knew that something had changed inside Jebalya, but they could not tell exactly what it was. By early December, the growing resentment against Israeli occupation policies had reached a flash point.

On the afternoon of December 8, 1987, a car filled with Palestinian workers was rammed by a vehicle driven by an Israeli, and four young Palestinian men were killed. Rumors spread quickly through Gaza that the accident was a purposeful act of revenge by a relative of an Israeli who was murdered in Gaza's central market two days earlier. Such accidents were not uncommon, but this time slogans blaming the Israelis for the "murder" began to appear on the walls of Jebalya. The first incident of the intifada occurred just a few hours later, when a crowd returning from the funeral for the men surrounded an Israeli outpost.

After taunting the Israelis with slogans, the crowd of mostly young Palestinians began to hurl stones. When the Israeli soldiers attempted to disperse them by firing their rifles into the air, the crowd responded with more stones. Thousands of Palestinians rushed from their homes in the camp and surrounded the military unit. That had never happened before. In a matter of minutes, the mob attempted to storm the outpost. The assault came out of nowhere, but it was sustained and stunning in its ferocity. By late evening, the rioting had spread eastward through the camp, and Israeli patrols were having difficulty tracking the groups of Palestinians who attacked them and then fled through Jebalya's maze of alleys.

When the sun rose on the morning of December 9, Jebalya was in full revolt. Burning barricades and other small fires set by Palestinian mobs had spread through the camp's narrow streets, and crowds of Palestinians controlled the major intersections. When Israeli soldiers entered the camp to put down the disturbances, they were met with a hail of stones. Ill equipped to deal with the crowds, the Israeli units quickly retreated, covering their withdrawal by shooting their weapons into the air. It was one of the few times that the people of Jebalya had seen Israeli soldiers in fear for their lives and a feeling of euphoria gripped the camp's residents. The success of the Jebalya rebellion forced thousands of ordinarily restrained Palestinians into the streets, where they joined the growing mobs.

On the afternoon of December 9, the uprising spread to the Islamic University in Gaza and then to the Shati camp, just up the road from Jebalya. Groups of young Palestinian students roamed the streets of Gaza City, shouting to the residents to either stay indoors and not go to work, or come into the streets to join the rebellion. The Shati camp, in particular, was in an uproar, as groups of Palestinian men engaged in hit-and-run tactics with Israeli patrols. Soon, the disturbances spread up and down the Gaza Strip, reaching the crowded Khan Younis camp near the Egyptian border by nightfall. But the growing uprising was still focused in Jebalya, where a patrol of Israeli soldiers shot and killed a young Palestinian boy during a particularly violent confrontation. When armored personnel carriers finally appeared inside the camp to reinforce the foot patrols, the first Molotov cocktail of the intifada was thrown. It was a portent of things to come.

By the morning of December 10, barricades of stones and tires had closed off major sections of the Gaza Strip. The uprising was remarkably contagious: In short order, West Bank Palestinians began to riot in sympathy with their cousins in Gaza. On December 11, the rioting spread to the refugee camps in the northern part of the West Bank, where crowds of Palestinians forced an Israeli patrol to give ground near Nablus, and the city was soon under the control of a patched-together committee of intifada leaders. A general business strike gripped East Jerusalem, where middle-class storekeepers—who the Israelis believed were the least likely to participate in any demonstration—closed their shops. But the scene of the worst troubles was in the far north, at the Balata refugee camp, which was promptly dubbed "the Jebalya of the West Bank."

Israeli authorities were stunned by the sudden outbreak of violence. The attacks had come without warning and had been pressed on all fronts. These factors convinced senior Israeli Defense Force officers that they were dealing with well-organized demonstrations planned by a small group of instigators; they simply did not believe that they were facing a spontaneous uprising. But the problem was that the IDF could not identify the Palestinians in charge of planning and coordinating the rebellion, and so the officers were forced to adopt a brutal strategy: They decided to meet the violence with over-

whelming force while simultaneously appealing for cooperation from the more moderate elements in the territories. But by
December 11, it was clear that large portions of the population
of the occupied territories, including the moderate elements,
were willing to join in the spreading disturbances. An unofficial
economic shutdown gripped Gaza City, and the thousands of
Palestinian workers who traveled to Israel each morning began
to diminish.

By mid-December, the increasing levels of violence had
touched all parts of Palestinian society. Rioting had broken out
in every refugee camp in the Gaza Strip and in every major city
of the West Bank; even normally quiet villages were becoming
dangerous battlegrounds for Israeli patrols. But the situation
was still at its worst in Jebalya, where crowds of protesters were
pressing the Israeli military and threatening to swamp its un-
dermanned posts. Inevitably, the young Israeli soldiers on occupation duty, most of whom had little or no training in
handling large unruly crowds, began to overreact to the ava-
lanche of demonstrations and attacks. This was a new situation:
In the past Israeli soldiers had been confronted by small groups
of taunting Palestinian youths, but now they were being forced
to quell protests that were in some cases led by housewives in
traditional dress.

Jebalya was the first place Palestinian women appeared on
the streets in elaborately embroidered black skirts and white
scarves—as if they were on their way to midday services at the
mosque—to hurl stones at the roving Israeli patrols. The soldiers had no idea what to do, and retreated. The American
media began to follow the uprising and pictures of Israeli soldiers fleeing from crowds of Palestinians were widely shown.
The specter of lone and elderly Palestinian women and their
children attempting to face down Israeli patrols with rocks,
weakly thrown, shocked Israeli citizens and the American
public. In just two short weeks, the political situation in the
occupied territories—and in Israel—had been completely transformed. The change was astonishing.

The Israeli government responded slowly to the challenge of

the uprising. When told of the troubles in Gaza, Israeli Defense Minister Yitzhak Rabin, a hero of the Six Day War and a former prime minister, dismissed the troubles as a temporary problem and refused to cancel a scheduled visit to the United States. Even after his return to Israel, on December 21, Rabin would not acknowledge that the IDF was facing a crisis in the occupied territories. Trained as a professional soldier, Rabin reacted to the highly volatile situation as he had reacted to other threats to Israel in the past: When confronted by violence, Rabin and his IDF colleagues reacted with force—a tactic that had always worked before. So it was no surprise that Rabin followed this same strategy in response to the intifada. He directed his senior military officers to double their patrols, and he sent more troops to Gaza.

Rabin was convinced that the demonstrations could be easily quelled if the IDF engaged in a campaign of sustained pressure against the Palestinian population. But by late December of 1987, Israeli units in the occupied territories were well past the point of merely trying to maintain order. In Jebalya and other camps, the soldiers were being forced to resort to the use of live ammunition simply to keep from being overpowered by the surging crowds. But the spectacle of Israeli soldiers shooting at unarmed men, women, and children appalled the Israeli public and, when the pictures appeared on Western television, brought protests from the United States and Israel's allies in Europe.

The intifada became an immediate sensation in the Western press. A series of editorials by leading American newspapers— some of whom were openly sympathetic to Israel's lone plight in the Middle East—criticized Rabin and the IDF. Less than four weeks after the outbreaks in the occupied territories, *The New York Times* published a cartoon that was a scathing indictment of Israeli policies. Its appearance would have been unthinkable just weeks before. The graphic depicted a group of Israeli soldiers beating defenseless Palestinians behind a sign that read: OCCUPIED TERRITORIES: YOUR AMERICAN TAX DOLLARS AT WORK.

Rabin stood fast against his critics. He stubbornly refused to curb the orders of his local commanders, defended the tactics of senior IDF officers who resorted to the use of live ammunition to cope with the deteriorating situation, and blamed the PLO for planning the uprising. Rabin then responded to the mounting political pressures in Israel by vowing that he would meet violence with violence. He ordered more riot control equipment sent to the occupied territories and approved the roundup and detention of hundreds and then thousands of Palestinians. Throughout the end of 1987 and well into the beginning of 1988, the use of rubber bullets, beatings, summary arrests, and mass detentions became widespread. Rabin applauded the work of his soldiers and reassured the Israeli public that the violence would eventually be suppressed.

But as the death toll among the Palestinian population mounted—at times averaging a death per day—Rabin began a desperate search for a way out of the crisis. Attempting to dampen concern over the use of combat tactics against unarmed civilians, he ordered his senior officers to begin employing a strategy of mass punishment. Instead of directing his soldiers to use the riot control equipment that he had shipped to Gaza and the West Bank, however, Rabin instructed his commanders to begin sealing off the most troublesome areas in the territories. Jebalya was the first camp to be sealed and placed under a twenty-four-hour curfew. Inside Jebalya, Rabin's order was taken as a sign of impending victory. For the first time in over twenty years, Palestinians had been officially separated from Israel—they were "liberated."

By the end of December, Jebalya was isolated from the outside world. The large double fence that surrounded the camp was topped by barbed wire, camp inhabitants were constantly monitored, and every road into Jebalya except for one was blocked. The few Israeli patrols that furtively entered the camp did so only to arrest Palestinians identified as leaders of the uprising. At the same time, the Israelis increased their efforts to recruit informants and collaborators. The prison in Gaza was expanded to include room for two hundred more Palestinians, a large portion of them from Jebalya. It was a desperate strategy.

In mid-January of 1988, Rabin visited Israel's troops in the territories. At his first stop in Gaza on January 12, he told Israeli soldiers that he understood the pressures they were under and reassured them that the government would defend their actions. But he cautioned them against using live ammunition, which was giving Israel and the IDF a bad reputation. He counseled senior officers to be more aggressive and to respond to rioting with immediate counterpressures. "Beat them during a demonstration," he said, "but not otherwise." Rabin underlined his concerns about the IDF's reputation several days later in the West Bank, where he told Israeli soldiers to "prevent violence by force, not by fire." Back in Tel Aviv, he held conferences with IDF commanders and once again admonished them about the dangers of lethal fire; the IDF, he repeated, should resort to mass beatings. "Beat them," he repeated. As his tour went on and he was exposed to the harshness of the intifada, Rabin's instructions became more and more emphatic. But he had a hard time getting his point across: His commanders told him that their soldiers were confused about how to react to the continued rioting.

Speaking with Israeli soldiers on the West Bank, Rabin tried to be more specific. "Use force during the course of the operation," he said, "whether it's coping with a demonstration, or breaking up a roadblock, or dispersing and chasing stone-throwers. But don't beat people in order to get them to open up shops, because business strikes don't constitute violence." But the soldiers were still unsure of what to do—when they beat Palestinian demonstrators, the news media criticized them, and when they responded to threats by retreating, the crowds became more and more unruly. Finally, on the verge of being routed, they responded with live ammunition; they thought they had no choice. In the face of this severe reality, Rabin's instructions were contradictory and actually seemed to fuel Palestinian anger. Nothing worked. In the midst of all this, Rabin was quoted as saying that his soldiers should respond to the uprising by "breaking bones."

When Rabin's directions "to beat" Palestinians and "break their bones" were publicized, a howl of protest went up from Israel's supporters around the world. It sounded as if Rabin was advocating the use of mass brutality against unarmed civilians. American Jewish leaders were particularly distressed by Rabin's apparent lack of compassion for unarmed people living in hovels under a harsh occupation, and they issued rare criticisms of the Israeli government. It was becoming more and more difficult to defend Israel from its critics, but Rabin's phrase made it nearly impossible. His words constituted a public relations disaster.

Rabin's defenders have since pleaded that the defense minister had been misunderstood and that he was simply attempting to deescalate a worsening situation. "Rabin is not fond of the Arabs, but he doesn't despise or hate them," a former IDF colleague of the defense minister argued at the time. "He's not a brutal man. The image was that he enjoyed breaking bones, but it's not true." But that explanation became less and less convincing as time went on. By the end of January 1988, seventeen Palestinians had died in the intifada and hundreds had been hospitalized.

Today, half a decade after the beginning of the intifada, it is clear that Rabin's words were a desperate attempt to keep the IDF from unraveling. He was not simply trying to suppress the uprising—which remained his first priority—he was also attempting to head off a vengeful mass slaughter of the kind that had taken place in Lebanon in 1982, where Israeli-backed Christian-Phalangist militias entered the Sabra and Shatila refugee camps and murdered over two thousand unarmed Palestinian men, women, and children. Another massive loss of Palestinian life like Sabra and Shatila, whether intended or not, Rabin knew, would be devastating to Israel. Throughout much of January, Rabin tried to hold together a swiftly deteriorating situation, but the more he looked for a policy that would end the uprising and bring calm back to the occupied territories, the more elusive that goal became.

After weeks of crisis, Rabin was slowly beginning to rethink the factors that were fueling the Palestinian uprising. By the end of January, he was convinced that the same variables that had undermined the fitness of the IDF in Lebanon were now coming into play in Gaza and the West Bank. Ceaselessly pressed by thousands of stone-wielding men, women, and children, Israel's soldiers were reacting as a brutal army of occupation. In addition to the worry that an Israeli unit somewhere in Gaza or the West Bank would get out of control was the very real fear that the IDF would fracture from inside. A growing but significant number of new recruits were beginning to protest Israeli tactics in the occupied territories and IDF officers were reporting that their soldiers were becoming more and more frustrated by their inability to respond effectively to the constant demonstrations.

This was a new kind of warfare for Yitzhak Rabin, who gloried in clear-cut military triumphs, unambiguous battlefield victories, and the calm and understated laurels that came with command. As chief of staff of the Israeli military in 1967, Rabin was credited with masterminding Israel's lightning victory during the Six Day War and while he was no longer on active duty during the crisis of the Yom Kippur War in 1973, he was buoyed by the resilience of the Israeli army in the face of insurmountable odds. Even during the darkest days of the Lebanon invasion in 1982, Rabin believed that Israel would survive and prosper—that its people could overcome despair and defeat to build a stronger nation.

But each of Israel's four major wars had been fought against outside aggressors, along the northern, southern, and eastern frontiers of the State of Israel. The intifada was starkly different. Starting in December 1987, and for five years thereafter, IDF soldiers were attempting to overpower masses of Palestinian civilians on a new and ever more fluid front that threatened at any moment to spill into the heart of Israel itself. The enemy was not at the gates, but inside the fortress—"in our midst," as

Rabin himself would later say—where hundreds of thousands of disaffected Palestinians went to work every day.

For all his public bluster, Rabin was deeply disturbed by the resilience of the uprising—the ability of its leaders to act with near impunity in the face of arrests and detentions, and the IDF's ineptitude at mounting an effective response. And while he dismissed any suggestion that the intifada could ever have a lasting impact on Israeli society (his wife, Leah, added to the bravado by quoting him as saying that "We've had our challenges; the intifada is not one of them"), the events of December 1987 and January 1988 brought about a startling shift in Rabin's own views of Israeli policies toward the people of the occupied territories.

In public, Rabin continued to play the confident soldier, but in private he was stunned by the ferocity of the Palestinian rebellion. By the end of January, Rabin decided that he had to prepare the Israeli public for a long battle or, as he finally admitted, "a complicated and long drawn out affair that cannot be taken care of in a few days." It was a surprising shift in tone from the combative one that he had adopted at the beginning of the troubles in December.

Finally, in late February, with the rebellion more than three months old, Rabin made his own personal doubts about the uprising public. His carefully measured words came during an otherwise innocuous address before Labor party members in Tel Aviv. Rabin had intended to present a straightforward account of the measures he was taking to respond to the uprising, but several minutes into his talk, his remarks turned into an unusually reflective, soul-searching exercise. His Labor party colleagues had rarely seen him so subdued and were shocked by the apparent depth of his frustration. "I've learned something in the last two and one half months," Rabin quietly admitted. "Among other things, that you can't rule by force over one and a half million Palestinians." He stopped speaking then, for a long silence, letting his words sink in.

Rabin's words were a startling and, up to this point, an unheard-of admission. For if he was right and what he said was true, then there was only one solution to the intifada—and it had nothing to do with force. Israel would have to leave the occupied territories, not because they wanted to, but because they had to. His words meant that the dream of creating a Greater Israel that included the West Bank and much of Gaza was simply out of reach.

Rabin was not yet willing to draw that lesson, or at least explicitly state it in public. But for anyone present on that February day, it was clear that the defense minister had come to a number of startling conclusions about how Israel should handle its Palestinian problem. Rabin set up a number of options for dealing with the intifada and then systematically rejected every one of them. Perhaps, he mused, Israel should annex the territories. "[But] what would we do with all the Palestinians?" he asked. Perhaps Israel should remove the Palestinian population—to Jordan and Lebanon, a listener in the crowd shouted. Rabin responded: "Transfer so far has only been done to Jews." The crowd sat in stunned silence, taking in the truth, and the implications, of the statement.

There was another option: to make the Palestinians citizens of Israel itself. But Rabin ruled that out. "If we make them citizens, they will have 25 to 30 seats in the Knesset," he said. "If we don't, we shall be a racist state, not a Jewish one."

By March, Rabin had transformed these personal reflections into a tentative political program, which he tested on one of his favorite audiences—a group of Israeli high school students. "I am opposed to a Palestinian PLO state between Israel and Jordan," Rabin told the group of students. "Since I am totally opposed to this, I am also totally opposed to negotiations with the PLO. I oppose, under any circumstances, withdrawing to the 1967 borders; I support the preservation of Greater Jerusalem, united, under Israeli sovereignty and serving as its capital. . . ."

At first glance it appeared that Rabin had not changed his opinions about the possibility of Palestinian self-rule. His address to the group of Israeli high school students, in fact, sounded like a retreat from his February position. But while Rabin remained adamant about a new Israeli policy toward the

Palestinians, he added an important caveat, saying that he would be willing to grant the Palestinians of the territories a measure of self-rule and the option of Jordanian citizenship.

That was new thinking for Rabin, who had once believed that, given the right pressures, the Palestinian population in the occupied territories might be permanently subdued or, better yet, might voluntarily seek exile in Jordan or Lebanon. Rabin knew that widespread abandonment of the territories by its inhabitants was a faint hope, but so long as the Palestinian population remained quiescent there was always a possibility that the strategy of just waiting might eventually work. Now, given the violent uprising, it was becoming more and more clear that Israel would have to deal creatively with its Palestinian problem—or be overwhelmed by it.

Following his remarks, Rabin discreetly opened discussions on self-rule with a small group of Palestinians from the occupied territories. In a series of highly unusual informal meetings in his Tel Aviv office and on the West Bank, Rabin told the Palestinians that he was certain that Israel might consider granting limited self-rule to an elected body of officials from the occupied territories, so long as the resulting council would leave security matters firmly in Israeli hands. Rabin also reiterated that if self-rule were to become a reality, it would be negotiated solely with those Palestinians who lived on the West Bank and Gaza, and not with the PLO. The Palestinians realized immediately that there had been an enormous shift in Israel's view of the territories. The intifada was working: For the first time ever, Israel was actively looking for a resolution of its conflict with the Palestinians.

At the same time that he was opening a dialogue with Palestinian leaders in the occupied territories, Rabin was gathering information about the PLO's increasing strength among the ad hoc Palestinian committees running the intifada. While he had abandoned his claim that the PLO was directing the uprising (the PLO was, in fact, as surprised by the sudden rebellion as the Israeli military), intelligence information he obtained in mid-March convinced him that Khalil al-Wazir, known as Abu

Jihad—the PLO's chief of intifada operations and Yasser Arafat's second-in-command—was gaining control of key intifada committees in the territories. Four months after the outbreak of the intifada, the intelligence reports said, the PLO was making a comeback.

That was just what Rabin was waiting for. While the PLO had been surprised by the intifada, Rabin could use the intelligence information to resuscitate the IDF's badly tarnished image. If Israeli military commandos could strike a high-profile blow against the PLO's leadership in Tunis by assassinating Abu Jihad, Rabin believed, then Israel might disrupt or even destroy the Tunis leadership's burgeoning intifada network. Such an operation would also reap benefits for the group of Palestinians with whom Rabin had been conducting discreet, but useful, political discussions. The assassination of Abu Jihad would prove to Palestinians in the occupied territories just how vulnerable the Tunis leadership had become, and how valuable the Israelis considered the local Palestinians' role as potential negotiators in a future settlement. Assassinating Abu Jihad was a gamble, but Rabin (and a number of Likud ministers and senior defense officials), thought it was one worth taking.

On April 15, a group of Israeli commandos put ashore on a beach outside Tunis and stealthily made their way to the home of Abu Jihad, which was located in a complex of villas near the ruins of ancient Carthage. Quickly and expertly the Israeli team blew the door of Abu Jihad's villa, vaulted up a nearby stairway, and assassinated the PLO leader while he slept. The commandos then made their way back to the Tunisian beach, where they were retrieved by Israeli navy speedboats. The most dangerous part of the entire operation took less than thirty seconds. Abu Jihad's assassination was trumpeted by Israeli officials in off-the-record conversations, while the government itself never admitted to playing any role in the operation. Nevertheless, it was clear that Rabin and his colleagues believed they had struck a blow against the intifada. But did it work? Within days, Rabin had his answer.

The Israeli raid dealt a crippling blow to the PLO, but it was not fatal. Abu Jihad's guiding hand and his genius for military operations was sorely missed at a crucial time in PLO history, but his death did not stop the intifada. Quite the contrary: As Abu Jihad was being laid to rest by Yasser Arafat in Tunis, Palestinians in the occupied territories were carrying placards bearing his picture through Gaza's teeming refugee camps. Within twenty-four hours of his murder, a new round of intense rioting broke out throughout the Gaza Strip. Jebalya, which had been sealed once and then unsealed, was closed off yet again.

The assassination of Abu Jihad was to be a new monument to the prowess of the IDF and yet another crowning achievement for Yitzhak Rabin. But within one week of the Israeli commando raid, the enthusiasm for the Israeli triumph had been quickly dampened by the escalating violence in the West Bank and Gaza. Even Rabin himself realized that the Tunis raid was only a temporary victory—now that Abu Jihad was gone, the emerging committees of the intifada (the self-proclaimed Unified Command) were free to act on their own. The good news was that the PLO's hand in the intifada had been crippled; the bad news was that it had not made one bit of difference.

On April 27, two weeks after the Abu Jihad assassination, Yitzhak Rabin—visibly exhausted from the crises of the last five months—broached the unthinkable. In an unusually specific answer during a television appearance in the United States, Rabin said that he would no longer discount negotiating with the PLO. "Allow me to say that if you get an announcement by any Palestinian who belongs to the PLO," Rabin explained, "that . . . he renounces the Palestinian covenant; that he is ready to accept Resolutions 242 and 338 . . . and that he is ready to stop violence and terror [then] I am ready to negotiate."

Yitzhak Rabin had not been totally transformed by the intifada, but he had begun the long period of personal questioning and reassessment that would reconstruct Israel's relations with the Palestinians. It was the first step on the path to peace.

*   *   *

The main road to Gaza begins at the Erza checkpoint, follows a broken and crowded highway through a barren wasteland, skirts the Jebalya camp for one mile, and then opens into Gaza City. Marna House is on the edge of the downtown market, just a short half-mile walk from Shifa Hospital—one of the most horrifying examples of inhumanity in the world. There were few drugs in the hospital in June of 1988, and the Palestinian doctors were forced to run a gauntlet of grieving families to treat the sick and injured. Bandaged bodies lay on soiled sheets while young Palestinian men patrolled the hallways.

Beyond the hospital Israeli soldiers walked an uneasy perimeter, checking passes, identity cards, and the occasional passport. Palestinian women stood in long lines outside the hospital, searching the faces of passing journalists for a friendly expression. One woman proffered the picture of a young man. "They have taken him," she cried shrilly. "They have taken him. Tell Mr. Kennedy, tell Mr. Kennedy. He will help." Even here, in the midst of the third world, the name of a famous American family carried a familiar cachet, as if the intervention of a distant senator could somehow make a difference.

Beyond the hospital, on a strangely quiet urban street, is the villa of seventy-year-old Dr. Haidar Abdul Shafi, the combative Palestinian nationalist who is held in such high esteem by Gazans. Born in Gaza City in 1919, Abdul Shafi graduated from the American University of Beirut and returned to Gaza in the early 1940s to practice medicine. He thereafter led the Communist party of Gaza, headed the Gaza Red Crescent Society, and, during the 1950s, was the leader of the National Front, a leftist Palestinian movement. An avowed Communist, Abdul Shafi supported the PLO's program and helped to found the Palestine National Council—the PLO's parliament. Even so, Abdul Shafi has remained one of the PLO's most constant, and fearless, critics. He always seems to be above partisan politics and, more than any other Palestinian leader, has been able to maintain a uniquely independent political position.

Abdul Shafi's hold on the Palestinian people is almost impossible to explain. In 1980, a group of Islamic fundamentalists burned the offices of the Gaza Red Crescent Society in Gaza City and marched on Abdul Shafi's home to protest his "godless" sympathies. He was protected then by Israeli units and a small core of young security guards, but later, on a quiet street nearby, he met the leaders of the demonstration. He raised his voice and shook his finger at them as they stood in silent humility, embarrassed at being berated by an aging warrior.

At every turn, Abdul Shafi seems to hold in thrall all who come into contact with him. Prior to the beginning of the intifada he could be seen walking through the city market surrounded by a group of Gazans, who followed him in admiration. From time to time, a hand would reach out to touch him, and he would turn and smile and then move away. Abdul Shafi could have unquestionably become a major figure in the PLO if he had only followed it into exile. Instead, he decided that he could serve his people best as a doctor in Gaza, and not as a politician in Tunis. He is viewed as a Palestinian political leader of such unquestioned honesty that many feel that he, and not Yasser Arafat, should head their national movement.

In June 1988, Abdul Shafi was the only openly acknowledged member of the Palestine Liberation Organization to live in the territories without being harassed by the Israeli authorities. The story that was passed from journalist to journalist was that the doctor was allowed to live unmolested because he remained under the protection of the American government; Secretary of State George Shultz, it was said, intervened on his behalf with the Israeli government to keep him from being arrested. The real story is probably less dramatic; Abdul Shafi was allowed to live in comparative peace because the Israelis knew that his arrest would set off a storm of protest far in excess of anything that was triggered by the assassination of Abu Jihad.

"If they deport me, what can I do?" Abdul Shafi told one group of journalists during an interview at the height of the intifada. "I do not want to leave here, I have lived here all my life, and I know the people of Gaza. I should be with them now, but this is out of my hands. There is nothing I can do. Besides, I am not afraid and I have some protection." Despite Israel's unspoken promise to leave Abdul Shafi alone, two young men regularly served as constant lookouts at the end of his street, while a platoon of three Palestinian men sifted carefully through the small crowd that came to visit him.

In May 1988, there were continual visitors to Abdul Shafi's home, and he greeted each group with renewed interest, including a group of American students seated in chairs set out along the walls of his home's main room. Taken with the political radicalism they had seen during their visit to the refugee camps, the students asked him what they could do to help the Palestinian cause. He was bemused by their questions, but answered each in turn. "The intifada was inevitable," he said. "It is the way that the people here in Gaza have defined themselves. The intifada is a national movement that has been brought on by the Israeli occupation. This occupation is not without pain, but not just for us. The troubles now must also have a very high cost for Israel." He nodded shortly, smiled, and wiped the top of his head. He appeared as a once physically imposing man who was now slightly slumped from age. He wore a formal, tailored gray suit. A watch fob peeked from behind a lapel and he fumbled with it from time to time, shining the back of the gold plate with his thumb, before he replaced the piece in his vest.

"You have come to ask me about the suffering of the Palestinian people," he said to the students. "You think that the story here is the story of the Palestinian uprising, and it is, but that is only part of the story. This is really a story about Israel." Someone tried to interrupt him with a question, but he raised his hand. "Listen to me," he said. "You must look into the eyes of these young Israeli soldiers to see what I see. They are such young men, young like you, and they are frightened. When they go back to Israel, they will tell the story of what is happening here in Gaza. I can see what is happening and you must see it too."

He fumbled with his watch again and then nodded. "This

intifada will eat away at the heart of Israel. It will destroy them. It is starting to do so now and they know it. This occupation is their tragedy, not ours.

"The intifada is a very important fact for two reasons," Abdul Shafi said. "The first reason is that it is making the Israelis much more than occupiers of our land. They are now very clearly our oppressors—they have become in fact what they were once in theory. And second, the intifada is defining our national character. We are discovering that we are all Palestinians." This last statement was a hallmark of Abdul Shafi's political beliefs, for while he remained a member of the PLO, he was skeptical that its hit-and-run tactics against Western interests could ever bring nationhood. That, he has felt, could only come when there was mass resistance—an intifada.

Abdul Shafi was on his way to address a group of Palestinians in East Jerusalem on the day that the uprising broke out in Jebalya. He guessed that there would be troubles in the Gaza Strip in 1987 and closely followed activities in the refugee camps throughout that summer. He told his top aides and members of his family that they could expect increased violence and he said that he expected that Israelis would overreact to the troubles. "It was a great mistake for them to assume that they could continue the occupation without pain," he confirmed. "It is difficult to sympathize with them, but we must remember the pain that they feel and the one simple fact of their existence— that the Arab nation can lose many wars, but Israel can only lose one. Sooner or later they will come to us with a peace proposal. And now it will be sooner."

Later, privately, Abdul Shafi talked about the results of the Palestinian uprising and was asked about the prospects for Palestinian statehood. "The intifada will not die," he said, "and the Israelis know it. Right now they are looking for a way out, but they cannot find a way." He wandered out onto his front porch to pose for photos. How soon will peace come? Can he see twenty-five years into the future?

"There will be a peace conference," he said, "in five years. And then there will be autonomy. I see this very clearly, I can see this happening. And five years after that there will be a Palestinian state here in Gaza and in the West Bank." Abdul Shafi was confident. "Five years after we gain our state, there will be a general economic union with Israel." He smiled again, a stooped man in a wrinkled gray suit. And then? "And then, who knows. But I think that Israelis and Palestinians working together would frighten very many people."

He waved off his words. "I do not have a crystal ball," he said, "but I think that I can see our future and it is not like this . . ." And he gestures at his surroundings, out beyond the wall that protects his house from the Gaza Strip. "We cannot continue like this. The Israelis are ready for peace, they are ready to meet with us. But the truth is that we are not yet ready to meet with them. But it will happen, it will happen." He nodded his head again, while shaking hands with his visitors: "There will be another major crisis and then it will happen," he said.

No one in 1988 could precisely analyze the reasons why the people of Jebalya had suddenly rebelled against Israeli occupation. While there was a long period of seething mistrust in the months before the December explosion, similar episodes over the past twenty years had come and gone without so much as a single sign of protest. The harshness of Israeli military rule had been unvarying from season to season and year to year, and 1987 was no different. But something had clearly changed. In looking back on the events of 1987 and 1988, it is now apparent to many observers that there was a distinct split between those Palestinians who lived inside the territories—under Israeli rule—and those who did not. The PLO leadership, once viewed as the unquestioned, sole leader of Palestinian nationalism, was being more widely criticized by the people of the territories.

It was not so much that the PLO's political program had failed as that it was increasingly irrelevant to the day-to-day struggle of living under Israeli rule. The PLO talked of "the return"—but the Palestinians of the territories talked of self-determination and "self-rule." For those Palestinians living in the occupied territories there was never any question of launching commando operations against Israeli military assets, or of targeting Israeli military leaders; the intifada was a minute-by-minute struggle for national survival. Every moment of every day contained its own rebellion and every individual—every man, woman, and child—was somehow involved. The PLO leaders in Tunis only understood this belatedly, and even then it was nearly too late. Their reaction was much like Yitzhak Rabin's; sooner or later, the men of the PLO believed, the pathetic little revolt would be crushed and then the national leadership would have to take over to wage the *real* war against Israel. As they always had.

But the simple and embarrassing truth for the PLO—"the sole, legitimate representative of the Palestinian people"—was that they knew as much about what was going on in Jebalya in December 1987 as the Israelis. Or less.

In May 1988, Jebalya had been closed to the outside world for forty days. The people of Gaza City were abuzz with the news that Islamic officials in Mecca would soon issue a *fatwa*—a religious decree, which would save the camp's inhabitants from starvation by allowing them to eat their dogs and cats. Israeli jeeps continued to patrol Jebalya's perimeter, the long rifles of IDF soldiers tipped by tear gas canisters.

The Erza checkpoint was usually quiet at night and the Palestinian taxis were waved through on their way back to the West Bank. They passed under the huge sign that spanned the road—WELCOME TO GAZA—and on into the green farmland of Israel. The taxi driver carrying the journalists past Jebalya, to the Marna House and back, was sighing in relief to be leaving the Strip in one piece. He muttered to himself in Arabic, then aimed his words at his passengers. His friend translated for the benefit of his American passengers. "It is an old Palestinian proverb," he said. "Literally it means, 'Everything that falls from the sky lands on the ground.' It means something like what you call fate, but what we mean by God's will."

For Americans who watched Yasser Arafat and Yitzhak Rabin on the White House lawn on September 13, 1993, the words of the Palestinian taxi driver take on added meaning. For while the handshake that sealed the Israeli-Palestinian agreement might have seemed somehow inevitable, the fact is that it took a confluence of many events spread over a period of five years to bring about the ultimate agreement. Abdul Shafi, then, was correct: The intifada proved that Israel could not rule the occupied territories; but that was only one half of the equation.

For while key Israeli leaders were persuaded by the intifada that they had to begin the search for peace, the Palestinian leadership was not. It would only be after the PLO itself was convinced that it could not defeat Israel—*ever*—that serious discussions on a new Palestinian-Israeli relationship would begin. Ironically, that shift in thinking would not come for another two years and, by then, the focus of Palestinian activities would have shifted from Jebalya to La Marsa, a small town in Tunisia.

CHAPTER TWO
LA MARSA

The Tunis suburb of La Marsa is not much different from any other modern North African town. The new villas being built on the hillsides are square and squat with wide windows to let in the desert breeze. Wedged between Tunis to the west, the large international airport to the east, and the wide Bay of Tunis to the south, La Marsa is beautiful in its own strange way. The air is dry and dusty and the high, barren, brown stone bluffs that rise out of the desert in the distance seem massively overpowering. At night, the desert sky over La Marsa is clear and quiet.

But unlike the other towns of North Africa, La Marsa has the unique distinction of being the home of the senior leadership of the Palestine Liberation Organization. It is difficult to believe that the small and simple collection of villas and modest homes serves as the headquarters of one of the most radical political movements in the world, yet it is here, in La Marsa, that Tunisian taxis and government limousines come carrying as their cargo important visitors from around the globe: diplomats, secret envoys, Arab businessmen, journalists, and PLO bureaucrats. The PLO came to La Marsa in 1982 after marching proudly out of Beirut under the watchful eyes of the Israeli military, which had invaded Lebanon to destroy them.

In the wake of the PLO's Lebanon disaster, the Tunisian government agreed to provide a home for the battered organization. It seemed the perfect location for the dying, past-its-prime liberation movement—it was quiet, out of the way, and, most important of all, far from Israel. At first, Tunisia balked at playing host to the Palestinian contingent: Wherever the PLO had gone in the previous two decades there had been trouble—first in Jordan in the early 1970s, and then just across the border from Jordan, in Lebanon, ten years later.

But after hasty consultations with the United States and a number of Arab governments, Tunisian officials agreed to the arrangement. The only proviso was that PLO Chairman Yasser Arafat and his associates would not be allowed to make any trouble, and Palestinian militias that he commanded would be interred in other parts of the Arab world. With nowhere else to turn, Arafat agreed to these conditions. But he knew that things had changed; Tunis was not Beirut and, unlike Lebanon, the Tunisian government had a well-trained, well-armed, and single-minded internal security service. Tunisian officials were less than sympathetic to the views of the leaders of international revolutionary movements and looked on Arafat and his entourage with suspicion.

The change in the PLO was remarkable. By 1983, the distinctive arrogance that so marked the organization's activities in Amman and Beirut was considerably dampened by the realities of Tunis; PLO "gunmen" were now called "security officials," and the speeding line of cars that accompanied Arafat and other leaders on their rounds was now called a "motorcade." While the young Palestinians whose job it was to guard PLO officials still entertained themselves by seeing who could drive the fastest through downtown Tunis (and poked fun at the "sleepy" Tunisian police), it was painfully evident their cocksure confidence was gone forever.

The most startling evidence that the PLO's loss of power and prestige had diminished came on April 15, 1988, when Yitzhak

Rabin's Israeli commandos put ashore near La Marsa and stealthily made their way to the home of Abu Jihad. After the specially trained military team assassinated the PLO official and escaped, the organization's leadership began to reassess their stay in Tunis and doubled and retrained their security guards. Abu Jihad's assassination was a damaging blow to the PLO, but it showed Arafat and his colleagues that the Tunisian security service was indeed "sleepy," but only when it suited its purpose. The Tunisian government tolerated the PLO—but that was all.

PLO leader Bassam Abu-Sharif admitted as much just weeks after Abu Jihad's death. "This was a heinous murder that was done in the dead of night when our enemy could not show his face," he said. "But it had one benefit in that it made us more careful. If we did not know that we had to provide our own security before, we knew it after what happened to Abu Jihad. Just because we are in Tunis doesn't mean anything. We are still the PLO—we are still fighters for our cause. As long as Israel opposes us, the Middle East will be a very dangerous place. No matter where we are."

Bassam Abu-Sharif has a house in La Marsa that is up a sandy road on a small hill that contains few other villas. Abu-Sharif, who is one of PLO leader Yasser Arafat's chief lieutenants and his closest personal aide, is proud of the home he has made. His dinners are prepared by a small staff and he often invites guests to dine with him.

"Come eat," he yells and moves down the hallway to a large dining room. He points to the pile of small fried red fish that are indigenous to the Bay of Tunis. "This is delicious. You cannot find this in America. No, I don't think so. Only here. Only here in Tunis."

Abu-Sharif is a comparative newcomer to Arafat's inner circle; a former deputy to George Habash—the head of the Syrian-based Popular Front for the Liberation of Palestine—Abu-Sharif abandoned the PFLP's more radical program and joined Arafat in the mid-1980s. Habash was stunned by the defection; Abu-Sharif had been like a son to him, supervised the planning of his most important operations (including the

elegantly planned mass hijacking and theatrical destruction of
three airliners in the Jordan desert in 1970), was designated as
his likely successor, and remained his closest confidant for
nearly fifteen years. At least part of the reason for Abu-Sharif's
decision to join Arafat, however, was his growing belief that
Habash's continuing terrorist war against Israel could not succeed. Like many other Palestinians, Abu-Sharif had come to the
realization that the Palestinian movement was being slowly destroyed by its brutal worldwide war against Israel.

Abu-Sharif still bears the scars of that battle. His right hand
and part of his face are deformed, the result of a letter bomb
that blew up when he opened it in Damascus in 1972. He laughs
about the incident now, but the bomb nearly killed him and the
explosion left him partially blind. He spent weeks in a Syrian
hospital hovering near death. He wears dark glasses as a cosmetic device and keeps his hands folded firmly in his lap to
disguise the effects of the bomb, but its scars are plainly visible.
Still, he is a handsome man who is given to casual, Western,
political jokes. He punctuates his comments with an explosive
"really," and regularly asks his American visitors to bring him
cartons of Marlboro cigarettes, which he smokes in an endless
cloudy chain. In exchange, he repeats tales from his dangerous
"terrorist" past, including how the Damascus letter bomb made
him a wiser man.

"You know how it happened?" he asks, a huge smile creasing
his face. "Here is how. Very simple: Ten years after the incident, I met an Israeli and I said to him, 'Listen, take a message
to [then-Israeli Defense Minister Ariel] Sharon. Tell him that I
want to talk to him. I will meet with him. Tell him that it is time
to stop this needless killing. Really.' But it was many months
before I saw the Israeli again. I was very intent to hear what
Sharon had to say, you can't imagine. The Israeli said that
Sharon was surprised by my request. Sharon said, 'I don't understand why Abu-Sharif would want to talk to me. Didn't he
receive my letter?' "

When Abu-Sharif ends the story, there is a silent hesitation
for a moment—and then he erupts in laughter. He does not

mind that the joke is on him. "Can you imagine the look on my face?" he asks. He shakes his head and implores his guest to try the fish. "That is the last time that I heard from Mr. Sharon," he says, still laughing, "but someday I would very much like to meet him."

Down an oak-paneled hall from the entrance to Abu-Sharif's house is a cluttered office where he spends most of his time. He is surrounded by his prized books, papers, personal mementos, pictures of his family (who live in London), and a television that is constantly tuned to CNN. There is a phone on the desk (the "hold" signal features the Christmas tune "O, Little Town of Bethlehem"—no matter what time of year), an answering machine, an intercom, and in the back by the window is a fax machine—the ubiquitous symbol of the PLO.

Journalists who travel to La Marsa soon become accustomed to the PLO's nocturnal schedule: Most of the interviews take place well after sunset or very early in the morning so that the organization's senior leaders can monitor the evening news broadcasts from America. As a result, it is impossible to get an interview with a PLO official after sunrise or in the early afternoon, since everyone is asleep. This is called "Palestinian time."

"It is not Palestinian time," Abu-Sharif protests. "It is American time. When your leaders are awake we have to be awake. Just to watch them, to see what they are going to do to us next. We have learned: That is the only way." Still, it is somewhat disconcerting to see the morning news from Atlanta beamed halfway across the world and into Abu-Sharif's study in the late afternoon. "You get used to it," he says.

On the wall to the right of Abu-Sharif's desk is a small wood painting of the Virgin Mary and Abu-Sharif smiles when he points to it. "It is always great fun to see the look of surprise on the face of an American when they realize that I am a Christian," he says. "But I am a Christian, yes. There are many Palestinian Christians. I was educated as a Christian and I live as a Christian."

*   *   *

In late August 1990, Abu-Sharif was seated comfortably in his small office in La Marsa with the desert heat radiating through the window behind him. He was in an expansive mood: Just one month earlier, Saddam Hussein had invaded Kuwait and driven the hated emirate's ruling family into exile in Saudi Arabia. Yasser Arafat visited the Baghdad strongman after the invasion and announced that the PLO supported Iraq's claim to Kuwait and would act as an intermediary in resolving the crisis peacefully. Arafat's announcement energized Palestinians living in the diaspora and in the Israeli occupied territories, many of whom believed that the newly "liberated" land of Kuwait, where Arafat himself had first gotten his start as a revolutionary, would become a temporary Palestine and a haven for their battered movement. Abu-Sharif expressed full support for Arafat's decision and claimed that Saddam Hussein's actions were the result of America's support for Israel—and the resentment that that had caused in the Arab world.

"One of the first things that you need to know is that Saddam Hussein has received the popular backing of the Arab world," Abu-Sharif said four weeks after the invasion. "Saddam has a great deal of political strength among the Arab peoples. He has overwhelming support among the masses and in the streets, which is where the politics of the Middle East is really made. In spite of efforts to keep this fact quiet it is true and cannot be denied. It is certainly true in Jordan and it is true in Algeria. There are one million people marching in the streets of Algiers in favor of what Saddam Hussein has done. I will tell you, the people of the Arab world are hungry and they want peace. Saddam Hussein is their hero."

Abu-Sharif was confident that the United States—which had just dispatched the first of hundreds of thousands of troops to Saudi Arabia—would find a way to peacefully resolve the crisis. Already, he claimed, Arafat was attempting to mediate a solution to the confrontation by contacting diplomats in Europe. The PLO chairman, he added, "is in constant contact with Saddam Hussein." But Abu-Sharif quickly dismissed any suggestion that the Bush administration would move militarily against the Iraqi leader. "That would be insane," he insisted, "and it would mean another Vietnam for you. You do not understand a man like Hussein. He kills people like you eat chicken." Abu-Sharif went on to paint an apocalyptic scenario in, as he said, "the very unlikely case that war breaks out."

"The first thing that Saddam will do if there is war is strike Israel," he predicted. "Ten thousand Israelis will die in five minutes from the chemical attack. Saddam Hussein is the kind of man who would do that. It will be a disaster for Israel. Can Israel take that? And if Israel retaliates there will be a Middle East war of everyone against everyone. The Arab masses will take to the streets. The Muslims will be infuriated. Iran and the Islamic republics of the USSR will rise up. Hosni Mubarak will be toppled because the Egyptian Army will move against him. Hafez al-Assad will have the same problem. He will have to move against Israel or be assassinated. And finally, [King] Fahd [of Saudi Arabia] will be torn to pieces."

Abu-Sharif was suddenly somber, reflecting on the American military deployment. In his heart, he said quietly, he was unsure about what the PLO should do. "A political solution is necessary," he said, "but we must keep in mind that the Palestinians are at the center of this controversy. The Palestinian problem is truly the one outstanding problem in the region and is the heart of the problem between Israel and the Arabs. And because we stand at the center of the controversy, we must find a way out. We must." Did everyone agree with Arafat's decision to support Saddam Hussein? "There is some discussion, yes of course," Abu-Sharif confirmed, but he waved off any suggestion of a split in the PLO's ranks. "There are some minor disagreements in our organization, at the margins as you Americans say, because we are democratic. We admit to that. But everyone agrees with the chairman. Everyone."

But Abu-Sharif was wrong. In August and September of 1990, the disagreements inside the PLO over Yasser Arafat's support for Saddam Hussein were neither "at the margins" nor "minor." They were serious, deep, divisive, and, at one point—

during a series of stormy and confrontational meetings on the
subject held in the first weeks following the Iraqi invasion—
they nearly shattered the organization.

The dispute involved a handful of Palestinian officials who
condemned Arafat for openly supporting Saddam Hussein
against the Arab nations of the Persian Gulf, which provided
the PLO with hundreds of millions of dollars in operating
funds. Arafat's judgment was faulted on two points: He was
criticized for his decision to send Saddam Hussein a telegram
congratulating him for "liberating" Kuwait (which was
promptly published, and then condemned, in the Arab and
Western press), and for publicly embracing the Iraqi leader
during an early August trip to Baghdad. The gesture was captured by television cameras and beamed around the world.
During the harsh exchange at Arafat's Tunis home, his critics
charged that his public support of Saddam Hussein was de-
stroying the credibility of the organization. If he insisted on
following this policy, the group of dissenters predicted, the
PLO would soon be broke. Its cadres would diminish and then
disappear, its support among diaspora Palestinians would evap-
orate, and the organization itself would be bankrupted. All that
they had worked for for years would be destroyed.

Arafat struck back in typical fashion. He cajoled, pleaded,
and angrily denounced his critics as "uninformed," "naive,"
and "disloyal." He demanded unity and summarily ordered his
colleagues to support his position. At one point, he even threatened to resign as head of the PLO and retire to Europe unless
his decision on Iraq met with unanimous support. Arafat argued that he had led the organization through two decades of
crisis and his decisions had almost always been right. He would
not stand by, he said, and allow the organization to be destroyed by "disunity and dissent." He had made his decision to
support Iraq after careful thought, he argued, and his decision
on the policy was final; what he was doing, he said, was in the
best interests of the Palestinian movement.

But Arafat's defense failed to calm his critics and, after several hours of debate, he was forced to resort to a second line of

argument. He finally admitted that his decision was controversial, and that it was hurting the Palestinian movement in the Arab world, but he maintained that the crisis provided the PLO with an unprecedented opportunity to show that it was interested in peace. After years of living in fading glory, he said, the movement now had one more opportunity—perhaps its last—to put the Palestinian question at the top of the Middle East agenda. The PLO, Arafat argued, was again at the center of events; if it could become an indispensable mediator between Iraq and the United States-led Gulf coalition—that is, if he could persuade the parties to negotiate an end to the crisis—the resulting agreement would revive the PLO's flagging fortunes.

After hours of contentious debate, the PLO's leaders said they would support Arafat's decision. But they insisted that he meet two conditions. First, he was required to keep everyone informed on the success of his diplomatic efforts; and, second, Arab leaders had to be persuaded that Arafat did not support Saddam Hussein, but was only trying to find a peaceful way to resolve the crisis. Above all, the dissenters insisted, the PLO must not appear as a public apologist for a foreign occupier.

Arafat readily agreed; in fact, he was ebullient. As far as he was concerned, the requirements set down by his critics meant that they had endorsed his diplomatic program. With this assurance in hand he again traveled to Baghdad to confer with the Iraqi leader.

Arafat's stunning support for Saddam Hussein should not have come as a surprise in the Arab world. The PLO leader had been leaning toward an alliance with Baghdad since the assassination of Abu Jihad, when Saddam Hussein told Arafat that he would be happy to provide the PLO with a new and more secure home. The Israelis could attack the PLO in La Marsa, Saddam Hussein said, but they would never dare to launch such an operation inside Iraq. The Iraqi leader then added an extra inducement by providing the PLO with a $20-million "personal gift" and he informed Arafat that there was more to come. Buoyed by this support, Arafat began to describe the Iraqi leader as a great military genius, and he argued that Saddam Hussein was the one regional leader capable of avenging the Arab world's humiliation at the hands of the United States and Israel. Saddam Hussein was "a new Saladin," Arafat said, and the best friend the PLO had.

Arafat's personal relationship with Saddam Hussein came to dominate his thinking. In March 1990, Arafat proposed moving the PLO's offices to Baghdad, and soon thereafter the organization's officials began the long process of shifting the Tunis-based headquarters staff to the Iraqi capital. Arafat was convinced that his friendship with Saddam Hussein would form the basis of an unbreakable PLO-Iraqi alliance. By moving its base of operations to Baghdad, Arafat reasoned, the organization would be closer to the center of events in the region. From Baghdad, the PLO would also be able to keep an eye on Iraq-based Palestinian factions that, despite their radicalism, carried considerable weight inside the PLO. "Saddam is our great protector," Arafat told his associates, "and he can be trusted."

Arafat's close relationship with Saddam Hussein had other benefits. Before the August invasion, Arafat acted as a high-profile mediator in the growing financial and territorial dispute between Saddam Hussein and Kuwait. During a meeting of the Arab League, he proposed a compromise to the crisis that he believed would satisfy both sides. After the proposal was rejected, Arafat went on a mission to Kuwait City to plead with the emir to agree to Iraq's demands. Through it all, the PLO chief was convinced that he was building his prestige as an indispensable diplomat who could successfully navigate the treacherous waters of Middle Eastern politics.

Arafat is one of the most confident men in the world, but he was never more self-assured than during the months leading up to the Gulf War. Even after the invasion of Kuwait and the subsequent deployment of American troops to Saudi Arabia, he was utterly persuaded that a negotiated settlement of the conflict was inevitable. "America will never attack Saddam, never, never," he told Abu-Sharif in one of the PLO's August meetings. "The Americans do not understand the Arab world. It is our job to help them."

The confrontation between Arafat and his critics in early August did little to dampen the PLO leader's enthusiasm for his ally in Baghdad. In meetings in Tunis after he returned from his second trip to Baghdad, in mid-August, Arafat again painted a luminous scenario. He argued that after much bluster and a mounting crescendo of military threats, the United States would come to its senses. Having tallied the possible death toll in a face-off with Saddam's Republican Guards, and the prospect that thousands of American soldiers would be slain in the deserts of Kuwait, George Bush and James Baker, Arafat argued, would look for a way to end the crisis. The only way for the Bush administration to save face then would be to engage in direct talks with Saddam Hussein; and Arafat was the only person who could get to the Iraqi leader, the only person whom he trusted. The price that Arafat would ask of the Americans in exchange for playing the role of peacemaker would be steep—direct negotiations with Israel leading to the establishment of a Palestinian state.

For all of Arafat's arguments, it is still difficult to comprehend why the PLO would support Saddam Hussein. Did Arafat really believe that he could negotiate an end to the crisis? Did he really suppose that he would become an indispensable international mediator, a kind of superdiplomat—a go-between who could win the trust of such diverse personalities as George Bush, James Baker, and Saddam Hussein? Was he truly convinced that someone like Israeli Prime Minister Yitzhak Shamir would turn over the future of the Middle East to the head of the PLO? It is almost impossible to understand now why Arafat took the position that he did then, but his supreme confidence and his ability to paint a vivid picture of his own power tells us much about what inspired him to take center stage during the Gulf crisis.

Yasser Arafat is an extremely complex personality whose actions and words have always defied easy explanation. He is a prodigiously talented leader with an incredible capacity to master detailed policies and programs. He rarely delegates authority and has mastered the minutiae of the PLO's most complicated and far-reaching programs. Despite these obvious talents, over the course of thirty years, Arafat has made an inordinate number of enemies and is the butt of common jokes on the part of a large number of Western and Arab leaders. Most Americans find his appearance distasteful and the mere mention of his name is often accompanied by questions on his uniform ("Why doesn't he wear a suit?"), his headdress ("Is he really bald?"), and his beard ("Why doesn't he shave?").

But for vast numbers of Palestinians, Yasser Arafat is an appealing symbol of their own national aspirations. His photo, complete with sunglasses, is a regular feature in many Palestinian homes, and his speeches and remarks are quoted and cited alike by students, professors, shopkeepers, and refugees. "Mao needed his little red book," a PLO partisan once said proudly, "but Arafat needs nothing." Arafat's very survival, after more than one dozen assassination attempts, is a matter of personal pride. He is single-minded, tireless, ascetic, and hardworking; he spends nearly every minute of every day working for the establishment of a Palestinian state. While he has made enormous mistakes (in Jordan and Lebanon) no one can doubt his political intuitions or his uncanny ability to turn certain defeat into victory. Yasser Arafat is a political phoenix: Just when everyone has counted him out, he returns stronger than ever. For this reason, he is the physical incarnation of Palestinian statehood—like the issue itself, he is an irritating problem that simply refuses to go away.

But Arafat has one Achilles' heel. The PLO chief is particularly susceptible to flattery and seems surprisingly incapable of seeing through the hypocrisy of official adulation. He craves attention and believes that such idolization is his due. Though he maintains a rigid schedule and shuns the retinue of fawning aides and assistants so common among other Arab national figures, Arafat fairly glistens with pride when he is greeted by long lines of heavyweight officials, touted at diplomatic receptions, or when he appears as the special guest at state dinners. He plays his role as a national fighter well: He lavishes attention

on widows, wounded fighters, and young children. He kisses
and hugs everyone. It is almost as if, after twenty-five years at
the center of the world's most perplexing conflict, Arafat fears
that he will be forgotten.

Critics and friends alike understand this one salient feature
of Arafat's personality. "He says he is married to the Palestinian
revolution," a longtime acquaintance says, "but he is really married to himself. This is a terrible thing to say about a person, but
you know, the marriage has worked." In his sixty-plus years,
Arafat has been a diplomat, bureaucrat, fighter, international
pariah, terrorist, and national leader. He is loathed by many
Arab national figures and passionately hated by hundreds of
thousands of Israelis. His closest friends and associates follow
him without question, though they are often stunned by his
decisions and maddened by his almost inexplicable mistakes
and his occasionally appallingly bad political judgments. But,
while no one likes to admit it, without Arafat there very well
might not have been a Palestinian revolution.

All of these attributes and personal foibles pushed Arafat
into the arms of Saddam Hussein, where he deluded himself
into thinking that he could somehow play the role of a humanitarian diplomat embarked on a tireless search for peace. His
decision was a major, nearly fatal mistake for the PLO, but it
was clear to his closest associates as early as September of 1990
that it could not be reversed. Arafat was in his element: The
Gulf crisis reminded him of the PLO's darkest days—its Black
September battle with Jordan, its knee-buckling nightmare in
Beirut, the humiliating hegira to Tunis, and the death of Abu
Jihad. But he was confident that he could beat all the odds, just
as he had before.

Unfortunately for Arafat, there were a number of powerful
PLO officials who still vehemently disagreed with his policy and
continued to criticize the wisdom of his strategy. Even after
Arafat had won the tentative approval of his closest associates in
August, vocal dissent was still being heard in a number of quar-
ters. By the beginning of September, three of his most powerful

associates were beginning to mount serious opposition to his program and recruit allies inside the organization to provide a united front in opposing him.

From his home near Tunis, Khalid al-Hassan viewed Arafat's political maneuvers with increasing alarm. Known inside the PLO as Abu Said, Hassan had years of experience in high-level diplomacy. In the mid-1960s, for instance, he shocked his colleagues by announcing that the PLO should accept a two-state solution to the Palestinian problem. In the mid-1970s, he gained the confidence of the United States during secret United States-PLO contacts initiated to protect Americans in Beirut. Hassan thereafter successfully pushed the PLO to a more moderate viewpoint and helped make the organization a respected member of the Arab world. He had long ago become persuaded that the United States would never abandon its alliance with Israel and that the PLO had to admit to that fact. The deployment of American troops to Saudi Arabia did nothing to dispel that belief.

Arafat's support for Saddam Hussein convinced Khalid al-Hassan that the PLO was on the verge of a major catastrophe. He had told that to the PLO leader in August. During the first week of September, Hassan, who was plagued by poor health and worried by the plight of his family who had fled Kuwait City after the Iraqi takeover ("That is my seventh library that has gone up in smoke," he commented), had another bitter confrontation with Arafat. The argument did not go well for the aging Hassan, who had never seen Arafat so convinced that he was right. Finally, after realizing that he could not change Arafat's mind, Hassan abruptly brought the discussion to a close. But he did not give up. Through all of September, Hassan warned Arafat that he must stand by the PLO's unstated founding principle: that the Palestinians could depend on no one but themselves to win their rights. It seemed to him that Arafat had forgotten that cardinal precept.

Khalid's brother Hani was another dissenter. In the mid-1960s, Hani Hassan had helped Arafat build Fatah with an infusion of Palestinian student power. It was chiefly through his efforts that the PLO became the vanguard revolutionary movement for a rising generation of young Palestinians. Hani Hassan further enhanced his standing in the PLO in the mid-1980s, when he served as the organization's trusted liaison with the oil-rich Arab states. His persistent work enabled the PLO to collect millions of dollars from diaspora Palestinians through a "PLO tax." Hassan also made sure that the Gulf states sent tens of millions of dollars of their own money to the PLO to show their support for the Palestinian cause. It had taken Hani Hassan years of work to build this impressive financial network, but now, he feared, all of his work would be destroyed: Arafat's open courtship of Saddam Hussein was making the PLO anathema in the capitals of the Middle East.

Khalid and Hani Hassan were important critics of Arafat's Iraq policy since both of them served on the PLO's highest decision-making body and retained considerable influence among the rank-and-file PLO membership. But it was Salah Khalaf—known as Abu Iyad—who provided the greatest challenge to Arafat's program. Abu Iyad had served with Arafat for three decades and, with him, helped to found Fatah, the mainline PLO group that dominated the organization's policies. In many ways, his life paralleled the organization's tumultuous history. As head of PLO intelligence operations, Abu Iyad was viewed as the movement's most uncompromising firebrand and its most fearless activist. He was blamed by some Israeli officials for planning the massacre of eleven Israeli athletes during the Munich Olympics in 1974.

While Abu Iyad denied that he played a central role in the incident, the Munich disaster kindled a deep emotional crisis in him. Like Khalid al-Hassan before him, Abu Iyad decided by the late 1970s that he would never see a Palestinian state in the land of Israel. He was sickened by the part he played in the continuing carnage and he was haunted by the vision of the debilitating war that was claiming the lives of his closest friends. He slowly began to revise his own views and decided that the only way the Palestinian people could regain their homeland was to renounce terrorism and recognize Israel's right to exist.

Abu Iyad thereafter argued vehemently for an opening to the United States and, with Khalid al-Hassan, worked behind the scenes to gain American recognition of the PLO.

Even with this personal transformation, Abu Iyad remained a deeply embittered man. The compromise of his own political views had not dissuaded him from the belief that the plight of the Palestinian people remained one of the greatest injustices of modern times. He renounced terrorism, hijackings, and assassinations, but he refused to compromise his own view of Israel, and remained convinced that the Palestinian people were being systematically liquidated. The years took a toll: By September 1990, Abu Iyad, who had once been an imposing physical presence, was visibly distraught over the PLO's support of Saddam Hussein and emotionally drained by the endless and violent disagreements that marred Palestinian politics. To some of his friends he seemed to be on the verge of a physical collapse.

Abu Iyad's physical deterioration can be attributed in part to the grueling intelligence operations that he supervised. Beginning in 1986, Abu Iyad had painstakingly recruited dozens of Palestinians aligned with the notorious terrorist Abu Nidal. After a period of training, Abu Iyad sent these new recruits to Nidal's base in Libya to destroy his organization. The program sowed discord in Nidal's ranks and nearly destroyed his organization, but the operation's success was purchased by scores of young lives that could not be replaced. The carnage of the war with Nidal was still on Abu Iyad's mind when the Gulf crisis broke out in 1990.

After the chaotic confrontation between Arafat and his opponents in Tunis in early August, Abu Iyad remained loyal to the PLO chairman because he believed that the movement could have only one leader—and follow only one policy. So while in private he castigated Arafat for cozying up to the Baghdad dictator, and even railed against Arafat in off-the-record interviews with foreign journalists, he diligently maintained a public stance that the organization remained unified. But six weeks after Saddam Hussein's invasion, Abu Iyad changed his mind, and concluded that Arafat was purposely flouting the requirements set down during their early August confrontation with the PLO leader. The PLO chairman, he decided, wanted a full-fledged alliance with Saddam Hussein and was not going to be curbed by any agreement he made with his colleagues. Therefore, with time running out, Iyad attempted to recruit a number of senior officials to his side in the hopes that he could once again divert Arafat from his dangerous course. Abu Iyad began his program in mid-September.

The first official Abu Iyad attempted to recruit was Hayel Abdel-Hamid, known as Abu Hol, the head of the PLO's security apparatus and the Tunis coordinator of Fatah operations in the occupied territories. Abu Hol had gained enormous power and influence from his tireless efforts to monitor the course of the Palestinian uprising and was a trusted intelligence and security officer. But Abu Hol refused to engage in a power struggle with Arafat. A decision had been made at the highest levels to back Saddam Hussein, he told Abu Iyad, and it was up to everyone to support that decision. He said that Abu Iyad would have to stand up to Arafat by himself.

Abu Iyad had his work cut out for him; he understood that Arafat was banking on other PLO officials outside of the tightly knit group of senior founders to support his position and that they were gaining power and prestige at the expense of the dissenters. Among these were Farouk Kaddoumi, the titular PLO foreign minister, and Mahmoud Abbas, known as Abu Mazin, an Arafat loyalist and the head of the PLO's political department. In late September, after carefully marshaling his arguments, Abu Iyad had an angry confrontation with Arafat over the Baghdad alliance. According to PLO officials, Abu Iyad told Arafat that his support of Saddam Hussein would destroy the organization. All that they had worked toward for thirty years was now being put in question, he said, including the belief that eventually the PLO would negotiate with Israel for a separate Palestinian state.

Arafat remained calm during Abu Iyad's presentation, but his anger grew when it became apparent that his top deputy would not be persuaded by Arafat's arguments. Arafat pointed

out that he knew that Abu Iyad and others had tried to approach the United States to find a solution to the crisis, but he
also knew that they had failed. That should prove that an eventual settlement of the crisis was not in the hands of Washington,
Arafat said, but in the hands of Saddam Hussein. Arafat concluded his argument by saying that he would continue to support Saddam Hussein, no matter what opposition he faced
inside the PLO. Distraught and drained by the endless argument, Abu Iyad pressed his final point: Saddam Hussein, he
contended, could not possibly win a military confrontation with
the United States. Surely Arafat could see that.

But Arafat laughingly dismissed this claim and clapped Abu
Iyad on the back. "It won't come to that," he said.

Seated in his office in Tunis in September 1990, Abu Iyad
smiled grimly at the mention of Yasser Arafat's unyielding support for Saddam Hussein and shook his head at the mention of
a PLO-Baghdad axis. "I know that in the mind of the world we
are now Saddamists," he said, "but I am telling you, we are not
Saddamists. We have met with Mr. Hussein several times and
we have told him that he should withdraw from Kuwait. During
the first few meetings he was hesitant, but now he is not so
silent. We have told him that he has made a great mistake and
that he is hurting the cause of the Arab world. I think that he
has started to listen."

As always, Abu Iyad was holding an American cigarette and
the room was wreathed in billowing blue smoke. Nearby was a
tray of cold water, a Tunisian necessity. Seated across the room
was Abu Iyad's oldest son, who had arrived home from school
in London to serve as his father's translator during the crisis. In
his early twenties and the pride of the family, which earned its
prominence as residents of Gaza, the young man was an articulate and worldly intellectual, just like many of the Khalafs
before him. Light-complexioned, with piercing eyes and a spray
of red hair ("a Crusader baby," according to Palestinian lore),
Abu Iyad's son tenaciously wiped his smoke-irritated eyes and
proudly translated his father's words, stopping only to flash a

smiling and quizzical look at the older man's occasional turn of phrase.

"We have been criticized in the Gulf, we have been criticized in Egypt; but our people have suffered because of this crisis," Abu Iyad said. "Four hundred thousand Palestinians live in Kuwait. Now what will happen to them? For them there is nowhere to go. So why would we support this unjustified invasion of Kuwait and the suppression of another people? We know what it is to be under occupation and hunted."

The interview reflected Abu Iyad's complex personality; he clearly liked journalists and was good-humored. Even under pressure he appeared relaxed and self-confident, although he was aged well beyond his fifty-seven years. His face was creased and his physique was that of a middle-aged man who refused exercise. He wheezed shortly, in gasps, and coughed. His fingers were tobacco-stained and calloused. Even in the air conditioning of his home, Abu Iyad perspired visibly and continually wiped the sweat from his forehead. He nodded briefly in answer to a question. "Yes, it has been a difficult time. But we are with Abu Amar [Yasser Arafat]. We are with him," he said.

Abu Iyad was telling only part of the story. After his last two-hour gut-wrenching clash with Arafat, he swallowed his pride and accompanied the PLO chairman on yet another trip to Baghdad, where he spent several hours with Saddam Hussein talking about the American deployment in Saudi Arabia. Saddam Hussein told Abu Iyad what he had already told Arafat: that the war against Kuwait and its allies was necessary and that it provided an opportunity to show the world how the Palestinians had suffered. The Americans and Israelis could not be talked into peace, he said, but had to be shown that there was no other alternative. Abu Iyad told Saddam Hussein that he agreed with his argument, especially when it came to Israel. Yes, he said, the Israelis would never compromise with the Palestinians. But he disagreed vehemently with Saddam Hussein's tactics and he said so. "You must withdraw from Kuwait right away, right now," Abu Iyad said, "and agree to talk with the Americans. Otherwise this crisis will end in disaster for you and Iraq." Later, when he recounted this exchange, Abu Iyad said that he knew that facing the Iraqi dictator would be difficult, but he had not anticipated his harsh reaction to his argument. Saddam Hussein stared at him for many moments in silence, Abu Iyad recounted, and then turned on his heel and walked away. Even for the hardened Palestinian revolutionary, Saddam Hussein's gesture was chilling.

But what disturbed the PLO official the most was that Arafat, seated nearby, remained silent throughout the discussion. For the rest of his stay in Baghdad, Abu Iyad was under virtual house arrest and he feared for his life. When he returned to Tunis, he was more convinced than ever that Saddam Hussein was using the Palestinian cause to mask his own aggression. Still, Abu Iyad kept his own counsel.

"We have accepted this as a complicated problem that needs a solution," he said while seated in his study in Tunis. "How could we accept war as an option? We would not be in keeping with our principles if we were to do so. I think that the PLO and Yasser Arafat are the only ones talking peace." Abu Iyad smiled and leaned forward in his chair. He shifted from his native Arabic and spoke in broken English. "There are three possible results to the crisis," he said. "The first is that there is a political solution and we are a part of it. The second is that there is a war and America wins and the third is that Saddam somehow succeeds." He again shook his head and then lowered his voice. "But I do not think that this will happen."

By the end of October 1990, not only was Abu Iyad convinced that Saddam Hussein would lose in his showdown with the United States, he was certain that the PLO would be shunted aside in any postwar settlement. He continued to warn Yasser Arafat about the consequences of siding with Iraq in the coming war, but Arafat continued to dismiss any suggestion that his strategy would fail. But by then, at least, Abu Iyad was not alone in opposing the PLO chief. Other voices were now being heard at the top of the organization, which was suddenly facing financial ruin.

When Arafat embraced Saddam Hussein, the PLO's funding

base in the Gulf slowed to a trickle and then stopped altogether. PLO officials were jolted by the cutoff in funds: $160 million was collected for the PLO in 1990, but under the new restrictions, only $60 million would be received in 1991. The prospects for the next year were even dimmer, with an expected income of just $10 million, much less than the PLO required to continue its programs. The financial crunch was more than a temporary setback: The PLO was forced to close a number of its offices in Tunis, as well as several of its foreign embassies, and nearly one dozen of its overseas programs. Worse news followed. The end of financial support from the Gulf countries meant that the social benefits provided by the PLO to both diaspora Palestinians and those living in the occupied territories—including money for health clinics, employment offices, payments to widows of PLO fighters, and the like—would be terminated.

The political news was also critical. After Arafat completed yet another round of diplomacy in early November, PLO officials in Tunis were told that he was no longer welcome in Arab countries that were members of the United States-led coalition. The welcome mat that traditionally greeted him was rolled up and put away. The worsening political situation was highlighted by a PLO crisis in Syria, where President Hafez al-Assad ordered his security services to crack down on PLO officials operating in the country. He then directed his military commanders in Beirut to mop up the remaining PLO strongholds in Lebanon. These moves should not have taken the PLO by surprise: Assad loathed Arafat and viewed him as a "pretend Palestinian," a "coward, braggart, and criminal." Cut off from his fighters and shunned by his fellow Arab leaders, Arafat was powerless to stop him.

By December 1990, the PLO was being shaken by its internal divisions and was increasingly isolated from the rest of the Arab world. Wherever Yasser Arafat looked, the Palestine Liberation Organization was on the run. With funding from the Gulf states cut off and its remaining military units in Lebanon impotent against the Syrian onslaught, Arafat might have been excused for distancing himself from his unwise alliance with Saddam Hussein, but he refused. Instead, he continued to insist that the PLO-Iraq alliance would result in an unprecedented diplomatic breakthrough that would guarantee the establishment of a Palestinian state.

Torn by their loyalty to Arafat and their judgment that Saddam Hussein could not possibly win in his confrontation with the United States, Khalid and Hani Hassan and Abu Iyad reluctantly went along with Arafat's strategy. They were under enormous pressure to do so. Bolstered by the pro-Iraq reactions of Palestinians, Arafat and his allies were gaining strength inside the organization. "To date, not a single Palestinian faction intends to defect from supporting him because they know that Arafat has really made the only choice possible," Nabil Shaath, the PLO's foreign minister, said at the time. "It was impossible for him to back any side in which the United States and Israel are fighting an Arab country." The Hassan brothers and Abu Iyad were also being outmaneuvered by senior officials, who were arguing that organizational unity was now a paramount concern. The PLO might suffer from siding with Saddam Hussein, they contended, but it would certainly perish if the Hassans and Abu Iyad continued to draw out their argument.

With the help of these political reinforcements, Arafat succeeded in drawing together the divided wings of his organization by the end of November. He eventually succeeded in exacting an uneasy loyalty from his top aides, and silence from his most vocal dissenters, but he paid a heavy price: His leadership would never again be as unquestioned as it had been when the PLO was at its strongest. The organization had survived a crippling internal battle—but it had barely done so, and only then because Arafat threw everything that he had into the battle. For five months, from August 1990 until January of the next year, Arafat debated, flattered, browbeat, and pleaded with his top associates to stand behind him. At the height of the crisis, on the eve of America's massive air assault on Iraq, he was at his most persuasive: He told Abu Iyad and Khalid al-Hassan that he had almost convinced Saddam Hussein to withdraw from Kuwait. Such an act, he argued, would constitute the diplomatic breakthrough he had always sought. After Saddam Hussein's retreat, the PLO would be credited with stopping a bloody war.

The long battle for statehood would be over, won.

Two months later, on the night of January 11, 1991, Arafat boarded his private jet for one last trip to Baghdad. Abu Iyad stayed behind in Tunis hoping that he could convince a number of European diplomats to schedule an international conference on the Gulf crisis. If Saddam Hussein agreed to allow European mediation, Abu Iyad reasoned, the resulting conference could postpone an American military invasion of Kuwait. The senior PLO leader spent the next seventy-two hours talking with Italian and French diplomats about the proposed summit.

Three days later, Abu Iyad decided to accept a dinner invitation with the head of PLO security, Abu Hol. The dinner would provide a good opportunity to review Abu Iyad's diplomatic initiative and to compare notes on Arafat's trip to Baghdad. When Abu Hol asked if senior PLO official Mohammed Fakr Omari could join them, Abu Iyad readily agreed. It was a simple Arabic meal: lamb, yogurt, bread, juice, and stuffed grape leaves. Abu Hol and Abu Iyad were close friends—they had served together at the top of the PLO for two decades and while Abu Iyad was the better known of the two, Abu Hol was a trusted PLO official in his own right. In addition to serving as liaison officer to the uprising in the occupied territories (a task he had inherited after the assassination of Abu Jihad), Abu Hol was responsible for the security of senior PLO officials.

Both men had plenty of enemies. Israel had once placed Abu Iyad on its assassination list, presumably because of his role in the Munich massacre. But there were others who wanted him dead: Abu Nidal, the Syrians, and of course, Saddam Hussein, who resented his blunt talk of withdrawal from Kuwait back in September. Still, there was no reason to be alarmed—both men lived with danger for many years and they were accustomed to the tension caused by the constant possibility of attack. After finishing their meal, the three moved away from the table to a spot near the television.

It was a special meeting. Just twenty-four hours earlier, Abu Hol had returned on a flight from Baghdad, leaving Arafat behind to conduct further meetings with Saddam Hussein. From accounts of Abu Hol's disposition prior to the dinner, the PLO head of security was not in a good mood. He reported to Abu Iyad that while Saddam Hussein said that he was now ready to consider withdrawing his troops from Kuwait, he would not do so until the United States agreed to an international conference on the Middle East. A quiet and unexcitable man, Hol reported the news in matter-of-fact tones.

Abu Iyad must have been intrigued by the report. His own contacts with European leaders, who also wanted to postpone the outbreak of fighting, gave cause for optimism. Abu Iyad briefed Abu Hol on his attempts to interest European leaders in a negotiated settlement to the crisis and the prospects for peace. After his upcoming meeting with the foreign minister of Italy, Abu Iyad believed, the Americans might be persuaded to allow Italy to negotiate an end to the crisis. The three men probably then discussed the shifting diplomatic environment in the region and speculated on Arafat's meetings in Baghdad.

About one half hour after they finished dinner, one of Abu Hol's heavily armed security guards, who was recently recruited as a defector from the Abu Nidal organization, appeared in the doorway. "Is everything okay?" he asked. Abu Hol nodded curtly and then, in keeping with PLO tradition, motioned to the man to help himself to what remained of the dinner. At this point the security guard, Hamza Abu Zeid, opened fire with the automatic weapon he was carrying. The first four shells struck Abu Iyad in the chest; a fifth penetrated his left temple. He was killed instantly.

Omari was next. After scrambling to get out of the way of the initial burst of gunfire, Omari tried to hide under a nearby sofa. Zeid stalked him across the room and shot him three times.

Abu Hol was last. After a moment's hesitation, Zeid fired off six shells that stitched a line of blood across his legs and left him moaning in the center of the room. He bled to death in a nearby hospital. The entire incident had taken no more than sixty seconds. After the shootings, the gunman hid in an upstairs room, taking Abu Hol's family as hostages. But after a standoff of four hours, he surrendered to the Tunisian police.

At the same time that the three PLO officials were having dinner in Tunis, Yasser Arafat was desperately trying to extricate himself from an increasingly dangerous situation in Baghdad. After all-day consultations with Saddam Hussein, the PLO chairman took his personal limousine to the airport where he planned to board a plane for the long overnight journey to Italy—where he was scheduled to meet with European diplomatic officials. But Arafat was told by the Iraqi government that he could not leave because they could not guarantee his safety. Surprised by this unexpected delay, Arafat insisted that he be allowed to depart and he boarded his aircraft.

Just before takeoff, Arafat's departure was again delayed, this time because Iraqi military officials reported mysterious flights over Baghdad. Exasperated by this further delay and worried that he might be detained if he waited much longer, Arafat told the Iraqi authorities that he would order his pilot into the air against their wishes. Iraqi security officials dismissed this threat. They warned Arafat of the dangers of flying out of Iraq and cautioned him against traveling over coalition territory. They said that they had information that he would be shot out of the sky by American aircraft. Arafat responded angrily to the warning: He said that he knew the dangers, but was willing to take his chances.

Finally, when more unexplained delays seemed imminent, Arafat issued a personal appeal to Saddam Hussein. He told Saddam Hussein that he had important meetings with European diplomats that could resolve the Gulf crisis and he insisted that he be allowed to leave. This appeal seemed to work: After hours of waiting, Arafat was finally given clearance to leave Baghdad. On the morning of January 15, Arafat's personal jet

lifted off from Saddam Hussein International Airport, headed
north, crossed into Turkey, and then flew west over the Mediterranean. It was a nerve-wracking journey: Arafat was only
allowed to cross coalition airspace at the sufferance of the
United States and its allies, whose combat aircraft shadowed his
flight.

Arafat directed his pilot to Italy, and while in the air he made
a vain attempt to expand the number of officials whom he
would be meeting in Rome. He was in constant contact with
both French and Italian diplomats, but none of them told him
about the murder of Abu Iyad. Nor had Arafat learned of the
assassinations from PLO officials in Tunis, who wanted him out
of Baghdad before giving him the news. Finally, after Arafat
had confirmed his meetings in Rome, he was informed of the
three killings. His aircraft was nearing the eastern coast of Italy.
The PLO chairman ordered his pilot to turn the plane south.

In Tunis, meanwhile, the murder of the three officials had
thrown the PLO into crisis. The organization was in chaos and
security guards whose loyalty remained unquestioned were ordered to disarm anyone who had joined the PLO during the
last three years. Friends of the assassin were questioned repeatedly on his motives, while senior organization officials penned
special alerts to PLO offices around the world. They feared that
a major internal coup was under way as part of an American-
Israeli plan to wage war against Iraq. Arafat's return exacerbated the situation; his guard was doubled and after his arrival
he was quickly driven to his villa where he closeted himself in
meetings with PLO leaders. There was now no question about
his next move—he postponed his meeting with European diplomats and made plans to attend Abu Iyad's funeral, which
would be held the next day.

A major investigation of the assassinations was under way,
but PLO officials were stymied by the incident and who might
be behind it. Even so, within twenty-four hours of Abu Iyad's
death, Bassam Abu-Sharif inexplicably issued a statement blaming Israel for the killings. The statement was dead wrong: Preliminary findings by PLO investigators indicated that Israel

probably had nothing to do with the murder, and further evidence indicated that they were as surprised by the murders as the Palestinians. Nevertheless, the outlines of a conspiracy by one of the PLO's greatest enemies *did* become clearer in the days and weeks that followed. The assassin, it was learned, had not given up his ties to Abu Nidal, even though he had been with the PLO for many months. He apparently killed Abu Iyad on Nidal's orders in an act of revenge against the one PLO official who was most responsible for dismembering his organization. But other, even more intriguing information was soon made available to the PLO about the true motives behind Zeid's actions.

According to senior PLO officials, Abu Iyad's death may well have been ordered by Saddam Hussein himself. The organization's security service gathered an impressive array of evidence to back their claim: The murder of the three PLO officials, they pointed out, was timed to produce the maximum impact inside the PLO at the very moment that it was making progress in finding a diplomatic resolution of the Iraq crisis. The assassinations also came when Arafat was under virtual arrest at the Baghdad airport. PLO leaders also decided that Zeid had targeted Abu Hol—who had returned from the Iraqi capital with news that Saddam Hussein was not going to withdraw his army from Kuwait—in addition to Abu Iyad. The most important piece of evidence, however, was common knowledge: If Saddam Hussein wanted to strike at his enemies in the PLO, the one person he would have to murder was Abu Iyad. In one brutal swoop, the PLO's ranking moderates—including one of the first PLO officials to call for a two-state solution with Israel—were eliminated.

Abu Iyad was buried in Tunis on the afternoon of January 15. Yasser Arafat and Abu Iyad's son served as pallbearers. The senior PLO leader had wanted to be buried in Jordan, on a hill overlooking the West Bank, but his wish could not be fulfilled— the Middle East was on the verge of a major conflict and transferring his body to Amman was out of the question. As his flag-draped coffin was taken from his home for burial, PLO leaders were already assessing the impact of his murder on the organization's leadership.

Abu Iyad's assassination had a profound effect on Arafat. He retreated to his villa on the outskirts of Tunis after the burial and remained secluded for many hours. Later on in the afternoon of the fifteenth, he spoke with Bassam Abu-Sharif and accepted an invitation to be his guest in La Marsa the next day. Abu-Sharif said that Arafat needed a rest and he brought him the most recent news from the Gulf, which he said was "all negative." The Americans, Abu-Sharif reported, were organizing a military push against Iraq. Arafat's aide was downcast: The war could start at any minute, he said. But this news seemed to invigorate Arafat, who dismissed Abu-Sharif's gloomy assessment and said that they must plan more meetings with European officials. It was still possible, he argued, to negotiate a solution to the crisis.

On the afternoon of January 16, Arafat met with a group of top assistants to outline another diplomatic blitz. After finishing this strategy session, Arafat took a limousine to La Marsa, where he joined Bassam Abu-Sharif for dinner. They talked about Arafat's friendship with Abu Iyad and reviewed the events of the last two days. Arafat was honest and blunt: He had had many disagreements over the years with his senior associate, he told Abu-Sharif, but his loss was a terrible blow. Abu Iyad had been one of the original founders of the organization.

After the dinner, Arafat announced to his security detail that he would stay in La Marsa for the night. That was not unusual; Arafat routinely made last-minute decisions about where he would sleep and he made a point of staying at the homes of his top lieutenants from time to time. Abu-Sharif said that he would stay awake to watch the news reports on CNN.

Several hours later, at 2:15 A.M., Abu-Sharif emerged from his office and shouted to his security guards. He ordered them to double their detail and he ran up the stairway to knock on Arafat's door. He told Arafat that the United States had launched a massive air bombardment of Iraq. Arafat came downstairs several minutes later and sat watching the news in stunned silence. He was dressed in khaki pants and shirt, but was not wearing his kaffiyeh. He was slumped onto the sofa beside Abu-Sharif's desk. He could barely believe what he saw.

The television screen across the room was filled with the tracer fire of Baghdad's antiaircraft weapons. In the distance, beyond the windows of Baghdad's Al-Rashid Hotel, the thud of bombs could be heard—the first of thousands that would be dropped on Iraqi military emplacements. Air raid sirens wailed over the voice of CNN reporter Peter Arnett. Arafat remained silent. Abu-Sharif's aides were scurrying in and out of the room, casting sidelong glances at Arafat, as they brought telefaxes from the PLO's worldwide offices. Abu-Sharif read them quickly and then gave them to Arafat.

After one hour, Arafat went back upstairs to bed. He was clearly stunned by the American military move against Iraq, but he was not depressed. He believed that the PLO would survive the crisis and emerge from it stronger than ever. That had always been true, even after the crises of Jordan and Beirut— and it would be true now. He told Abu-Sharif that they would discuss the situation in the morning, when things were clearer. They would have to set out on a new course. Arafat said that he was convinced that after the war was over the United States would finally move to resolve the Palestinian problem. As always, they would have to turn to the PLO to find a solution: The United States, he said, simply had no other choice.

CHAPTER THREE
WASHINGTON

Yasser Arafat may have been convinced that the United States would turn to the PLO to find peace in the Middle East, but James Baker was not. After America's effortless triumph in the Gulf War, the secretary of state moved quickly to reap the benefits of the victory—and to make certain that the PLO had no role in a Middle East peace settlement. Baker was enraged by Arafat's support of Saddam Hussein and believed that his decision had so tarnished the PLO's standing in the region that it could no longer claim to represent the Palestinians.

Baker's views were colored by his personal animosity toward Arafat; he believed the PLO chairman's support of Iraq had prolonged the crisis. If Arafat had not allowed Saddam Hussein to use the Palestinian cause for his own ends, Baker concluded, the United States-Iraq confrontation might have been settled without a military clash. He held Arafat indirectly responsible for the loss of hundreds of American lives and thousands more in Kuwait, Iraq, and Saudi Arabia.

Arafat's mistake was Baker's gain: The PLO was no longer an obstacle to convening an international conference. Instead of having to cajole Israeli Prime Minister Yitzhak Shamir into negotiating with the Tunis leadership, Baker could now simply not bother to invite them. At one time such a purposeful slight would have been unthinkable, but in the wake of the American victory, Baker had little to fear from Arab leaders—especially those who had been part of the United States-led coalition. The leaders of Syria, Saudi Arabia, and Egypt, in particular, were as disgusted with Arafat's leadership as Baker was. The PLO had become the Middle East's newest pariah, a role that had once been reserved solely for Israel.

The PLO's dreary state was reflected by the Palestinian community in the occupied territories, which emerged from the war in a precarious position. In the weeks leading up to the American attack on Iraq, large numbers of Palestinians believed the Persian Gulf confrontation would result in an ignominious American retreat from the Middle East, Israel's humiliating withdrawal from the occupied territories, and the establishment of a Palestinian state. Iraq's collapse shattered these delusions; Saddam Hussein's destruction had been so complete that Palestinian leaders wondered how Arafat could have supported him in the first place.

Within days of the end of the war, the euphoria that had gripped the occupied territories during Iraq's missile attacks on Tel Aviv was replaced by fears of Israeli revenge. After twenty years of occupation, Palestinians feared that their national aspirations could now be ignored altogether. This sobering thought gave life to innumerable rumors: that the United States would move to break up the PLO, that the American government would stand aside as Israel abandoned Gaza to Muslim fundamentalists, or that Israel would transfer the Palestinian population of the West Bank to Jordan.

The anxiety produced by Iraq's defeat also led to mounting disputes about what policy the Palestinian community should adopt. A number of leading figures in the West Bank privately urged a complete political break between the occupied territories and the PLO leadership in Tunis; the separation would make dealing with the Americans much easier, and was inevitable in any event. Such advice was unsettling, however, for

Faisal Husseini, Sari Nusseibeh, Hanan Ashrawi, and a handful of other West Bank leaders who were Arafat partisans and who were viewed as the leading moderates in the occupied territories. Even more disturbing, those moderates—who were organized around Husseini's think tank in East Jerusalem—now found themselves caught between the sullen Palestinian populace, on the one hand, and a group of liberal Israeli officials whom Husseini and his colleagues had embraced as allies, on the other. The territories' moderates had spent years convincing these Israelis that the PLO wanted peace, but now that argument was discredited.

For Faisal Husseini, the heir to the political legacy of the West Bank's leading patrician family, the PLO's position in the Gulf War was especially painful. As a former student at Baghdad University, Husseini befriended a number of Iraqis who kept him informed about the kind of regime that Saddam Hussein was running. He was incensed, but not surprised, by Iraq's invasion of Kuwait. But while he abhorred Saddam Hussein's actions, he found it difficult to disregard the wishes of the vast number of Palestinians who supported Iraq and found it impossible to break with Arafat.

Sari Nusseibeh, the Oxford- and Harvard-educated philosopher, high-profile Fatah adherent, and Husseini's closest colleague at the Arab Studies Society, held the same view. Nusseibeh was an intellectual with a bent for radical politics whose articulate defense of Palestinian rights inflamed Israeli conservatives: During the Gulf War, the Shamir government arrested him as an Iraqi spy. The flimsy accusation eliminated whatever doubts Nusseibeh harbored about Arafat's leadership and reinforced his suspicion that Israel and the United States were acting in league to destroy the PLO. He later held the United States responsible for its "refusal to understand the real position" of the PLO regarding Saddam Hussein. The Tunis leadership had never supported Iraq's invasion, he argued, but only advocated that the crisis be resolved through negotiations.

Hanan Ashrawi, the cosmopolitan, American-educated Ramallah Christian, was caught in the same quandary as Husseini and Nusseibeh. She privately acknowledged that the PLO had badly mismanaged its own political position and she admitted that Arafat had underestimated American resolve in the Gulf War. When Iraqi missiles flew over Ramallah on their way to Israel, she shook her head in outraged frustration at the reaction of Palestinians, who appeared on the rooftops of their West Bank homes to watch and cheer the incoming missiles.

All three of these Palestinian leaders had little sympathy for Saddam Hussein and found the PLO's support of the Iraqi regime difficult to defend. But each was also trapped by the emotions of their community and their desire to remain loyal to the PLO's program. The frustration of Palestinian moderates was best summarized by Saeb Erakat, a prominent Jericho intellectual whose passionate argument for Palestinian rights during an appearance on United States television touched a nerve with the American public and made him an instant celebrity. "Everyone criticized the Palestinians by saying that no one in their right minds could choose to cheer for such a man [as Saddam Hussein]," Erakat said just after the end of the war, "but that is just the point. We have been under occupation for over twenty years. Who did the Americans expect us to cheer for? Israel?"

The Israeli response was unsympathetic. In the first weeks after the end of the Gulf War, Husseini, Nusseibeh, Ashrawi, and Erakat all noticed a distinct cooling of relations with their Israeli allies. Their support of the PLO was now questioned by those who had once taken it for granted. Their Israeli friends now argued that their refusal to break with Tunis bared their own moral and political weakness—they did not remain silent because the Palestinian people cheered the incoming missiles, these Israelis argued, but the Palestinian people cheered the incoming missiles *because* they remained silent.

The argument hit its target: In the months that followed the end of the Gulf War, Palestinian moderates in the occupied territories began to distance themselves from PLO leaders in Tunis. But the stain of the PLO's decision to support Saddam Hussein remained. As a result, Israeli leftists who opposed the occupation were no longer frequent visitors to their Palestinian friends in East Jerusalem. Palestinian moderates were caught in a dangerous high-wire act: While Husseini, Nusseibeh, Ashrawi, Erakat—and many others—still publicly recognized the PLO's authority, they decided they could no longer afford to remain junior partners in the struggle to create a Palestinian state. They had few other options; from their unofficial headquarters at Husseini's New Orient House, the leadership of the occupied territories surveyed a hostile political landscape inhabited by an increasingly militant population and an utterly indifferent group of former allies. They were alone and isolated.

Faisal Husseini was forced to face these obstacles without the PLO's help or support, since Tunis seemed as unsympathetic to the views of those in the occupied territories—the "insiders" as the press dubbed them—as were Husseini's moderate Israeli friends. Faced with this political puzzle, and knowing that he was reversing long-standing PLO policy, Husseini made a fateful and courageous decision: If James Baker came calling during his many trips to the Middle East, Husseini would lead a delegation to meet with him. And if the secretary of state invited a group of West Bank and Gaza Palestinians to attend a peace conference, Husseini would do that too. He would act first, and deal with Arafat later.

While Baker could bypass Arafat in his search for peace, he knew that he could not ignore the Palestinian problem. He had gone to great lengths to impress this point on George Bush, whose triumphant postwar speech to the U.S. Congress on March 6 contained a uniquely Bakerlike formulation. "A comprehensive peace must be grounded in United Nations Security Council Resolutions 242 and 338 and the principle of territory for peace," Bush said. "This principle must be elaborated to provide for Israel's security and recognition, and at the same time for legitimate Palestinian political rights."

Bush's statement was filled with a number of immediately recognizable phrases—the most important of which had to do with Resolution 242. Passed after the end of the Six Day War in 1967, 242 called on Israel to give up the lands it had conquered. Six years later, Resolution 338 reinforced this principle. But Bush and Baker knew that the resolutions were purposely ambiguous; they did not require Israel to give up *all* of the land it had occupied in 1967—that detail was to be decided in the negotiations themselves. This subtle point was an important piece of ammunition in James Baker's arsenal when it came to talking with Israeli Prime Minister Yitzhak Shamir, who believed that the West Bank was part of Greater Israel.

In the months ahead, Baker argued to Shamir that 242 and 338 did not mean that Israel had to give up any piece of the occupied territories, but only that they were required to negotiate with their enemies. (Or, in the blunt linguistic construction of Likud party member Benny Begin: "We are negotiating the final status of the territories—just as the resolutions say we should. And these negotiations will have one result: the territories belong to us. Period.") At the same time that Baker was using the resolutions in an attempt to bring Israel to the negotiating table, he was also using them as an inducement for the Syrians, Jordanians, Lebanese, and Palestinians, who could only hope to regain their territories by negotiating with their Israeli enemies.

Baker wanted to make sure that the UN resolutions became an essential touchstone for Israel and its Arab antagonists, not because of what they required, but because of what they did *not* require. Baker was a master of the ambiguous and the UN resolutions seemed ready-made for the kind of diplomacy that he practiced. "That a legal document could seem to say two different things and still make everyone happy appealed to Baker," a State Department assistant who worked with him said. "To Baker, such obscurity seemed to be the essence of diplomacy."

Baker's use of the UN resolutions symbolized his style. While the secretary of state went out of his way to argue that he was a simple Texas lawyer who just happened to find himself involved in the single most important feud of modern times, his special talent for breaking through intensely volatile confrontations made him the one indispensable personality of the peace process. "Jim Baker has only two deeply held convictions," a friend of many years says. "The first is that the free market system is probably better than government control and the second is that talking is probably better than fighting."

The operative word is "probably," a term that Baker used to great effect in his travels through the Middle East in the five months after the end of the United States-Iraq war. Would the Israelis attend the conference if the Palestinians included members from Jerusalem? Did Israel's latest statement on settlements help or hinder the negotiations? "We can probably deal with that in good time," Baker would say. Was that a yes? Or a no? In many ways, the negotiations over the conference—who would attend, under what conditions, where it would be held, and who would speak—appealed to Baker's deeply held legal convictions, which were honed through twenty years of service with the upscale Houston law firm of Andrews Kurth, then refined by fifteen years as a Cabinet member in two separate administrations.

Baker had three other qualities that seemed to make him particularly well suited to dealing with the Israelis and Palestinians. The first was that he always gave the impression that he would never board an airplane that was about to crash and burn. That was good news for those on both sides who wanted peace—it meant that so long as he was on the job there was always a chance that his plan for a Middle East conference just might work. Baker, the Israelis and Palestinians knew, hated failure and was an optimist in a tradition that defined American diplomacy: He believed that if he could just get the Israelis and Palestinians to sit down together, they would both gain a stake in the negotiations. It would then be in their interest to make them succeed.

Baker's second quality was that he was enormously tough when he wanted to be—as he was when Faisal Husseini balked at a proposal that the Palestinians should attend an international conference as part of a Jordanian delegation ("Well then,

don't come," Baker said quietly)—and sympathetic when necessary (as he was with Yitzhak Shamir during his first postwar
trip to the region. "I know how difficult this is," he said, "but no
one is going to make you do something you don't want to do").
These emotional swings were deliberate; Baker knew that the
Palestinians would agree to be part of a Jordanian delegation
(since they had no choice) just as he knew that he could force
the Israelis to do exactly what they had no intention of doing,
like sitting across from their enemies.

But Baker's single-minded patience, his third essential quality, was his most important. It was gained through years of
experience as George Bush's political eyes and ears and his
almost single-handed molding of the Texas Republican into a
national political figure. While Baker hated playing second fid-
dle to Bush and sometimes wondered aloud why he would do
for his close friend what he would not do for himself, he rev-
eled in his reputation as a Washington insider. Much to his
credit, Baker never gained a reputation for being ruthless, despite his years in the American capital. That description was left
to White House assistants—and to the President himself.

In an attempt to explain Baker's singular talent for accomplishment, and his fame as a patient negotiator, the American
media turned to his love of turkey hunting (there were no less
than a half-dozen major news stories on the topic during the
Bush presidency). Baker loved to go turkey hunting during his
off hours at his Rock Pile Ranch, located just south of San
Antonio. The secret to successful turkey hunting is to remain
absolutely silent for long periods of time, waiting for the quarry
to make its appearance. When it does, the hunter springs up
from behind a blind and expertly blows the turkey's head off.
But, in a revealing interview in *Time* magazine in 1988, Baker
rejected the "easy pickings" theory of "the turkey shoot."

"The thing is getting them in," he said. "They're smart as
hell. Their eyesight and hearing are incredible, about ten times
better than a human's. The trick is in getting them where you
want them, on your terms. Then you control the situation, not
them. The important thing is knowing that it's in your hands,

that you can do whatever you determine is in your interest to do."

That the United States gained considerable prestige from its victory in the Gulf War and that Baker was a man of prodigious talents was no guarantee, however, that Israel and its enemies would sit down to talk peace. This point was brought home to Baker during his first trip to the Middle East, in early March of 1991. During his meeting with Faisal Husseini and other Palestinian leaders in East Jerusalem, Baker was astonished to hear that they would only agree to attend an international conference if they were officially designated as representatives of the PLO. Even making allowance for this demand as nothing more than an opening gambit in a long series of meetings, the secretary of state still found it hard to believe that the representatives from the territories refused to make even a symbolic break with the Palestinian leadership in Tunis. But Baker's response was laconic; he patiently explained that Israel would never agree to meet with a Palestinian delegation under such conditions, and he left it at that.

Baker's next stop was across town, to talk with Yitzhak Shamir. The meeting did not go well. Shamir reiterated his opposition to talking to anyone representing the PLO and he then added that Israel would not attend an international conference until the Palestinians had agreed to put an end to the intifada. Baker responded that he did not believe that the Palestinian leadership would agree to end the uprising, even if they could. But he pointedly suggested to Shamir that both sides could take measures to lessen tensions; Israel, for instance, could put an end to the building of settlements in the territories. Shamir was noncommittal, but answered that he might be willing to take that step—which was an unexpectedly surprising concession.

Shamir's statement on Israeli settlements fueled Baker's feeling that his trip had been successful and that real progress had been made toward convening an international peace conference on the region. But Baker's confidence was short-lived:

When he returned to the United States, he learned that Shamir had announced that new housing units would be built on the Golan Heights and that the prime minister had issued new restrictions on the movement of Palestinians in the occupied territories.

Any plans for convening an international conference on the Middle East might have ended there, but Baker refused to give up. Rather, he publicly emphasized the positive aspects of his meetings and accentuated the personal relationship he had struck up with Palestinian and Israeli officials. But Baker also leaked word to the press that Husseini's demand that the PLO be included in the talks would not be honored, and that Shamir's intransigent attitude on the settlement issue was unacceptable. Baker then repeated an interesting anecdote on his private meeting with the Israeli prime minister to the press: He told a number of reporters that, just as the meeting was ending, he had pulled out a recent Israeli newspaper poll that showed that nearly half of the Israeli public approved of trading land for peace. Baker's leak was perfectly timed; he wanted to show Shamir that he was not the only one who could use the tactic of surprise to send diplomatic messages.

Two more trips to the Middle East followed these initial meetings, but with very little progress. Throughout March and April, Baker did everything that he could to bring each of the parties to an agreement on the fundamental principles that would lead to a meeting to begin the process of resolving the Arab-Israeli conflict. While he had little to show for his efforts, Baker remained surprisingly optimistic that his mission would eventually succeed. This remained true even after the low point of his fourth trip to the region, during the middle of May. It was during that fourth journey that Baker learned that the Shamir government would expand its settlements in the occupied territories, over American objections. Baker interpreted the disclosure as a direct personal slap at his diplomatic efforts and he warned Shamir that the decision would harm Israel's standing in the international community. Baker also issued a personal warning—the United States would not stand by while

Israel built settlements in violation of United States wishes and international law. Baker was as blunt with Shamir as he had ever been. The Bush administration, he said, would actively oppose the approval of $10 billion in loan guarantees to Israel, which Shamir desperately wanted, if the Israeli government persisted in its settlements policy.

Baker was speaking from a position of strength not only in the United States, but also in Israel, where he received unexpected help from conservative Israeli politicians. Foreign Minister David Levy, for instance, announced during an official visit to Great Britain that he believed Israel should agree to attend an international peace conference. Levy's surprise statement showed that Shamir was vulnerable in his own party.

Ironically, Shamir's political exposure was also pointed up by Israel's ambassador to the United States, Zalmon Shoval—a very conservative, telegenic Likud party member and Shamir partisan who had a habit of putting his foot in his mouth. "Israel," he conceded during an American television interview, "will have at some point to choose between U.S. aid to absorb Soviet and Ethiopian immigrants and continuing the settlement drive in the territories." Shamir was aghast at Shoval's blunt admission; he had carefully maintained a diligent silence on the loan question since March, so that he could couch his request for the guarantee as a "humanitarian issue." The last thing he wanted was to tie the pledge to the Middle East peace process and, by indirection, to the building of new settlements in the occupied territories. While Shamir did not believe that the Bush administration would engage in a legislative showdown on the guarantees question, he did not want to take any chances.

Shoval issued a hasty apology for his remark and quickly corrected the record. It was all a big misunderstanding: What he had meant to say was that the two issues were *not* related.

But they were, and Baker could not have described the link any more accurately. The secretary of state's position on the question of the $10-billion loan guarantee was suddenly out in the open—and he had not had to say anything at all. If Israel wanted American help in absorbing the flood of refugees coming from the Soviet Union, then Shamir would have to abandon his settlement scheme and attend an international peace conference. Privately, Baker went even further. As far as the United States was concerned, he told a number of reporters, the only way that Israel could continue to maintain its security was to pursue peace with its enemies. If the Israeli government did not believe that was true, then the Bush administration was willing to take the steps necessary to make it abundantly clear.

The opening shot in the Baker-Shamir feud came on May 23, when Baker testified on the loan guarantee question before the House Foreign Affairs Committee. The showdown was marked by a bitter exchange between Israel's supporters and the secretary of state. "Every time I have gone to Israel in connection with the peace process, I have been met with the announcement of new settlement activity," Baker said. "Nothing has made my job of trying to find Arab and Palestinian partners for Israel more difficult than being greeted by a new settlement every time I arrive. I don't think there is any bigger obstacle to peace than [Israeli] settlement activity." In all the previous months of negotiation, Baker had not once used such harsh words to characterize his views on the Shamir government.

While there were no public clues as to why Baker chose his testimony in Congress to put pressure on Shamir, there were a number of private signals that the secretary of state was running out of patience with the Israeli government. The first hint came during his fourth shuttle to the region, when Baker broke his customary habit of traveling by air and decided to journey overland from Amman, Jordan, to Israel via the Allenby Bridge. "He wanted to get a look at the lay of the land for himself, without any of us [his aides] present," a senior State Department official said. "Baker wanted to see the occupied territories close up."

Upon his arrival in Jerusalem, Baker ordered several hundred copies of Elias Chacour's well-known defense of the Palestinian cause, *We Belong to the Land,* and directed that they be distributed to senior officials in the United States government, including Israel's most devoted supporters on Capitol Hill. "I know a lot of people in Washington who ought to read it," Baker said.

But the incident that convinced Baker that he had to challenge Shamir on the loan guarantee issue came during his visit with the prime minister in Jerusalem. While the meeting opened cordially, Baker and Shamir were soon engaged in a verbal standoff. At one point, Shamir even seemed to be setting new conditions for Israel's attendance at the proposed Middle East conference. Visibly frustrated by the Israeli prime minister's refusal to talk specifics, Baker fired off a number of questions that he said needed an immediate answer, and he removed a three-by-five-inch card from his suit coat pocket.

Shamir's answers to Baker's questions made it clear that after nearly four months of intense negotiations, he was unwilling to concede a single point. Instead, he reiterated his demand that Israel be allowed to veto the name of any Palestinian attending the conference (a condition he previously indicated he would be willing to drop) and he adamantly refused to put an end to settlement activity. As for Syria's recent request that the United Nations host the conference, Shamir was just as adamant.

The Syrian government wanted the UN to play a major role, Baker said.

No, Shamir responded.

By the time he returned to Washington, the exasperated secretary of state had made up his mind—he would take on Israel in public. After a meeting with President Bush, Baker blasted Shamir in the press and then kept up the public pressure throughout the remainder of the month. On June 1, Baker dispatched a compromise proposal to Shamir and Arab leaders on an international conference. The proposition was summarily rejected by the Israeli prime minister, who repeated his demand that Israel be allowed to dictate the composition of the Palestinian delegation. Baker was again maddened by the Israeli government's inability to compromise on even the smallest point and he informed a number of foreign diplomats that his relationship with Shamir was nearing the breaking point. One of them, Prince Bandar bin Sultan, Saudi Arabia's ambassador to the United States, was startled by the apparent depth of Baker's anger. "July is going to be a very important month," he said after a meeting with the secretary of state. "Either the parties will come to a consensus and meet each other halfway, or there will be a line drawn."

The line was drawn on July 1, when President Bush publicly criticized Israel's settlement policy. This statement was followed by a unanimous communiqué issued by America's European allies calling on Israel to cease construction on all settlements in the occupied territories. Finally, on July 20, during his fifth mission to the region, Baker presented a proposal for face-to-face talks between Israel and its Arab neighbors to Syrian President Hafez al-Assad, who praised it as "a firm basis for peace." Two days later, Assad formally accepted the American proposal and, on July 21, Baker obtained Jordan's agreement. Palestinians in the occupied territories also made it clear that they would join the conference, even if that meant being part of a Jordanian delegation.

The pressure was now on Shamir. Faced with a unanimous response from the Arab governments, a near revolt in the Knesset, the possibility of major defections from his own party, and a rising tide of public sentiment in favor of a peace conference, Shamir began slowly to yield to Baker's pressure. But the Israeli prime minister had still not surrendered and he moved quickly to regain the psychological initiative.

Within days of Baker's July 20 proposal, Shamir issued a statement that said that even if Israel were to attend a conference, it would make "no territorial concessions" and, days later—as Baker was concluding another round of discussions in Jerusalem—he announced the construction of another 380 new residences in the occupied territories. Shamir had still not lost his impeccable sense of timing, but when the secretary of state returned to Washington on July 31, he knew that while Israel had not yet committed itself to attending an international conference on the Middle East, it was slowly edging that way. The pressure was now on Shamir.

Baker had successfully coaxed the Israeli prime minister into

participating in a process that he opposed by winning concessions on demands that were enshrined as part of the Likud
party's political principles, and that Shamir was imperiously
certain would never meet with Arab approval. The first principle was that the PLO would not be represented at the conference and that the Palestinians would attend under the
auspices of Jordan. When it appeared that the Palestinians
would attend the conference under these conditions, Shamir
made a new demand. He said that there would be no negotiations on the status of Jerusalem and that the Jordanian delegation could not include any Palestinians from the city. When
this stipulation was met with grudging Arab approval, Shamir
made yet another demand. Israel's attendance at the conference, he insisted, did not commit his nation to making any kind
of compromise. The Israeli prime minister obviously hoped
that this demand would scuttle the proposed talks, but Syrian,
Jordanian, Lebanese, and Palestinian leaders, who were un-
doubtedly acting on the advice of Baker, remained silent. Only
Egyptian President Hosni Mubarak offered an understated response, saying that he thought that Shamir should be "more
positive" and "flexible."

It was now Shamir's turn to be exasperated. Faced with an
increasingly hostile Israeli electorate and a prospective national
election that would be decided on the peace issue, Shamir accepted Baker's proposal. With the American President ready to
issue public invitations, Shamir believed that Israel could not
afford to appear unwilling to participate in the negotiations.
Even Shamir's hard-line supporters in the American Jewish
community were beginning to worry that his stubbornness
would start to erode public support for Israel. Added to that
were the ineffable gains that Israel would obtain by agreeing
with Baker: Its attendance at an international conference would
be a de facto recognition of Israel's right to exist by its Arab
enemies—Shamir could gain a major victory just by showing up.

Shamir was predictably upbeat at the end of Baker's final
journey to Jerusalem. "For the first time the president of Syria

is ready to negotiate with Israel," he said, and he implied that
there would be an early Israeli cabinet vote approving Baker's
proposal. "As the situation stands now," he said, "we are approaching the beginning of negotiations." Despite these optimistic words, Shamir was still trying to find a way to delay the
conference past the October date suggested by Baker and was
still intent on exploring ways to make the Israeli occupation of
the West Bank permanent. More specifically, however, Shamir
wanted to win congressional approval for the $10 billion in loan
guarantees to help Israel settle its Jewish immigrants from
Russia.

On August 1, the Israeli cabinet voted "in principle" to attend
a Middle East peace conference cohosted by Russia and the
United States. The endorsement was a major victory for James
Baker, who had spent five arduous months molding a series of
difficult and complex compromises. But even as Baker celebrated, he had one last piece to put into place. When he left
Israel after his last discussion with Shamir, the Palestinians had
not yet agreed to attend the international meeting. Nevertheless, Baker was persuaded that, after taking stock of their situation, they would see that they had no choice. Even given
Israel's demands—that no Palestinian from Jerusalem, from
the PLO, or from outside the occupied territories be part of a
joint Jordanian-Palestinian delegation—Baker knew that the
Palestinian leadership of the territories would be in Madrid.
Faisal Husseini himself had said as much during Baker's last
meeting with him in East Jerusalem.

Baker and Husseini had struck up a fragile friendship over
the previous five months, in part because, while they came
from different worlds, they shared a number of important
traits. Like Baker, Husseini was an adept diplomat and a
strong believer in compromise, and, like Baker, he resolutely
refused to flaunt for personal gain his family name, his legacy, his riches, or his vast influences. Whatever power Husseini had in the West Bank—and it was considerable—he kept
largely in reserve, as if fearful that once used it would be

quickly depleted. He preferred to work quietly behind the scenes, seldom lost his temper in public, and rarely allowed his frustrations to show.

There were other odd similarities. As Baker publicly deferred to Bush, so Husseini deferred to Yasser Arafat; but, like Baker, he spent a considerable amount of energy maneuvering his chief past his own political blunders. To draw the comparison more exactly, Husseini was to Arafat what Baker had often been to Bush. Just as Bush was about to guarantee his own political destruction by blasting Ronald Reagan at the Republican convention in 1980, Baker convinced him to remain silent and, in so doing, won him second place on the Republican ticket. Without Baker, Bush would have never been President. In August 1991, Husseini filled the same role for Arafat. Faced with Shamir's demands on Palestinian representation at an international conference, Arafat angrily told his aides that he would never agree to such an arrangement. It was another humiliation, he said. But Husseini disagreed and, during his last meeting with Baker in East Jerusalem, he signaled that the Palestinians would attend the proposed conference—no matter what Arafat said. He and Baker then devised a plan; the Palestinians would not agree to the Israeli demand, but they would submit a list of attendees to a conference that would meet with Israeli approval.

Husseini was one of the few Palestinians with enough prestige to stand up to the PLO chairman. As the sovereign of one of the West Bank's leading families, Husseini had gained early experience in the sometimes perilous world of Palestinian politics. Husseini's father was Abdel Kader Husseini, the commander of the central district of Jerusalem during the Palestinian fight to retain the city during Israel's 1948 War of Independence. In April of that year, Abdel Kader and his men took control of the main Jerusalem-to-Tel Aviv highway, effectively isolating Jewish forces in the holy city. Fearing that Jerusalem would be lost, the Jewish forces launched an offensive against Abdel Kader in April 1948, attacking his positions at the village of Kastel. Husseini was killed on the morning of April 5.

He was immediately accorded the honorific "first martyr of Palestine." Faisal Husseini was eight years old.

Husseini's great-uncle was Haj Amin Husseini, the grand mufti of Jerusalem who had gained fame by leading the Arab Revolt against Jewish immigration in the 1930s. During World War II, in his desperation to reverse the British policy of allowing Jewish immigration to Palestine, Haj Amin openly supported the Axis powers. He visited Mussolini in Italy and gained his support for a Palestinian homeland. The German and Italian foreign ministers sent Haj Amin a letter promising backing for "the abolition of the Jewish National Homeland in Palestine." In Berlin in 1942, Haj Amin called on Arabs to fight the British, and declared a "holy war against the British yoke of injustice, indecency, and tyranny." At the end of the war, he eluded Allied authorities and slipped into Egypt in disguise.

While Haj Amin was a controversial figure, his claim to leadership of the Palestinian community after World War II was unquestioned. In a society that revered its leading families, Haj Amin's home in Cairo became a rallying point for Palestinian nationalists. In part, that was due not simply to Haj Amin's claim as a military leader but also to the Husseini family's tracing its roots to the original Husseini mufti of Jerusalem, Abdel Kader ibn Karim al-Din Husseini, in the seventeenth century. From there, the family tradition reports, Faisal Husseini's line could be traced directly to the Prophet Mohammed.

After the death of his father, Faisal Husseini joined his great-uncle at his home in Cairo, where he spent his early years. The Husseini residence was a hotbed of Palestinian nationalism, with well-known Arab officials constantly visiting Haj Amin to receive advice and assistance. But the Husseini home was also a gathering place for the large Husseini clan; uncles, aunts, and cousins visited and sometimes came to stay indefinitely. A distant cousin came to visit after the Israeli War of Independence—a bright-eyed, flamboyant, and fearless adolescent who wanted to meet the son of the famous Abdel Kader Husseini. It was Faisal Husseini's sixth cousin, Yasser Arafat. Following this visit, and on and off for the next two decades, Husseini's and

Arafat's paths crossed, as they both worked to build a Palestinian national movement.

Despite this personal relationship, Baker knew that Husseini was making a courageous move in committing the Palestinian community to an international conference. His meetings with Baker, and his temperate public statements, had drawn fire from Tunis. Husseini spent much of his time negotiating with the PLO leadership, and reassuring them that he would not make too many concessions to the Americans. There were other dangers: During the previous months, the fifty-one-year-old West Bank leader received death threats from radical elements in the occupied territories. Husseini had also become embroiled with Palestinian radicals in the West Bank. The pressures were mounting on Husseini, and many other moderate Palestinians, to show that they could stand up to the United States and Israel.

Never one to show fear, Husseini was nevertheless shaken by the step he was about to take. While he remained confident that once the peace process was under way the Palestinian leadership could gain concessions from Israel, and a perceptible improvement in living conditions in the territories, he did not underestimate the challenge or the dangers that he faced. At one point in his last meeting with Baker, he grimly shook his head at the American secretary of state. "You are talking to a dead man," he said. "Israeli extremists or Arab radicals will get to me. I want something in my hand so the peace process can continue."

Baker nodded. "I will do my best," he said.

There was one more obstacle to overcome. While Yitzhak Shamir promised Baker that Israel would postpone its request for the $10 billion in loan guarantees it needed to resettle its flood of Russian immigrants for 120 days, on September 6 the Israeli prime minister directed his government to submit the petition to the U.S. Congress. Shamir's defiance infuriated Baker and sparked the most bitter and divisive debate between the United States and Israel in its forty-year friendship. Before the battle was over, the relationship between the Bush administration and the Shamir government had been transformed, and Baker had committed himself to making certain that Israel's governing Likud administration would receive no help from the United States in fighting its own domestic political battles.

Baker interpreted Shamir's action as a bald attempt to derail his carefully crafted search for peace. By resurrecting the loan guarantee issue, and claiming that it should not be linked to a cutback in Israeli construction of new settlements, Shamir was out to prove that his own American political network was more influential than the administration's. But Shamir's request was also viewed by Baker as a personal affront that was intentionally conceived to cause Bush political problems at home. The Shamir request not only set the administration against Israel, it placed the Bush White House on a collision course with a formidable array of powerful pro-Israel lobbying groups in the United States.

Perhaps Shamir believed that Bush and Baker's opposition to the guarantees would prove to be embarrassing: He hoped that by casting the administration as obstructing Israel's need to absorb Soviet Jews, the White House would be forced to yield on what Shamir described as "a humanitarian issue." Or, Shamir might have reasoned that Bush's recent silence on the issue would be interpreted as an endorsement of the Israeli government's settlement policies in the occupied territories. If so, then Baker's claim that the loans could actually harm the peace process would be disproved, and it would be seen that there was no link between the search for peace and Israeli policies in the occupied territories. Either way, with the American election just over one year away, Shamir did not think that the administration would risk alienating a large number of Jewish voters. It was a colossal miscalculation.

On September 8 Shamir said that delaying the loan proposal was "impossible" and on September 10 he told Israeli journalists that Bush had broken his promise to support the guarantees. On September 13, in a statement intended to increase the pressure on the administration, Shamir said that he saw "no reason to change" his position on building new settlements in the occupied territories. Each of these statements was carefully timed to obtain the maximum impact in Washington, and solidify support for the wave of pro-Israel lobbyists that soon flooded the Senate. But the more that Shamir attempted to muscle the guarantees through the American political system, the more the administration worked behind the scenes to ensure that the loan question was postponed.

In mid-September, Baker's anger boiled over. In a conversation with his top assistants, Baker said that Shamir's actions were "a direct challenge to the independence of the American political system" and "an affront" to American foreign policy. He said he was committed to defeating Shamir's loan petition.

While Shamir called on the combined might of conservative and pro-Likud Jewish leaders in the United States, Baker lined up support on Capitol Hill, including an agreement to postpone the loans from a few powerful and influential pro-Israel senators. He also convinced a number of other congressional leaders to dampen the impact of the pro-Shamir forces by arguing that the peace process should be the first priority of the Israeli government. To those who were wavering in their support for Shamir, Baker promised that he would take up the loan guarantee question as soon as Israel proved that it was interested in peace. Postponing the loan guarantee question, he said, would not harm Israel, but dealing with it before an international conference might make such a meeting impossible. Baker sounded rational, low-key, and moderate. He was not against the loan guarantees, he was only against them at this time. In comparison, Shamir sounded shrill and demanding.

It was almost as if Baker had led him into a trap: The Israeli leader simply had not realized the depth of the goodwill that Bush had gained in the Congress as a result of his victory in the Persian Gulf—for the first time since World War II, America had won a foreign conflict. That was something that Congress was not likely to forget.

Baker was gambling that the Congress would agree with Bush that Israel owed the United States a debt of gratitude for de-stroying Iraq. Baker was also gambling that when faced with the question of whether to support America's vision of peace or Shamir's vision of Greater Israel, the majority of the American Jewish community would support the administration. Having lured his quarry into the snare, Baker placed Shamir firmly in his sights.

If the Israeli prime minister had done his homework, he might have realized just how far Baker was willing to challenge his government. The tip-off to Baker's reaction to the Shamir ploy had come in a speech that Baker gave to the American-Israel Public Affairs Committee (AIPAC), the most powerful pro-Israel organization in the country, just after Bush took office. In his speech, Baker put Shamir on notice: After saying that Israel was the "foundation of the U.S. approach to the Middle East," the newly appointed secretary of state told his stunned listeners that the Jerusalem government should "lay aside" the "unrealistic vision" of a Greater Israel. "Forswear annexation," he urged. "Stop settlement activity [and] reach out to the Palestinians as neighbors who deserve political rights."

The AIPAC speech established principles that Baker was to follow over the next four years: the convening of an international conference on the region, face-to-face negotiations between Israel and its enemies, the exchange of land for peace, and the recognition of Palestinian political rights. Baker had worked for six months in 1991 to reconfirm those views.

Baker had not wanted an open, public fight with Shamir, but, once engaged, he showed why he had gained a reputation for being one of Washington's most adept political alley fighters. "It is my recommendation that the president go to the American people on the issue if that's what it takes," he said, "because it is their tax dollars that will be supporting settlement activity that we used to characterize as illegal, and which we now moderately characterize as an obstacle to peace." Shamir had never asked himself the obvious question: If Baker was not afraid of alienating a powerful American voting bloc, why would he be intimidated by the Israeli government?

Having set the trap, Baker now sprung it. In a press conference in mid-September, President Bush pointedly criticized the
lobbying efforts of the American Jewish community and lost his
temper when his support of Israel was questioned. "Just months
ago," he said at a news conference, "American men and women
in uniform risked their lives to defend Israelis in the face of
Iraq's Scud missiles and . . . while winning a war against aggression, also achieved the defeat of Israel's most dangerous adver-
sary." Bush's argument had the desired effect: Over the next
two weeks, most members of Congress (even those Democrats
who had steadfastly supported Israel in the past) took sides
with the President against Shamir. In the end, Shamir's most
obstinate allies in Congress could not even bring the loan guarantee proposal to a vote and, on October 2, the U.S. Senate
formally agreed to postpone the request for 120 days.

It had been the single most bruising battle in American-
Israeli relations and it led to bitter feelings in Israel and the
United States. In the wake of the congressional decision, one
former AIPAC official called Bush "anti-Israeli" and "a servant
of Arab interests." Likud cabinet minister Rehavam Ze'evi said
that Bush was exhibiting "anti-Semitic symptoms" and wanted
to cause "something that will bring a second Holocaust upon
the Jewish people." Shamir was stunned by the congressional
decision and blurted out a statement that reflected his own
surprise and hurt. "I think that what we see and hear in recent
days isn't correct," he said. "It isn't realistic, this isn't the American people."

But it was: A national poll taken after the decision to postpone the loan guarantees showed that 86 percent of the American people supported the President. The shift in public
opinion was especially discernible among Israel's supporters in
Congress. In just two short weeks in September, support for
Shamir's position had been transformed from an asset into a
liability. The shift in American attitudes, however, could be
perceived long before the congressional decision. During the
Gulf War, for instance, a number of national polls showed that
the majority of Americans believed that Israel should be pres-

sured to reach a peace agreement with the Palestinians, and, even more surprising, a majority said they favored the establishment of a Palestinian homeland.

At the end of September, it was clear that Shamir and his allies in Washington had been dealt a severe blow; they had misread the American electorate and overestimated their own influence. In the wake of the guarantee debacle, pro-Israeli groups that traditionally carried Israel's message on Capitol Hill were blamed for misleading Shamir and for forcing him into a showdown that he could not win. Now, shaken by the defeat and the public relations disaster it generated, the American Jewish community's major political organizations engaged in a painful examination of their own ties to Shamir and their own views of the peace process.

In Israel, meanwhile, Prime Minister Shamir and his cabinet attempted to swiftly rebuild its badly damaged relationship with the United States. Shamir realized that there was little he could do to heal the breach between himself and Baker, but he attempted to put the United States-Israeli relationship on a more predictable course. During a six-hour meeting with Baker on October 17, Shamir mentioned the loan guarantee debate in passing and said that he hoped that any misunderstandings would not harm long-term United States-Israeli relations. Having won the debate, Baker could afford to be gracious; he said that he had always been a strong supporter of Israel and that Shamir could be assured that the United States would always remain Israel's strongest ally. The next day, Russia and the United States issued invitations to an international conference on the Middle East to be held at the end of the month in Madrid, Spain. On October 20, the Israeli cabinet voted to attend the conference.

In the eighteen months that followed the end of Jim Baker's last mission to Israel, diplomats, foreign policy analysts, and journalists all weighed in with their views on why Baker was successful in bringing together Arabs and Israelis, especially when so many of his predecessors had failed. It is a question worth asking, if for no other reason than to reexamine the causes of the Arab-Israeli conflict and to reflect on whether—at any point in the past—the thousands of lives that were lost in the endless wars between the antagonists might have been saved. Before Madrid, there was much talk of peace, but few substantive steps were ever taken to follow up the almost endless initiatives designed to bring together Israel and its neighbors.

It is now part of conventional wisdom to associate the Madrid Conference with the end of the cold war. The collapse of the Soviet Union deprived Israel's major Arab enemies of a superpower supporter who supplied weapons, expertise, and economic help to the Arab world. When that largesse ended, Syria and the PLO, in particular, were forced to turn to the United States as the region's only arbiter. The attempted coup in the Soviet Union in August 1991—as Baker was immersed in the round of shuttle diplomacy to woo Israel and the Arabs to the bargaining table—underscored the uncertainty of Moscow's continuation as a significant force in the region. For all intents and purposes, what little influence the Soviet Union had in the Middle East ended with *glasnost* and was sealed forever by the unsuccessful August coup.

It is also nearly universally accepted that America's victory against Iraq brought to a close the forty years of confrontation between Israel and its Arab neighbors. The war was followed by a significant, but still largely unexplored, intellectual shift among Israel's political elite, who realized that the politics of the region had been transformed—by choosing not to fight against Iraq, Israel implicitly made itself an ally of Saudi Arabia, Kuwait, and even Syria. The Gulf War made Israel a part of the Middle East as no other event had in its forty-year history.

While Iraq's defeat eliminated the last major military threat to Israel's survival, the horrifying specter of missiles landing on Tel Aviv had a profound impact on the Israeli public. The prospect that future missiles might be armed with weapons of mass destruction placed an almost intolerable psychological burden on the Israeli populace. For four decades, Israelis had been concerned with surviving in the midst of their enemies, but by 1990 that obsession had clearly passed. It was no longer enough for Israel to survive; its inhabitants wanted their nation to prosper. The Israeli public's reaction to Iraq's Scud attacks made it clear that, after all the political analyses, commentaries, polls, and studies had been written, the one overwhelming truth was that, forty years after Israel's founding, the Israeli people wanted peace.

There is no doubt that the fall of the Soviet Union and the American victory in the Persian Gulf were important factors in pushing Israel and its Arab neighbors to the peace table. But there are other, far more significant reasons why the search for a comprehensive resolution of the Middle East conflict began in October 1991, and not sooner. For Israel, peace had almost always come as a result of a great military victory. Now that had changed. The Palestinian uprising posed a unique challenge to the Jewish state, and, in many ways, the incidents in Jebalya represented the gravest threat that Israel had ever faced. For the first time in its history, the Israeli government was involved in a war that it would not lose, but could not win.

Similarly, the Gulf War was a defining moment for the Palestine Liberation Organization. Through more than two decades of conflict, the PLO's senior leaders, and especially Yasser Arafat, had never abandoned the dream of reclaiming the land of Palestine—all of it. Even after opening a tentative dialogue with the United States at the end of the Reagan years, Arafat's organization found it nearly impossible to end its war with Israel. The American war with Iraq changed all of that. From the moment that American warplanes dropped their bombs on Baghdad, Yasser Arafat was committed to the search for peace.

On October 24, Arab delegates to the Middle East peace conference met in Damascus, Syria, to chart a common strategy. They agreed that none of the Arab participants would make a separate agreement with Israel, a significant decision that was to have an enormous impact on later events. Any peace treaty would have to be—in a word that would be used again and again in the months ahead—"comprehensive." After the meeting, the Arab delegates returned to their capitals to make final preparations for the trip to Madrid.

In Jerusalem, Yitzhak Shamir announced that he would personally lead the Israeli delegation to the peace talks. His decision was a sign of things to come. For the next eight months, the Israeli prime minister—his beliefs, attitudes, and his commitment to the establishment of Greater Israel—would dominate his government's policy on negotiating with its enemies. Shamir viewed the coming international meeting with suspicion and he gave his top assistants strict instructions to keep contacts with Arab delegates to a minimum; there would be no back-room or hallway diplomacy in Madrid, only an appeal to Arab leaders that they demonstrate their commitment to the negotiating process. And there would be no talk of land for peace.

CHAPTER FOUR
MADRID

On the first morning of the Madrid Conference, David Kimche, a former Israeli intelligence official, walked down a long hallway of Madrid's Royal Palace and into a room that contained members of the Jordanian and Palestinian delegations. The Jordanians and Palestinians had met to relax, talk, and have coffee together before the opening of the momentous events that they hoped would transform the face of the Middle East. They were virtually sequestered for nearly thirty minutes. But that did not stop Kimche, who was known to them as one of the living symbols of Israeli power. They stopped to stare at the Israeli as he strode across the room, nodded to a small knot of Arabs in front of him, and quietly and self-consciously poured himself a cup of coffee.

Kimche was a former journalist who had spent years in the netherworld of Israeli intelligence activities. He spent much of the 1950s and 1960s operating for the Mossad in Asia and Africa, and then, in the 1970s, in Iran, where he developed close relations with the Shah. When Menachem Begin became Israeli prime minister, Kimche's career took off. While he was a member of the Labor party defense establishment, Begin admired the Mossad and sent Kimche to Morocco to help persuade King Hassan to act as an intermediary in Israeli talks with Anwar Sadat.

But Kimche's career as an intelligence officer was cut short by an internal battle over who would head the Mossad after its then-director Yitzhak Hofi retired. Kimche resigned, but took on the job of Shamir's director general of the foreign ministry. He soon aligned himself with Ariel Sharon and members of his shadowy cadre of wise men, who were dubbed "Arik's kitchen." Even though he never realized his cherished dream to become the head of the Mossad, Kimche became a powerful figure in the Israeli establishment, was close to Shamir, and was admired by the Israelis as the tough embodiment of their pragmatic foreign policy. He was the supersleuth, and was known as "the man with the suitcase."

Now, here he was, quietly pouring himself coffee in a crowded room of stunned and disbelieving Arabs, who were watching him suspiciously. He turned to the room, smiled, and raised his cup. "I just thought," he later said to a journalist, "that I would come and share a moment with some old friends—and wish them luck." After his demitoast, the delegates from Jordan and the territories crowded around to meet him. If Kimche's action was any indication, then the days of talks that lay just ahead would be filled with surprises.

James Baker had done the impossible. He had convinced the Arabs and Israelis to discuss peace at an international conference. His success marked the biggest breakthrough in the Arab-Israeli conflict since Egyptian President Anwar Sadat and Israeli Prime Minister Menachem Begin had signed the Camp David Accords, back in 1978. It was no wonder then that when delegates from Israel and its Arab enemies agreed to meet for the first time across a table in the ornate and massive Royal Palace in Madrid on October 30, 1991, literally thousands of members of the press from all over the world were in attendance. Baker's accomplishment was so extraordinary that some journalists, and a handful of diplomats, thought that it might be possible for the Arabs and Israelis to negotiate a breakthrough in the peace process right away, while they were meeting in Madrid. All that needed to happen was for the delegates to translate the palpable sense that something extraordinary was taking place into a new reality. It was possible and, given the amazing meeting, anything was possible.

Baker was under no such delusion. While he had negotiated the attendance of the parties to the conference, and issued letters of invitation, it was the unwritten, private stipulations that Baker wanted to enforce—and that he thought were the most important part of the conference. Primarily, the American secretary of state hoped that the Arab and Israeli delegates would set a conciliatory tone and not revisit past incidents that divided them. That would be a good start and also be a break with the past. It was important for each side to look forward to building a new regional order and, to do this, he thought, they had to get out of what one State Department official dubbed "the blame business." He urged this stance in meetings with each of the delegations. "Don't point fingers," he urged the Palestinians, "don't point fingers."

At one point Baker purposely took aside the Syrian foreign minister, Farouk al-Sharaa, for a short private discussion on just this point. Baker liked Sharaa personally—he was tough and opinionated, but intelligent—and he knew that the Syrians believed that they had gone out of their way to help to make Madrid a reality. Now, he feared, they would take the opportunity to wage a verbal campaign against Israel, painting it as an aggressor and an obstacle to peace. Nothing would be accomplished. Such a position would only make Israeli Prime Minister Yitzhak Shamir more intransigent, Baker told the Syrian foreign minister. The conversation was short, and pleasant. Sharaa nodded his agreement, but said nothing. Baker went away worried.

Baker was also concerned by the acrimony left over from the months of negotiations he had conducted in getting everyone to Madrid. Having engaged the Shamir government in a bruising battle over the $10 billion in loan guarantees, he was especially worried that the Arab delegates would start to depend on the United States to promote their own positions, and pressure Israel to make concessions. Baker made it clear that he would not do so. Israel was still America's primary ally in the region, and the United States had staked its Middle East policy on its continued strength and survival. He made this position clear in his last go-round in the Middle East: Israeli concessions would not be delivered by Washington, he told Hafez al-Assad, but result from hard bargaining between the parties. He delivered the same message to Palestinian Faisal Husseini (who was barred from being a member of the delegation, but was a member of its "advisory group") and King Hussein of Jordan. The Arab states, he told them, had to come to accept that Israel was a fact of life and that it had legitimate security concerns.

If anyone missed the message, George Bush made it clear in his opening statement, during the morning session of the first day of the conference, on October 30. Speaking before a hushed room of dignitaries, with a bank of cameras from television networks around the world trained on him, the American President reviewed the steps that had brought the parties to the negotiating table. He cautioned against impatience. "We come here to Madrid as realists," he said. "We don't expect peace to be negotiated in a day, or a week, or a month, or even a year. It will take time." Both sides, he said, should reach for compromise. So far, at least, his message contained no surprises.

But later in his remarks, Bush said that the United States believed that the Arab delegations should do more than simply focus on bargaining for the return of lands occupied by the Israeli government. There was more at stake. Normalization of relations between Israel and the Arab states, Bush implied, must include Arab guarantees assuring Israel's security. Bush's statement on Israeli security was blunt. "For too long," he said, "the Israeli people have lived in fear, surrounded by an unaccepting Arab world. Now is the ideal moment for the Arab world to demonstrate that attitudes have changed, that the Arab world is willing to live in peace with Israel and make allowances for Israel's reasonable security needs."

Bush's message was not only intended as a warning to the Arab delegation, it was also intended to calm Israeli anxieties. Those anxieties were raised in the days before the Madrid session by Baker himself. On the eve of the conference, the United States secretary of state decided to give the Palestinians of the joint Jordanian-Palestinian delegation equal time in Madrid, not only during the opening statements, but also during the time set aside for responses. The decision placed new pressures on Shamir, who was adamantly opposed to giving the Palestinian delegation equal status with Jordan, Syria, and Lebanon. If Shamir had had his way, the Palestinian delegation's position would have been staked out by the Jordanians and they would be relegated to mere onlookers, with no official standing at all.

Shamir was so angered by Baker's decision that he confronted him on the Tuesday evening before the opening session. Baker could tell that Shamir was mad, and he attempted to sell his decision by saying that giving the Palestinians a chance to present their views would help to get the negotiations off on the right foot. Shamir wasn't buying. "Enough is enough," the Israeli prime minister reportedly told Baker. "We have done enough." He told Baker that he wanted "no more surprises" during the Madrid meeting. Shamir then issued a new requirement: He insisted that the first round of negotiations following the conference take place in the Middle East and not, as the Syrians insisted, at a neutral site in Europe. To drive his point home, Shamir told Baker that the Israelis would not stay in Madrid for further talks following the opening discussions—they would be going home for the Sabbath.

The Palestinians, of course, were delighted by Baker's decision. "The Israelis would have you believe that they are the only ones who compromised their principles to be here," a Palestinian delegate said on the eve of the Madrid Conference, "but this is absolutely preposterous. We are the ones who had to accept being part of another delegation, not them." But that was not all the Palestinian delegation had given up. For ten years, the PLO had spurned the Camp David Accords, which called for the negotiation of a step-by-step, three-stage process that would slowly give them autonomy in the West Bank and Gaza.

What the Palestinians agreed to was important in the negotiations with Israel that would follow the Madrid meeting. By attending the conference, the Palestinian delegation confirmed the agreement signed by Menachem Begin and Anwar Sadat in 1978. They had never done that before. According to Camp David, the Palestinians would slowly take control of their own lands over a period of five years. Israel would withdraw from parts of the West Bank and Gaza after a Palestinian "self-governing authority" was elected. Talks would then take place over the "final status" of the territories. The whole point of the Madrid Conference was to begin that step-by-step process. The Camp David Accords did not detail which territories Israel would withdraw from, they did not stipulate how large would be the "self-governing authority" or who would be a member, and they did not guarantee the establishment of a Palestinian state. Everything was up for grabs—except for the principle that the West Bank and Gaza were occupied lands. All of this meant that the final status of the territories would be decided in the far future. Even with an agreement in Madrid, the Palestinians could not expect to receive the benefits of the process until 1996—at the earliest.

But what the Palestinians had agreed to and what they actually thought were two different things. In exchange for coming to Madrid as part of the Jordanian delegation (and agreeing to negotiate on the basis of the Camp David Accords), they wanted assurances that the outcome of their talks with Israel would not be prejudiced by any prior arrangements. They wanted to make sure that every issue was on the table, that they could negotiate anything they wanted. Baker agreed. The Palestinians, he said, could make an opening statement at the conference, could choose their own delegation (so long as those delegates were not from the diaspora or East Jerusalem), raise any issue that they wanted, and could even put the status of Jerusalem (which had been annexed by Israel) on the table.

"The United States understands that Palestinians must be free, in opening statements at the conference, and in the negotiations that follow, to raise any issue of importance to them," Baker said in his letter of assurance. "Thus, Palestinians are free to argue for whatever outcome they believe best meets their requirements." He added: "The United States has long believed that no party should take unilateral actions that seek to predetermine issues that can only be resolved through negotiations. In this regard, the United States has opposed and will continue to oppose settlement activity in the territories occupied in 1967, which remains an obstacle to peace."

That is exactly what the Palestinians wanted to hear: Baker's letter, they believed, had placed the status of the settlements and Jerusalem on the negotiating table—and they intended to make them a part of their talks with Israel. But, in fact, Baker's letter was not intended to set conditions for the talks. All he wanted to do was bring the Palestinians to the table. After that, it was up to them to see if they could win any concessions from Israel. He had committed himself to nothing. The status of the settlements and Jerusalem was a fit subject for negotiations—no doubt—but that did not mean that the Israelis would agree that the settlements would be dismantled (they would not) or that East Jerusalem should revert to Palestinian control; Israel annexed Jerusalem and considered it a united city and their capital.

Palestinian views on what Baker had agreed to would cause enormous problems in the bilateral discussions to follow. The Palestinian delegates insisted that Israel should negotiate the two most controversial issues (of settlements and Jerusalem) right away. The Israelis disagreed and went one step further: The most important issues should be left for negotiations on the final status of the territories, and not before; all that was being negotiated now were the interim arrangements, to decide the form of Palestinian self-rule. The Palestinians could talk about the settlements and Jerusalem, but the Israelis would not listen.

Israel's formula for negotiating with the Palestinians had been established long before Madrid by Shamir himself. And his view was predicated on two strong beliefs: Nothing could interfere with the eventual establishment of Eretz Yisra'el—with Greater Israel—and nothing could interfere with his decision to build settlements in the occupied territories. "Judea" and "Samaria," he said, were Jewish lands; they were part of the ancient promise made to the Jewish people.

Israeli Prime Minister Yitzhak Shamir staked out this position in his address to the delegates during the second morning of the Madrid Conference. He called on the Arab delegates to recognize Israel's right to exist and to begin to speak "the language of reconciliation, coexistence and peace with Israel." He made a formal bow to peace and confirmed the basic belief of most of Israel's citizens. "In Israel," Shamir said, "there is an almost total consensus for the need for peace. We only differ on the best ways to achieve it."

Shamir went on to imply, however, that he by no means accepted the "terms of reference" set down in UN Resolutions 242 and 338, or in the letters of invitation by the conference's cosponsors, the United States and the Soviet Union. "We hope that Arab consent to direct, bilateral talks indicates an understanding that there is no other way to peace," he said. "It will be regrettable if the talks focus primarily and exclusively on territory. It is the quickest way to an impasse."

Shamir's speech was widely interpreted as a conciliatory gesture for peace. He wanted simple recognition of Israel's right to exist, to live secure inside of its own borders, and to normalize relations with its Arab neighbors. But few Arab delegates viewed his speech in such optimistic tones. "If we are not going to negotiate for an end to Israeli occupation of our land, then why are we here?" Palestinian delegate Saeb Erakat asked. The same question was posed by Syrian delegates, who were especially angered by Shamir's description of the Damascus government. "To this day," Shamir said, "Syria is the home of a host of terrorist organizations that spread violence and death to all kinds of innocent targets, including civil aviation, and women and children of many nations. I could go on and recite a litany of facts that demonstrate the extent to which Syria merits the dubious honor of being one of the most oppressive, tyrannical regimes, but this is not what we have come here for. . . . " Baker listened impassively to Shamir's address, but he could not have missed the slap directed at him. Shamir was giving him his due: They were not in Madrid to revisit the past, but he mentioned it anyway.

James Baker sat impassively listening to Shamir's address and looked up only occasionally to survey the room—and to cast a furtive glance at the Syrian delegation. No one to his right, where the Syrians, Palestinians, and Jordanians were seated, looked in the least bit disturbed by Shamir's remarks, but he knew that the Syrians, especially, were seething. After Baker's talk with Farouk al-Sharaa on the need for conciliation, Shamir's opening address to the conference would make him look like he was playing an Israeli game; either that, or Sharaa would conclude that Baker actually believed that it was necessary for the Syrians to appear reasonable, but not the Israelis.

"That old taboo that Arabs and Israelis cannot meet and cannot talk is now something that we want to relegate to history," Baker had said the day before, but now it seemed that he had lost control of the situation; and the conference had just begun. The Israelis were talking alright, but they were not using the language that Baker would have preferred. "Not a good start," an American official said after Shamir's speech. "Nope, this is not a good start at all."

No one should have been surprised. Nothing in Shamir's previous statements indicated that he was actually willing to exchange "land for peace." Instead, he firmly believed that Israel's place in the Middle East could only be guaranteed by its continued strength. For Shamir, there was never any question of granting the Palestinians full autonomy in the West Bank or Gaza Strip—such a program, he believed, would inevitably lead to the establishment of a Palestinian state, and then, the destruction of Israel. Rather, what Shamir advocated was a very strict form of limited autonomy—what the Palestinians later called a "cantonment" policy, which would split their lands into small self-contained areas surrounded by Israeli settlements.

Shamir's position, however, was not considered unreasonable by many Israelis, a large number of whom had voted for the Likud party on just such a platform in the past. Shamir's views were based on Israeli fears built over forty years of mistrust of its neighbors, every one of whom was an enemy. "We're a very, very small land," he told an American interviewer on the eve of the conference. "Why have we to give up our small land? Where will we live, on the moon? It's my land, it's our land. How could we give up this land? There is a conflict between us and the Arabs. They say this land belonged to them. I think they are wrong."

In addition, despite the harsh words, the Israeli prime minister did not underestimate the importance of the conference or dismiss the effect it would have on his own political future. It was with this reality firmly in mind that, the week before his speech to the delegates, he had taken matters into his own hands. He told his cabinet that the Israeli position in the talks would reflect the views of the Likud party—that is, that the views expressed in Madrid would be his own, and no one else's. He told Foreign Minister David Levy that he would be leading the Israeli delegation (thereby ignoring Baker's suggestion that foreign ministers should be the ranking officials in Madrid) and he appointed Levy's deputy, Benyamin Netanyahu, as the delegation's primary spokesman.

Shamir then hand-picked a bevy of tough Israeli politicians to head the delegations to each of the bilateral talks—or "tracks," as they were called—that would follow the conference. The Lebanese track would be left in the hands of the brilliant and ebullient Uri Lubrani (who could talk for hours on Israel and the Arab world), the Syrian track would be under Yosef Ben Aharon (whose personality was the opposite of Lubrani's), and the Jordanian-Palestinian track would be placed in the hands of his trusted adviser, Elyakim Rubinstein. There were also multilateral discussions on key issues—water, economic development, refugees, arms control and regional security, and the environment—that would be discussed outside of the bilateral negotiations. Shamir appointed foreign ministry official Eitan Ben-Tsur.

The personalities of the Israeli delegation meshed well. Almost every one of Shamir's team owed his political future to Shamir's success, and each of them agreed with the broad outlines of his conservative foreign policy program. In fact, the most powerful influence arrayed against Shamir was Levy—who was unceremoniously dumped from the Madrid team. But of the four major personalities in Madrid, the two most important were Benyamin Netanyahu and Elyakim Rubinstein. In many ways, they were a study in contrasts.

Rubinstein was soft-spoken, but argumentative. He was accustomed to presenting his position in well-formed phrases, as if they had been meticulously outlined and committed to memory beforehand. That habit was the result of a sterling career as a lawyer and diplomat. His habit of speaking gave him an appearance of being overly serious, but in person he could be warm and cooperative. In later negotiations—during the bilateral talks held in Washington—he often made himself available to passing journalists by standing in the lobby of the headquarters hotel of the Israeli delegation.

"Did you get the story you wanted?" he would ask. "Perhaps I can help." He would wink when he said it, knowing that he never had any intention of revealing anything beyond what was released by Israeli press officials. "I am not being underhanded," he would say. "This *is* what I think."

Benyamin Netanyahu, on the other hand, had gained a reputation for saying exactly what he meant and not caring what anyone thought. Since Shamir had taken office as prime minister, he had become more and more accessible to the press and appeared often as the designated Israeli official on American television. In many parts of Israeli society, he was lionized as the quintessential Israeli technocrat-hero, as a handsome, westernized, accessible, and sophisticated young conservative whose political views were beyond dispute. Shamir chose him precisely because of his media capabilities, but there was never any question of his own political position: He stood with Shamir on the important issues. There would be no talk of land for peace. The formulation, instead, was much more simply put as a peace-for-peace exchange. "We want peace with our neighbors," Netanyahu said, "and we think that they should want peace with us."

The Palestinian delegates who arrived in Madrid for the conference never had any doubt about the usefulness of an international conference, but that was not true for a large percentage of the Palestinian population. During the last week of September, Yasser Arafat gave his blessing to Palestinian attendance, and then called a meeting of the Palestine National Council, in Algiers, to ratify his decision. The PLO leader did not think that he would have any problems in bringing the PNC into agreement with his position. But Arafat had underestimated the strength of opposition to the Madrid meeting. In Algiers, Arafat was attacked from both left and right—from those who were disgusted by his manhandling of the PLO foreign policy positions (symbolized by his disastrous support of Saddam Hussein), and by those who did not think he was being tough enough.

The PNC meeting in Algiers featured the appearance of the hardest of the hard-liners: the suddenly ailing old warrior George Habash, the head of the Popular Front for the Liberation of Palestine, the strident Nayef Hawatmeh of the Democratic Front for the Liberation of Palestine, and Mohammad Abu Abbas, the mastermind of the *Achille Lauro* attack and the leader of the Palestine Liberation Front. Habash and Hawatmeh were especially critical of Arafat's decision to attend the international conference and they staged a floor fight on the question that jeopardized his position. Even Arafat's trusted assistant, Bassam Abu-Sharif, was fearful of the outcome of the debate. "I thought throughout that we had the situation in hand," he later said, "but frankly, in all truth, there was much more opposition than I had anticipated."

That was Abu-Sharif's way of saying that Arafat had not only miscalculated the strength of his own moderate position, he was slowly losing power inside the PNC—even among his allies. But the attack in Algiers was not led by his friends; it was led primarily by PLO groups based in Damascus, the so-called rejectionists, his enemies. The PLO, they said, was caving in to "Zionist demands." These critics were even more disparaging when it came to the composition of the Madrid delegation. Baker's formula had excluded everyone from the conference except those from the occupied territories, leaving large segments of the Palestinian populace on the outside of the negotiations. "We have no guarantees that those negotiating on behalf of the Palestinian people will actually negotiate on behalf of all the Palestinian people," Hawatmeh said. "We call them the notables. But their time is past. Who are these people who think that they can take our futures into their hands?"

Arafat's counterattack, and his defense of the delegation, only fueled the arguments of his critics. He assured the PNC delegates that the Madrid negotiators would be monitored by the PLO ("Yes, this is true," he said, to catcalls) and that their honesty should not be questioned. "They are Palestinians," he said, surprised by the criticism. "They will not bargain away their own rights. Who says they will? Who says? Why would they do so?" The reassurances did not convince PFLP delegates who, egged on by Hawatmeh, engaged in a series of outspoken attacks on Arafat when he was temporarily away from the podium. At one point just prior to the vote on whether the delegation should actually attend the conference, it seemed almost as if Arafat had lost control of the proceedings. It was the first time that anyone in the PLO had seen that happen.

It took a last-minute plea from the PLO leader to win the vote. Informed of the attack on his leadership by Hawatmeh, Arafat made an unscheduled appearance on the podium, which brought the hall to a sudden silence. He leaned forward, turned aside the microphone, stood up, and spread his hands in a wide embrace. He demanded that the PNC fall in line with his views and he argued for their support. Stabbing his single index finger into the air—a personal quirk he had adopted from years of speaking to Palestinian audiences—he demanded full unity. The speech went on for many minutes but, at its end, Arafat could sense that he had not yet convinced the doubters. So he took an unusual tack: He admitted to his past mistakes and acknowledged that the PLO—and the Palestinian people—were facing "a great crisis." He added, "Yes. We are facing a catastrophe, and what weapons do I have? I have no chemical weapons. May God help us," he said, "the only missile I can give to my people, the only bomb I can give to my people, is your unity."

Arafat's dramatic speech was the turning point in the Algiers PNC summit and it paved the way for Palestinian participation in the Madrid Conference. But the vote did not give Arafat a free hand. He cautioned Palestinians attending the conference that, while they would be charged with representing the views of the Palestinian people, their status as true negotiators was likely to be judged in the diaspora on their ability to represent the PLO's position. "Any Palestinian anywhere is a representative of the PLO," Arafat said. "The PLO is not an organization. The PLO is the identity of the Palestinian people."

The cautionary note was unnecessary. Seven of the fourteen members of the delegation were members of Fatah and the others were all members of PLO groups. All the members of the delegation owed their own political base in the territories to the PLO's influence and power. They had no base of political support of their own. They agreed with Arafat; they were coming to Madrid to represent the PLO because the PLO *was* the Palestinian people. They owed their allegiance to the PLO, as did hundreds of thousands of others. In this sense, they were as unlikely to cut a separate deal with the Israelis as Hawatmeh. "They had PLO written all over them," Palestinian adviser Daoud Kuttab said, after the Madrid Conference.

Even so, even if the Palestinian delegation actually represented the PLO (and made no secret of it), the Palestine delegates who attended the Madrid meetings appeared to be far more pragmatic, and moderate, than the PLO leadership in Tunis; and they insisted on presenting a position that was in keeping with their own pragmatic beliefs. While they would consult with Tunis, ask for its guidance (they had set up a series of interlocking committees to do so), and promote its positions, they emphasized the important role that they played inside the organization; they were not marionettes. Most important of all, the Palestinian delegates made it clear to Arafat that they had decided that they would present a new Palestinian face to the world that was divorced from the stereotypes that had been set by the Palestinian revolution. They wanted to be respected as leaders who could take on the Israelis on their own, as they had done in the streets of Hebron, Nablus, and Ramallah.

The Madrid Conference provided the Palestinian delegation with an unprecedented opportunity to present their point of view to the world. "We have never had this opportunity, ever," delegation spokeswoman Hanan Ashrawi said before the opening ceremony in the Royal Palace. "I do not think that people believe that we even have a point of view. We have been invisible for so long that that is what we have become: 'the invisible Palestinians.' So because no one would listen to us, the Israelis assumed that we would just disappear. But we have not." Privately, a number of Palestinian delegates went much further. "All you hear in America is one side of the story," a delegate who had spent considerable time in the United States said. "I know of those images. I have seen them on your television. We are always presented as masked terrorists or anti-Semites. You are so tied to Israel that you have not even bothered to find out who we are. You don't care who we are."

It was with this in mind that the Palestinians took such care in choosing who would be in Madrid. Their delegation, fourteen members in all, was composed of doctors, dentists, lawyers, engineers, and scholars—the cream of Palestinian society in the West Bank and Gaza. None of the delegates was well-known (though some of them would become so) and none of them had ever appeared in an international forum. Some of them, like Saeb Erakat, had appeared on American television, but none of them had had to present detailed papers on the kind of society that they wanted to create. They were untrained in the ways of international diplomacy and inexperienced when it came to the rough-and-tumble, give-and-take of high-level negotiations. They were untried and untested. They had to create their own bureaucracy and support staff from the ground up. They had no think tanks and no prior position on which to draw. In many ways, they were disarmed, and they were clearly the weakest delegation at the table.

Worse yet, the Palestinians were novices when it came to influencing public opinion. They had tried to do so, in fits and starts, by establishing a Washington office (ostensibly independent of the PLO, because it had to be), but their efforts were amateurish and shrill. They complained endlessly about the "pro-Israel" views of the American media and they deeply resented and were frustrated by their own inability to change their public image. For many of them—even for the most sophisticated and educated Palestinians in the Madrid delegation—it was a given that Israel was an oppressor and they were the oppressed. It was as if the terms "oppressor" and "oppressed" were themselves an argument. They did not yet have a clear conception of how to conduct a sophisticated public political campaign.

One Palestinian who worked hard to change this outlook was Hanan Ashrawi, the delegation's spokesperson. Of all the public figures to emerge from the Madrid talks, Ashrawi was clearly the most influential and effective. While not a member of the Palestinian delegation, Ashrawi did more over the next year to change the world's view of the Palestinian people, and their problems, than had been done in the previous forty. Serious, soft-spoken, articulate, and obviously intelligent, Ashrawi was the first Palestinian ever to communicate the views of the Palestinian people without using the political slogans and chilling code words of a revolutionary. She was quick and never at a loss for words, and she spoke with authority.

There were obviously other factors that made Ashrawi such an important figure. Her very appearance broke through American stereotypes of Palestinians: She was an American-educated woman, a scholar (who taught literature at Bir Zeit University), and a Christian (she was married at St. George's Cathedral in Jerusalem). As a resident of Ramallah (a Christian city on the West Bank founded by her ancestors six hundred years before), she had lived under Israeli occupation. She could speak about the hardships of the Palestinian people from personal experience. So when she told the press that "Israel is practicing state terrorism and not being held accountable," there was a tendency to at least investigate what she said.

Ashrawi's presence in Madrid was immediately interpreted as a Palestinian bow to moderation, and a rejection of the maximalist, hard-line political positions held by the PLO. Ashrawi rejected the label. "When people say that we are moderates, what they really mean to say is that we have adopted the position of our enemies, the Israelis," she said. "I would disabuse them of that position. We are a real people fighting for our legitimate rights to our own country. We take not one stance or another according to any prevailing philosophy. We are here representing the Palestinian people."

Ashrawi's inclusion as a member of the Palestinian team in Madrid, and her understanding of American society, placed her in a position of influence with Faisal Husseini and especially Haidar Abdul Shafi. Abdul Shafi came to rely on Ashrawi's sense of what would work with the American and European media, and what would not. The strategy of influencing public opinion was not left totally in her hands, but she played a central role, as a spokesperson, adviser, and speechwriter. In the week leading up to the Madrid Conference, she and Abdul Shafi carefully crafted his opening statement that would both present the Palestinian political position and review the hardships of the Israeli occupation. If the speech succeeded, Ashrawi knew, the Palestinian people would be transformed from wild, bomb-throwing fanatics into reasonable people with a legitimate claim to their own land and identity. The whole world would be watching.

Abdul Shafi's speech was also important to other Arab delegations. While the American media had been promoting the Madrid Conference as a confrontation primarily between Israel and Syria, American diplomats knew that the Palestinian problem was "the core issue" of the Middle East conflict and much more difficult to solve than any other. The Palestinian problem was also much less amenable to negotiation than, say, an Israeli withdrawal from the Golan Heights, or exchange of ambassadors between Jordan and Israel. Those were difficult problems, but at least there were governments in place to deal with them. That was not the case with the Palestinians. They had no government.

For American officials, then, Abdul Shafi's speech was the first test to see whether the Palestinians were up to negotiating their own future. It was key. So when the Gaza physician stepped to the lectern at the international meeting hall in the Royal Palace, the moment was as electrifying as many had predicted. Abdul Shafi began speaking in Arabic, but then bowed to the realities of the international setting and gave the rest of his speech in English. He welcomed the parties to Madrid, repeated the predictable gracious remarks on the significance of the occasion, and then launched into an eloquent defense of Palestinian rights. Abdul Shafi's heartfelt plea for recognition and his proud retelling of Palestinian history was clearly the most captivating moment of the conference.

"The issue here is land, and what is at stake here is the survival of the Palestinian people on what is left of our olive groves and orchards, our terraced hills and peaceful valleys, our ancestral homes, villages and cities," Abdul Shafi said. "Security can never be obtained through the acquisition of other people's territory, and geography is not the criterion for security. We, the people of Palestine, hereby offer the Israelis an alternative path to peace and security: abandon mutual fear and mistrust, approach us as equals within a two-state solution and let us work for the development and prosperity of our region based on mutual benefit and well being." Abdul Shafi paused then, and lifted his head to look directly at Yitzhak Shamir. "We wish to directly address the Israeli people with whom we have had a prolonged exchange of pain: let us share hope instead."

Appearing on a national news show later, Benyamin Netanyahu acknowledged what he called "the flowery language" of Abdul Shafi's words, but he did not shift his position on Shamir's rejection of a straight land-for-peace exchange. "My problem and the problem of all of us [in the Israeli delegation] who heard the speech was that, sandwiched between the flowery language . . . this was a speech of confrontation and called for the dismantling of Israel. This was like coming to someone and saying, 'I'm going to pull off both your arms, peel off both your legs, and rip out your heart, but I'm going to make peace with you.' " The commentator was surprised by Netanyahu's reaction: "That's not what I heard," she said.

Worse was to follow. While many observers felt that the Israeli and Palestinian exchange might be the harshest of any of the Madrid speeches, they had not counted on the views of Farouk al-Sharaa, the Syrian foreign minister. A former airline executive who had turned to politics, Sharaa had become one of Hafez al-Assad's most trusted aides. He was escorted to Madrid by Walid al-Moualem, the Syrian ambassador to the United States, and Mowafaq al-Allaf, the chief delegate of Syria in its talks with Israel. Like his Israeli counterpart, Assad had put together a high-powered team. Moualem was no more a diplomat than Abdul Shafi, but he understood the nuances of American society, and the importance of influencing American public opinion. Al-Allaf, on the other hand, was a hard-liner for whom Israel's withdrawal from Syrian territory was a matter of personal pride, and international principle.

But it was Assad, and Sharaa, who dictated the tone taken by the Syrian delegation. Both held out some small hope that Shamir might be less intransigent than his previous positions indicated, but the prime minister's opening speech was persuasive evidence that that was not to be the case. So when Sharaa took the podium to present the Syrian viewpoint, the delegates in the hall around him leaned forward to listen to what they all predicted would be an indictment of Israeli policies. They were not disappointed: Sharaa, an otherwise almost diminutive, smiling man, issued one of the most blistering verbal assaults on Israel ever heard in an international forum.

Sharaa's speech began with a review of the Islamic world's contribution to modern civilization. For him, Israel was an interloper on Arab land, the living evidence of a new Crusade, and an imperialist design whose object was to subdue the independence of the Arab world. He was as single-minded in his own views as Shamir, and he even condemned the very idea of having to negotiate with Israel for a withdrawal of forces from occupied lands. "Security Council Resolutions 242 and 338, on the basis of which this peace conference is being convened, were adopted as a compromise between the permanent member states of the Security Council," he said, then added, darkly: "As is well known, the majority of those states have been sympathetic to Israel since its creation. Hence, the implementation of these two resolutions should not be the subject of new bargaining during the bilateral negotiations."

Baker thought otherwise. After the conference was recessed, he confronted the members of both the Israeli and Syrian delegations, telling them that the use of such inflammatory language could not continue. But Sharaa and Shamir ignored the advice. The die was cast.

In the responses given on the fifth day of the conference, Sharaa turned up the temperature. He was prepared for the Israeli accusation that Syria sponsored terrorism and he brought a prop with him to help make a counterargument. So, in the middle of his remarks, he held up a WANTED poster of Shamir that had been issued more than forty years before by the Palestine authorities of the British Mandate. The picture showed a scowling Shamir who was wanted for carrying out terrorist acts against British soldiers. James Baker now perceptibly squirmed in his seat, looking fully at Yitzhak Shamir, who sat impassively looking at his papers in front of him.

Sharaa had made his point, but it backfired. "Here was the Arab that Shamir's Likud party has come to know, hate and rely on," *Washington Post* columnist Jim Hoagland wrote of the incident. Israel's ambassador to the United States, Zalman Shoval, however, could hardly contain his glee. "I want to deny the rumor that we paid them to help our information effort," he said.

The response by Sharaa effectively ended the Madrid Conference. Shamir and his delegation held no last, conciliatory press briefing, and instead returned home for the Sabbath. But they did not walk out, as Jim Baker had once feared they would.

The Palestinians won the public relations battle of Madrid, but the Arab delegation lost. Abdul Shafi's dramatic call for peace and his emotional defense of Palestinian rights were drowned in the controversy that followed the Shamir-Sharaa exchange. But the Palestinians realized that, despite this, they had won an important early skirmish: They had suddenly transformed themselves from stepchildren in the proposed Israeli-Syrian dialogue to center-stage participants. As a result of this, in the months that followed the Madrid meeting, it was clear that the greatest chance for an agreement was on the Palestinian-Israeli track. As the Syrians and Israelis exchanged icy glares during the bilateral talks, the Palestinians and Israelis began the long, slow process of staking out diplomatic claims.

The first round of bilateral talks convened in Madrid just days after the Israeli delegation had returned to Israel. Not surprisingly, the Syrian-Israeli track nearly collapsed on the first day of meetings, held on November 3. While little was accomplished in the next six days, the Palestinians and Israelis agreed that they would exchange proposals for Palestinian autonomy on the West Bank and Gaza.

The second round of talks was scheduled to begin in Washington on December 3, but Israel refused to attend, saying that the negotiations should take place in the Middle East. American officials were exasperated by Israel's refusal to come to Washington, and even Jerusalem's friends in the United States questioned Shamir's strategy. Writing in *Washington Jewish Week*, Douglas Bloomfield, a former official of the pro-Israel American-Israel Public Affairs Committee, said that Shamir's strategy was counterproductive: "By appearing to be consumed with procedural wrangling, Shamir reinforces those who say his objections are designed to postpone discussing substantive issues. As a result, he makes his enemies look good."

On December 10, the talks finally began—but they did not follow the course laid out during the first round. The problem had to do with the position taken by the Palestinians, who insisted that the Jordanian-Palestinian track be split in two and that the Israelis negotiate with them separately. Israel refused. The Palestinian delegation then virtually boycotted the rest of the talks, sitting silently on a group of benches in a State Department hallway. It was a ludicrous scene.

Pressure was mounting on all the parties to show progress. Secretary of State Baker was especially impatient, for while he knew that the peace negotiations would take time, he did not believe that anything could be gained by "negotiating the size of the table" (as he described what was happening to one reporter) as had been done for one year during the United States-Vietnam talks in Paris in the early 1970s. But he was loath to break the impasse. He had told each of the Arab delegations that they should not rely on the United States to force concessions from Israel and he wanted to stick to that position. Nor did he want to engage in another standoff with the Israelis. Instead, he said, the Americans would provide "bridging proposals" and act as "an honest broker" in the process. The problem was that there were not yet any proposals for the United States to bridge.

A breakthrough seemed to come in the third round of the talks, in January of 1992, when the Israelis and Palestinians agreed to a split in the Palestinian-Jordanian delegation. One track would be composed of nine Palestinians and two Jordanians while the other track would be comprised of nine Jordanians and two Palestinians. One track would meet in the morning, the second in the afternoon. But the change was not merely cosmetic. Despite the time that it had taken to come to this point, the Israelis seemed genuinely interested in negotiating the interim arrangement for Palestinian self-rule in the occupied territories, and their agreement to split the tracks implied that they looked on the Palestinians as a distinct national identity. The chance of progress was enhanced when the Palestinians finally produced a plan for a Palestinian Interim Self-Governing Authority. It called for a 180-seat legislative assembly and required a phased withdrawal of the Israeli army.

The Israeli government responded with a plan of their own, which would slowly turn over domestic affairs in the territories to a Palestinian authority whose full responsibilities were yet to be detailed. In the fourth round of talks, convened in late February, Israel expanded on its program: The Palestinians would control their own affairs in twelve distinct areas. But the proposal left Israeli settlements in place and designated the Israeli army as the sole institution responsible for security. The plan was rejected by the Palestinians as "not serious."

"The problem is that the Israeli government has refused to engage in these talks on the basis of the terms of reference and on the letter of assurance given to the Palestinian delegation by the United States," Hanan Ashrawi said at the end of the fourth round. "Israel simply will not give up its occupation. They insist on negotiating peace for peace. We give them peace and they give us nothing." In essence, Ashrawi said, "these talks have stalled."

Not surprisingly, it was events away from the negotiating table that turned out to be the most significant and that would have the greatest impact on the Israeli-Palestinian search for peace. In early January, the 120-day postponement of congressional consideration of the $10 billion in loan guarantees ran out and Israel quickly petitioned the Bush administration for the funding. Yitzhak Shamir was convinced that he could now win approval for the guarantee or, at least, make it very difficult for the Bush administration to oppose them.

Shamir was right. Baker and Bush did not want to risk an-

other showdown over the guarantees. With the American election only eleven months away, both men wanted to shore up
their support among Jewish voters. Baker, however, feared that
giving Israel the loans outright would ruin the peace process.
But there was trade-off: With Bush's popularity in American
opinion polls wavering, the secretary of state was also concerned
that a disastrous collapse of the talks would harm Bush even
more than opposing the guarantees. Once again, Baker was
forced to walk a fine line—he wanted to put pressure on Shamir
to stop building settlements, but he did not want to spark a
partisan battle with Israel's supporters in Congress.

By mid-January, at Baker's suggestion, congressional leaders
were exploring a number of compromises on the guarantees
question. Baker had proposed an interesting formula. He
wanted to give Israel $2 billion outright, but he wanted all
future loans to be predicated on the Shamir government's willingness to dampen its settlement policy. Any settlement building after the first year, Baker suggested, would mean a
deduction in the guarantees that Israel would be granted.
Shamir did not like the idea of compromising on settlements,
however, and he once again threw down the gauntlet on the
Bush proposal. Speaking to a group of settlers in the West Bank
on January 20, the Israeli prime minister defiantly pledged that
"the Gentiles of the world" would never stop the construction
of settlements "in Judea and Samaria."

Shamir's promise injected a new tone into his relations with
Bush and Baker that had not been seen before—not even at the
height of the loan debate in the weeks leading up to the Madrid
Conference. The reason for the escalating confrontation, at
least in part, was Shamir's desire to take a high-profile proset-
tlement stance. He was staking out a domestic political position
that would increase his prestige with Israel's voters. There was
good reason to do so. On the day before his announcement,
Shamir's governing coalition lost its majority in the Knesset, as
two right-wing parties resigned over his program of limited
autonomy for the Palestinians.

Shamir could not win: He was buffeted by the Americans for

his settlement policy and his hard-line attitudes in the Middle
East negotiations on one side, and on the other by conservatives
in Israel who thought he was giving up too much. Frustrated by
his inability to keep his government together, he lashed out at
the United States. "At the very least, we have to protect our
principles," is how one Israeli official in Washington put it. "We
have to stand by the Likud party position." Roughly translated,
Shamir was gambling that he could win an Israeli election based
on fears of the establishment of a Palestinian state. He knew
that, at a minimum, he had the votes of the settlement community. And he had time. The elections were not scheduled
until late June.

The possibility of another confrontation with the Bush administration was thereby almost predictable. Though Baker
desperately tried to fashion a compromise, it appeared that
Israel did not want one. After a meeting with Israel's ambassador on January 24, Baker hardened his stance: He made it clear
to a number of important senators that the Bush administration
had not changed the views it had held before the Madrid Conference. The key was Vermont Senator Patrick Leahy, whom
Baker had enlisted in the loan guarantee fight back in September 1991. He publicly adopted Baker's compromise position.
There would be guarantees, Leahy said, but there were three
conditions: The guarantees would be no more than $2 billion
for the first year; second, the Israeli government would have to
agree to "significant economic reforms" in order to assure the
United States that it could repay the loans; and third, the guarantees would include provisions penalizing Israel for building
more settlements.

"I want to make clear to everybody on both sides of this issue
of Israeli loan guarantees that I do not intend to give a foreign
blank check drawn on the American taxpayers to any country
for any reason," Leahy said publicly. "Those who want the loan
guarantees without any conditions on them, frankly, are fool-
ing themselves. I will do everything possible to block such a
move." This was all that Baker could have hoped for.

The loan debate heated up in February, however, during the

secretary of state's appearance before a House subcommittee dealing with the issue. The Baker appearance featured a major media face-off between the secretary of state and Florida Congressman Larry Smith, who accused Baker of siding with the Arab delegations in the peace process: "Why must you insist on a loan guarantee that is coupled with a freeze on settlements when you in fact are not putting any conditions on anyone else on the Arab side . . . ? Aren't you presupposing and putting yourself in the position of negotiating for one side, putting the other side at a significant disadvantage?" Baker denied the charge.

The exchange then became very heated. Smith and Baker got into a near shouting match, after which Baker said that he had answered Smith's questions. Smith replied, "You know, you've done that before . . . and I find it extremely offensive." Baker reiterated that he had finished his answer.

"I hope some day," Smith responded, "the American public is going to determine whether you finish the answers or not. Disgraceful!"

After the hearing, Smith admitted, ruefully, that the Bush administration "probably has the votes to stop this thing [the loan guarantees], if it ever really comes up" and he went on to confirm that "my mail is running against the guarantees." The pressure on Baker mounted throughout March and by early April the pressure and verbal assaults on Baker were getting nasty, and went well beyond anything that Shamir himself would have wanted. As at the end of 1991, the loan debate had now polarized American Jewish community opinion. In early April, the pressure was so intense that the administration and the Jewish community in the United States were in a state of nearly open war that included charges that Baker had slurred Israel during a White House meeting.

According to the report, during a discussion of Jewish votes, Baker burst out, "Fuck them. They don't vote for us." The secretary of state issued an angry denial, but many voices inside the American Jewish community were convinced that he had used the epithet.

New York Times columnist William Safire, for instance, told his readers on April 2: "I can confirm that Mr. Baker did say that, with the same vulgarism that made it so memorable, to two high officials on two different occasions. President Bush and his top staff know he did; it has been agreed that everybody would deny it was ever said. But James Baker said it—twice—and meant it." AIPAC executive director Thomas Dine vowed that the Bush administration would pay for its opposition to the guarantees and cited Baker's statement in calling for a full press for the guarantees in Congress. "There are those who dismiss us with four-letter vulgarities who think somehow we will be intimidated and just go away," he said. "But we won't."

Nearly lost in this clamor was an event that deeply affected the Palestinian community and nearly changed the course of Middle East history. On Tuesday night, April 7, Yasser Arafat's jet crashed in the Libyan desert in the middle of a sandstorm. The pilots of the craft had apparently lost control of the plane while trying to make an emergency landing. The craft was running out of fuel and its engines were being fouled by the desert storm. Arafat was lucky. Three of the thirteen people on board were killed and five were seriously injured. But Arafat survived. As the craft went down over the desert, Arafat's chief aides formed a human wall around the PLO leader in the back of the plane. Arafat was convinced that he was going to be killed, and as the Russian-built turboprop descended over the darkening sands, he chanted, "I am coming to see you, Abu Jihad," over and over.

A rescue team searching for the aircraft finally found it, nine hours after it landed in the desert. Arafat's first words when he saw his rescuers were "Thank God, thank God." Arafat then appeared in Misratah, in northern Libya, for treatment. He was wearing a patch over his eye but otherwise seemed to be in good health. The news of his disappearance had no discernible effect on anyone outside of the Palestinian community. In Israel, citizens on the street neither celebrated nor mourned his loss:

With the bilateral negotiations under way, his influence was thought to be nearing its end.

The disappearance of Arafat's plane threw the Tunis headquarters of the PLO into a crisis. No one knew what would happen to the organization if he was killed, or who would become its leader. Bassam Abu-Sharif spent the day of his disappearance issuing contradictory statements to the press, while members of the Fatah executive committee present in Tunis held an emergency meeting. When Arafat was found alive, nearly everyone was relieved. But they were also suddenly faced with the eventual inevitability of his death and they planned to ask him to make permanent arrangements for his succession. He had escaped many such scrapes before, but he could not go on forever.

Arafat was injured much more seriously than he originally believed. He suffered a concussion on impact that led to dizzy spells. He needed to rest. Taken from Libya, he was diagnosed as having a disorder that would require surgery and he was later taken to Jordan for medical treatment. But if Arafat was physically impaired, his political standing was not. If anything, his hold on the PLO was reinforced. When he disappeared, his assistants realized just how much they relied on his leadership. Faisal Husseini, for one, was visibly relieved that he had survived the crash. "He is our brother, our leader," he said. "I would not even like to think about what would happen to us without him."

The Arafat crash was merely an interlude in the explosive loan guarantee debate. By mid-April, it was clear that the debate over the loan guarantees was not simply damaging United States-Israel relations; it was dividing the Jewish community. With American-Israeli relations nearing a breaking point, moderate American Jewish community leaders tried to calm the antiadministration rhetoric of its most pro-Israel activists. They believed that not only was the face-off harming American relations with Israel, it was working against the Shamir government. Letters to Congress showed that the vast majority of

Americans supported Bush. The loan guarantee issue was lost. It was time, Jewish leaders said, for reason to prevail.

One of those leaders was Jacob Stein, a New York realtor and American Jewish activist who served as Bush's liaison to the Jewish community. "I have talked with the president personally," Stein said, "and he told me bluntly that James Baker did not say those words. And I believe him. I think that we need to take a step back from this fight. This administration supports Israel and it supports the peace process." Stein was hardly a liberal when it came to supporting Israel: He opposed the establishment of a Palestinian state, said that Israeli settlements must be guaranteed "and not just removed wholesale," and called for "a special kind of autonomy for the Palestinians that could guarantee Israel's security."

The two extremes of the American Jewish community had been pulling at the Bush administration since the end of the Gulf War, but in April the great, uncounted middle ground seemed to intervene in a way that it had not before. While the overwhelming number of American Jews supported Israel, they were less committed to the Shamir government's continuing settlement policy, and they did not want to see a break in Israel's good relations with the United States.

That view was best expressed during a stormy meeting of the American Jewish Congress, when its members voted to endorse a settlement freeze. While a tougher measure was deferred, AJC President Henry Seigman spoke for the majority of the delegates. "The majority of our membership support the view that Israel ought to suspend settlement during the peace process," Seigman said. The only question now was whether that was also true in Israel, where a national election campaign was focusing almost solely on the issue of peace.

CHAPTER FIVE
TEL AVIV

If Yitzhak Shamir was worried about losing the election, he didn't show it. At the beginning of the fifth round of the Washington talks in late April, the Israeli prime minister held a series of interviews that inaugurated one of the hardest-fought election contests in Israeli history. Shamir's campaign pronouncements were vituperative and defensive—and they were aimed squarely at the Bush administration. Unemployment was high because America had failed to provide for Israel's faltering economy, he implied. Recent immigrants were unhappy, he claimed, because the United States failed to understand their needs. The Israeli state was surrounded and endangered. It could only count on itself.

Shamir warned voters that Labor party standard-bearer Yitzhak Rabin would give away the occupied territories and he bitingly described the former defense minister as a worn-out warrior who had grown soft. At one point in the campaign, his partisans even suggested that Rabin was a drunk. (When the claim backfired, the prime minister put a stop to it. "I oppose all slandering," he later said.) But Shamir always saved his harshest criticism for George Bush and James Baker.

In one interview, Shamir condemned Bush for failing to hand over the $10 billion in loan guarantees that he claimed would have assured Israel's economic health. In another, he intimated that the United States was a shill for Israel's Arab neighbors. "In the beginning we were under the impression that the Americans were interested in reaching a compromise [on the loan issue]," he declared. "Afterwards, it materialized that they were not. And why? Because apparently in the meantime they promised the Arabs, so the Arabs say, that the guarantees would not be granted." The State Department reacted harshly to Shamir's allegations, calling his claim of American-Arab collusion "garbage."

Shamir believed he could win Israeli votes by drawing a stark line between Washington and Jerusalem. If victory meant offending Bush, he was willing to do it. "Look, when the Arabs say that there has never been a better American administration, they are referring to the guarantees and nothing else," he said angrily. "You have to take into account that Bush has a specific philosophy. For him, land for peace is not just a slogan—he believes in it." Shamir's combative style caused controversy among the Israeli electorate, and it sparked an uprising among Likud party stalwarts. But after the prime minister denied David Levy, his government's foreign minister, the second spot on the ticket for openly criticizing him, his opponents swallowed their doubts and followed his lead.

The Labor party leader, Yitzhak Rabin, ran an entirely different campaign, promising Israeli voters that he would work for peace by negotiating a Palestinian agreement within the first six to twelve months after the election, improve relations with the United States, reorganize the Israeli government's budget, privatize industry, and bring down the soaring unemployment rate. Compared with Shamir, Rabin sounded like a humanitarian. After winning the leadership of the Labor party in a heated contest with his old competitor, Shimon Peres, Rabin highlighted his military career as a hero of the Six Day War, his foreign policy experience, and his reputation for toughness. He wanted to come to an agreement with the Palestinians, but he would protect Israel's security: The velvet glove covered an iron fist.

Rabin tirelessly toured Israel to sell his program, and his campaign soon took on a Trumanesque whistle-stop quality: He visited farms, factories, shopkeepers, and posed with recent Russian immigrants. The differences between "the two Yitzhaks," as the Israeli press dubbed them, could not have been more starkly drawn: Shamir emphasized his arguments with the United States; Rabin reminded the voters that he had good relations with American officials. Shamir said he would never give up the idea of Greater Israel; Rabin said he would trade land for peace. Shamir was combative; Rabin was temperate.

Shamir's divisive tactics and combative tone gave him an early lead in electoral polls, and Israeli commentators initially predicted that his Likud-dominated political bloc would win enough votes to ensure his return as prime minister. At the very least, they predicted, the vote would result in a deadlock in the Israeli parliament, and a unity government (with Shamir as its head) would take office. Nothing would change. "We are living in great days, the battle is for the future of the Land of Israel," Shamir said at the outset of his campaign. "The notion of territorial compromise will fade away like a bad dream." He promised that after a few more years with the Likud in power, "hundreds of thousands of Jews will be living" in new settlements on the West Bank and Gaza.

Rabin was just as adamant in emphasizing his own toughness. But there was a difference: While Rabin vowed that there would never be a Palestinian state, he promised to move away from the confrontational policies of the Likud government. "I am against throwing billions away on settlements which are not part of greater Jerusalem," he said and then pointedly added that he would "rehabilitate" Israel's relations with Washington. Shamir was astonished by Rabin's pledge to end subsidies for West Bank and Gaza settlements and deal with the Palestinians. In a national television debate held just days before the final vote, Shamir lectured Rabin on his views. "In this small country there is no possibility to achieve peace through territorial concessions," he said. "Do you really want a Palestinian state inside Eretz Yisra'el?"

"I don't want 1.7 million Arabs to be citizens of Israel," Rabin shot back. Then, looking directly into the camera, Rabin told Israeli voters that Shamir's opposition to compromise would actually bring more Arabs into Israel, adding hundreds of thousands of new Arab citizens to the eight hundred thousand who already lived inside the state's borders. The Jewish state would be transformed into a Jewish-Palestinian state. "That's why I supported [former Prime Minister Menachem] Begin when he signed the [Camp David] autonomy agreement," Rabin said, reminding voters that Shamir had voted against Begin's Egypt agreement. "There are three points I adhere to: 'no' to a Palestinian state; 'no' to a return to the 1967 lines; and a united Jerusalem under Israeli sovereignty."

The June 1992 election was a face-off between the two grand old men of Israeli politics: one moderate, one conservative; each with a different view of Israel. But in fact, the competition between the two was more than a contest between different political parties. In a much more fundamental way, the Shamir-Rabin election of 1992 was a battle over two competing visions of Israel that had been at war since before the state was established. While many of Israel's young voters seemed alienated as a result of having to choose between two men who were members of a generation whose time had long since passed, by early June it was becoming apparent that this contest would finally resolve the debate over the borders of the Jewish homeland—a question that was at the heart of the one-hundred-year controversy that had divided Zionism.

The Zionist movement was founded by Theodor Herzl, a late-nineteenth-century Budapest journalist who became obsessed with the idea of establishing a Jewish state in the land of Palestine. He put his thoughts into a pamphlet entitled *Der Judenstaat* and convened the First Zionist Congress in 1897 in

Basel, Switzerland. "We are here to lay the foundation stone of the house which is to shelter the Jewish nation," he proclaimed to the two hundred-plus delegates. The Zionist Congress endorsed Herzl's proclamation and its delegates fanned out through Europe, spreading Herzl's words to the millions of Jews living in the diaspora. From 1897 on, the agents of Zionism pushed European Jews to emigrate from their homes to the Middle East. The political movement had a special appeal to Jews living in the shtetls of Eastern Europe, where it gained most of its early adherents. By 1920, Herzl's cause had been transformed from a small movement to an international political crusade that appealed to millions of Jews.

But not all was well with Zionism. The British government, which was assigned the Mandate in Palestine, wanted to strictly limit the number of Jewish immigrants arriving there. While movement moderates went along with the gradualist British policy, which was overseen by an internationally controlled Jewish agency, a small but significant number of radical Zionist leaders opposed it. The most prominent of them was a brilliant Russian poet by the name of Vladimir Jabotinsky, who believed that European Jewry was facing a crisis and that Zionists had only a limited time to realize their dream. For Jabotinsky, opposition to the British became a litmus tests of Zionist patriotism. "If you do not put an end to the diaspora," he warned his colleagues, "it will put an end to you." He called for armed opposition to the British program.

Jabotinsky not only opposed the British; he was an inflexible foe of the socialist, secular, and largely Western European policies that gave the Jewish national movement its initial impetus and its first converts. As an ardent follower of Italian nationalism, he adopted the tactics of the romantic revolutionary, and attacked his opponents as drawing-room leftists, fair-weather radicals, and British collaborators, who scorned the Jews of the Eastern European ghettos. In large part he was right: Herzl and his moderate followers had roots in the European political mainstream and were contemptuous of Jewish provincials.

They counted on political and financial support from cosmopolitan industrialists and philanthropists who had no intention of immigrating to Palestine.

Jabotinsky believed in Jewish self-reliance and built a following of dedicated radicals. He advocated a war of national liberation in Palestine and promulgated an extremism that viewed anyone who was not a friend as a potentially murderous enemy. (One of his earliest essays was entitled "Man Is a Wolf to Man.") The more that the British stalled, the more extreme Jabotinsky's language became, until his writings rang with the commonplace cadences of early-twentieth-century militarism. "It is the highest achievement of a multitude of free human beings to be able to act together with the absolute precision of a machine," he wrote. Jabotinsky's rapier pen rebuked those among his followers who praised the strength of the Nazi movement ("a knife in the back," he wrote, "a disgrace"), but his own black-booted language suggested a new and frightening form of Jewish nationalism. "There is no value in the world higher than the nation and the fatherland," he wrote, and some among his followers called him Il Duce.

For Jabotinsky, it was simply not important that Arabs inhabited Palestine. "It is impossible to dream of a voluntary agreement between us and the Arabs of Eretz Yisrael," he said, and called for an "iron wall of Jewish bayonets" to create the new Jewish nation. When he was criticized by the British for his radical tone, he defended himself by saying that the Arabs had many countries they could go to—but the Jews only had one. He initiated a program of arms smuggling from Turkey and Eastern Europe to Palestine (he was arrested, jailed, and finally released) and helped Jewish settlements organize armed resistance to Arab attacks.

Jabotinsky's Polish-based Zionist youth movement, Betar, reflected this extremism. Betar recruits wore brown uniforms, black riding boots, engaged in complex ceremonies, and conducted elaborate military rituals. While Jabotinsky firmly rejected fascism's endemic anti-Semitism, Betar's anthem mimicked the chilling sentiments of Germany's most virulent right-wing movements: "With blood and sweat we will create a race, proud and generous and cruel." Jabotinsky's extremism was repellent to Zionist leaders like Chaim Weizmann (Herzl's successor) and David Ben-Gurion (who once angrily called Jabotinsky "Vladimir Hitler"), but for Jews bending under the ruthless realities of Eastern European anti-Semitism, Jabotinsky's call for militant self-defense had a special appeal.

Jabotinsky carried his militant crusade into the Zionist congress in 1931. Zionism could no longer compromise with the British, he said, because European Jews were facing a desperate situation. But his program was repudiated and his call for the creation of a Jewish army to protect the community in the diaspora was rejected. Zionism's moderate leadership feared Jabotinsky, were repulsed by his strutting legions with their blood oaths and his ferocious maximalist talk of Jewish purity— "Man's superiority over the beast is the ceremony," he once claimed. After a vicious internal feud, Jabotinsky left the Zionist Organization and, in 1933, formed the Union of Zionist Revisionists. Jabotinsky's followers were true believers in Eretz Yisrael: They wanted to "revise" the Zionist movement's call for a homeland in Palestine so that the future state would include the land on both banks of the Jordan River.

Yitzhak Shamir inherited Jabotinsky's vision of "muscular Judaism." As the Betar recruit Yitzhak Yzernitsky, Shamir (from Ezekiel: "I will make your head like adamant [*shamir*], harder than flint") emigrated from Poland in 1935 to study at Jerusalem's Hebrew University. But even Jabotinsky was too moderate for the young Zionist, who was more influenced by ideologically driven ultranationalists, like the poet Uri Zvi Greenberg, who celebrated the ideal of the Jewish warrior. "The country conquered by blood, and only her conquered by blood," Greenberg wrote, "is made holy for a people of holy blood." After arriving in Palestine, Shamir abandoned his academic career and joined the Irgun Zvai Leumi (the revisionists' National Military Organization), known among Jews by its acronym—Etzel—and among the British simply as the Irgun.

Shamir took Jabotinsky's opposition to moderate Zionism to

new extremes: The gradualists of the Zionist movement, he believed, were more dangerous to the dream of a Jewish state than the Jewish people's most implacable enemies. Shamir rejected anti-Semitism as the motive force behind the Jewish movement and advocated the violent struggle for a national homeland that would transform Jews from victims to warriors. In 1940, a group of extremists with similar views split from the Irgun to form their own organization, under the leadership of Avraham Stern. Shamir joined them.

Lohamey Herut Israel (Fighters for the Freedom of Israel), better known as Lehi—or, more popularly, the Stern Gang— inaugurated a new chapter in the struggle for Palestine. Lehi began to plan and carry out a violent campaign against the British "occupiers." Stern, Shamir, and their followers acted on the belief that the British were their primary enemy and, conversely, that anyone who opposed them was an ally—even the German Reich. Lehi did not openly support the Nazis, but they were unwilling to drop their war against the British in Palestine to fight them. In the summer of 1941, the Lehi leadership passed a note to a senior Nazi official in Beirut that proposed an alliance in exchange for guns and political support. In their note, Lehi called for "the establishment of the historical Jewish state, on a national and totalitarian basis, tied by treaty to the German Reich, in accordance with the preservation and strengthening of future German power positions in the Near East."

The Lehi-German agreement was never consummated, but it showed how radical Lehi had become. Lehi leaders were not above using the tactics of their moderate enemies in the Zionist establishment to further their own cause: At the same time that Lehi representatives were attempting to contact German officials in Beirut, its agents in Palestine were smearing Zionist moderates as collaborationists with the Reich. When Stern was killed by the British in Tel Aviv in 1942, Shamir became the de facto captain of the underground group, planned its operations, and enforced a strict internal discipline against traitors and informers. He helped draft the organization's call for a revolutionary war against the British that consisted of propaganda, sabotage, and terror. By the end of World War II, when Shamir was captured by the British and sent to a prison camp in Eritrea, he had become an ascetic revolutionary. He returned to Israel in 1948 to lead an illegal underground movement.

By 1949, Shamir was beginning to emerge from the shadows of Jewish radicalism, but he was shunned by the new Ben-Gurion–dominated Israeli establishment. When he applied for a job in the ministry of the interior, Ben-Gurion made sure he did not get it. "I understand that you intend to employ the terrorist Yzernitsky. I oppose it," the new prime minister wrote in a short memo. Ben-Gurion's little note may well explain why, much to James Baker's relief, Shamir did not stalk out of the Madrid Conference when Syrian Foreign Minister Farouk al-Sharaa held up a British wanted poster of him. After you have been called a terrorist by the George Washington of Israel, what does it matter what Farouk al-Sharaa says?

After a career in the Mossad, Israel's intelligence service, Shamir joined Menachem Begin's Herut party, the forerunner to the Likud, in 1970. While the two were not on good terms (Begin disdained the Stern Gang's anti-British complicity with the Germans), Begin took great glee in Shamir's political success. When Begin became prime minister he appointed Shamir to be speaker of the parliament. "We appointed the head of Lehi to be speaker of the Jewish Parliament," he marveled in delight. "What a revenge of history." Shamir bided his time, having learned in the school of politics to defer to a strong and popular leader until it was his turn to lead. He was often seen, smiling and stooped, emerging from cabinet meetings with a file under his arm. But he said very little.

Shamir served as Begin's successor for eight months in 1983, before becoming a minister in a national unity government (the result of a parliamentary agreement) headed by Shimon Peres, in 1984. Shamir finally won outright election in 1988 and he served longer than any prime minister since Ben-Gurion. Shamir seemed to care little for the everyday concerns of governing, choosing instead to follow a vision of Israel that was formed from his days as a revisionist Zionist and member of the Stern Gang. While he learned the art of compromise, he never totally abandoned his past attitudes as a Stern Gang operative and continued to embrace the inflammatory language and habits of the Jewish underground: His opponents were traitors who had to be destroyed, party discipline must be maintained, and informers rooted out. Yitzhak Shamir was the same man as prime minister that he had been when he came to Palestine sixty years before as a young student—he remained obsessed with the dream of Greater Israel.

Yitzhak Rabin was made of different stuff. Unlike Shamir, Rabin was born in Tel Aviv, in the *yishuv,* the native Jewish community of Palestine, in 1922. His father had come to Palestine from the Ukraine by way of the United States, and his mother had come from Odessa after having settled for a short time in Scandinavia. His parents' odyssey was not unusual: Despite their strong support for Zionism, many of Eastern Europe's middle-class Jews were not ready to trade the harsh conditions of their original homes for the increasingly violent environment of the Arab-dominated British Mandate and had, therefore, first settled elsewhere. Eventually, however, Rabin's parents came to Israel. Their decision had a profound effect on Rabin's life: Unlike many of his contemporaries who arrived from Eastern Europe in later years, he grew up with Arabs and traded stones with them on the streets of Tel Aviv.

Rabin began his life in the small Jewish metropolis of some thirty-five thousand residents, but his heart has always been in the kibbutz. He learned Zionism from his mother and father, who leavened it with large doses of socialism: The two ideologies were closely tied together in the yishuv community, and when Rabin marched with his classmates in school parades their blue-and-white Zionist banners were adorned with red socialist pendants. He went off to Kadoorie Agricultural High School in Galilee, where he gained high marks in zoology, botany, and chemistry and began to plan a career as a farmer. He became fascinated by politics, however, and with the coming of war in Europe, decided to join the Palmach, the military arm of the National Jewish Council of Palestine—the Hagana. His recruiter was a young Palestinian Jew named Moshe Dayan, who later rose to prominence as the premier military commander of the Israel Defense Forces.

Rabin and Dayan became competitors and critics: Rabin questioned his commander's grasp of tactics, while Dayan thought Rabin too quick to start a fight and too slow to stop one. When Rabin joined the Palmach in 1941, he was placed under Dayan's supervision and was involved in British-coordinated military operations against the Nazis. At the end of the war, he led a military campaign against the British and was arrested during a roundup of Jewish militants during "Black Monday," in June of 1946. After his release, Rabin rejoined the Palmach in the War for Independence and at the age of twenty-six led a unit of Jewish fighters against Arabs holding the roads to Jerusalem.

Rabin's bravery is well-known, but his personality is more difficult to assess. He coveted military promotion and his swift climb through the IDF's officer ranks was furthered by his serious, nearly humorless nature. He became known as a deft bureaucratic infighter and was not above labeling his enemies in public. He broke with Dayan during a particularly hostile military dispute over command of the IDF in the early 1960s, when Dayan was competing with Yigal Alon, one of Rabin's mentors. Dayan never forgave this personal betrayal and criticized Rabin's work as chief of staff in the mid-1960s. In the weeks preceding the Six Day War, Dayan accused Rabin of putting Israel in an untenable military position. The criticism, combined with the enormous pressures brought by Arab vows to destroy Israel, had a debilitating effect on Rabin, who was exhausted by the endless days of planning Israel's defense. Just when Arab armies seemed poised for attack, on the eve of the war, Rabin suddenly excused himself from duty and disappeared. Dayan claimed that Rabin had "cracked"—but he soon returned to duty to lead Israel's armies to their greatest victory. (Rabin later claimed that he simply needed rest, but his absence contributed to rumors that he had gone on a twenty-four-hour drinking binge.)

Rabin's public distaste for Israeli politician Shimon Peres dates from the mid-1960s, when the two found themselves on the opposite sides of several critically important military questions. These policy disagreements led to chilly relations and an open breach during the fight to determine who would succeed Golda Meir as prime minister, in 1974. When the competition for the succession began in earnest, Peres called on Rabin and pledged that, despite their past differences, he would wage a fair fight. But several days before the Labor party convention, Ezer Weizmann, at Peres's instigation, dusted off the story of Rabin's unexplained absence in 1967 and gave it to the Israeli press. Weizmann portrayed Rabin's absence as a nervous breakdown brought on by the impending war.

Rabin thereafter portrayed Peres as a power-hungry and underhanded opponent who refused to play by the rules. But he had his revenge when he was elected as Golda Meir's successor and the first native-born prime minister of Israel. Unfortunately, his tenure was marked by controversy and the tragic suicide of a cabinet minister brought on by corruption charges. He fared poorly in comparison with other prime ministers, especially the widely revered Golda Meir, and was victimized by years of economic mismanagement. When his government lost a vote of confidence in the Israeli parliament, in 1977, he turned the party leadership over to Shimon Peres. Rabin's nemesis campaigned hard, but he had little chance of winning the election and Menachem Begin's Likud party took the reins of government. For the first time in Israel's history, the nation was turned over to the successors of Vladimir Jabotinsky.

Rabin's checkered political past makes it difficult to think of him as a great politician, a view that is reinforced by his bland personality. He is painfully ill at ease in front of crowds, self-conscious in personal meetings, impatient with reporters, and moody with aides. He seems to have lost the vibrancy and self-command of his youth—when he was looked on as a handsome and personable military commander with an attractive flair for understatement. The attention to detail, the tactical creativity, and the mechanical self-discipline that he brought to Israel's military campaigns have not served him well in the political arena: He is awkward, monotoned, and uncharismatic.

Rabin represents the quintessential native-born Israeli, or *sabra*—a Hebrew word that means "prickly pear" (a native fruit that is tough on the outside and soft on the inside)—and the term seems a particularly appropriate description. Rabin is neither personable nor social and he seems constantly poised on the edge of an explosive outburst. Nevertheless, he has shown remarkable flexibility in moments of crisis and is comfortable in situations where a person like Shamir would never be found: as when he secretly met with Palestinian leaders at the height of the intifada, or had his picture taken with two elderly kaffiyeh-clad Palestinian men in the midst of his election fight with Shamir. But could he bring peace?

Two weeks before the national election, Yitzhak Shamir's hold on the Israeli electorate started to slip. Likud party leaders could sense the shift. Unemployment remained at 11 percent, and his program to maintain party discipline was starting to cost him votes. The absence of David Levy from the ticket cost him valuable votes with Sephardic voters—among the Likud's staunchest supporters. In a Jerusalem shopping mall in early June, Shamir was greeted by Sephardic protesters singing, "Rabin, king of Israel." These Israelis, immigrants from small Jewish communities in the Middle East, had once been the heart of his party; now they proclaimed, "Rabin is king." Shamir ignored the protesters. In his gray, pin-striped suit, the seventy-six-year-old prime minister looked like a small town politician, out stumping for a city council seat. "We're in trouble," a Likud strategist said. "Rabin is catching us."

The former prime minister and retired general, meanwhile, was running the campaign of his life. Sensing Shamir's uncertainty and inability to excite voters, and capitalizing on worries about increased unemployment and a sluggish economy, Rabin brought a new urgency to his message, pushing himself and aides into eighteen-hour campaigning marathons. He crossed paths with Shamir a half-dozen times in June, but shook his hand only at the urging of reporters. His deep personal dislike of the old Stern Gang warrior and his Likud followers was obvious to everyone. "Throw them out, throw them out," Rabin implored his supporters at stop after stop. Everywhere he went he was greeted with the Labor party's newest posters and his campaign slogan: ISRAEL IS WAITING FOR RABIN.

Shamir scrambled to recover his lost momentum. In the last week of the campaign, he attacked Rabin as an appeaser who would turn Israel over to its enemies and directed his own supporters to portray him as "a man of iron." Aware that recent polls showed that over 40 percent of all voters were still undecided, Shamir reminded Israelis that he had overseen the largest influx of immigrants in Israel's forty-year history—nearly five hundred thousand new Jewish residents of the former Soviet Union. Shamir had not lost his old radicalism: He spoke passionately about his past in an Ethiopian prison camp and, when interrupted by hecklers, he pointed an accusing finger: "Terrorists," he shouted back. "Terrorists." But his emotional appeal could not defeat Rabin, who closed and then passed Shamir in the national polls.

On the night of June 23, it was evident that Rabin's Labor party was headed for victory, though it would fall short of a clear majority in the Israeli parliament. But Rabin's triumph was not the biggest surprise. By 11:00 P.M., Shamir and his followers were headed for an electoral disaster. When all the votes were counted, the Likud party had polled its lowest totals in nearly twenty years, losing seven Knesset seats and collecting over fifty thousand fewer votes than in the 1988 election. "We're going to change the national priorities," Rabin said to a cheering throng of supporters after it was clear that the Labor party would form the new government. "First of all, employment for the unemployed, and hope for the young."

The final results showed that Labor had outpolled Likud by some three hundred thousand votes and won 44 seats in the

Israeli Prime Minister David Ben-Gurion

The Israeli Knesset

Egyptian President Anwar Sadat and Israeli Prime Minister Menachem
Begin seal the Camp David Accord with President Jimmy Carter.

The beginnings of the intifada, 1988

Jebalya refugee camp

Gaza City in October 1992

George Bush and James Baker

Israeli Prime Minister Yitzhak Shamir and George Bush in
December of 1990

Secretary of State James Baker and George Bush

Hanan Ashrawi

Palestinian leader Faisal Husseini

Yitzhak Rabin and George Bush in August of 1992

DAVID VALDEZ, THE WHITE HOUSE

Yasser Arafat and King Hussein of Jordan

Israeli Prime Minister Yitzhak Shamir

Israeli Prime Minister Yitzhak Rabin

Secretary of State James Baker
confronts Yitzhak Shamir in
Madrid.
(Benjamin Netanyahu stands
behind Shamir.)

Vladimir Jabotinsky

Israel's Ambassador to the United States,
Itamar Rabinovich

F. LESLIE BARRON

Deputy Foreign Minister Yossi Beilin

Haidar Abdul Shafi

Haidar Abdul Shafi

Norwegian Foreign Minister Johan Jørgen
Holst

Palestinian militiamen praise the Oslo accord in graffiti in
a refugee camp in Lebanon.

Foreign Minister Shimon Peres on his way
to the Washington signing on the morning of September 13

Left to right: Stanley Fischer, Anna Karasik, and Leonard Hausman

Salah Ta´mari (*in profile*) with Khalil Jahshan (*closest to camera*) on the night of the signing

A triumphant Yasser Arafat in Washington

Rabin as Arafat: protesters outside the prime minister's residence in Jerusalem. The placard reads: "The Liar. Elections Now!"

Palestinian Abu Mazin

September 13

The handshake

Celebrating in Gaza (the boy's gun is not real)

Knesset. Rabin's party lost in the Likud stronghold of Jerusalem and in the occupied territories, but won in Tel Aviv and Haifa. Most striking of all was Labor's victory among soldiers (taking 32 percent of the vote to Likud's 28 percent) and immigrants—where the Labor party and its left-wing ally, Meretz, won over 50 percent of the vote. The election was a repudiation of Shamir's policies. Meretz party official Dedi Zucker, a supporter of the peace talks and a more favorable climate between Israel and the United States, was elated by the Rabin victory. "Israel has voted for peace," he said. "The old idea of a Greater Israel is finally discredited, dead."

The defeated Likud party chief reacted to the election by announcing that he was retiring from political life. In a widely disseminated interview, Shamir then confirmed what many had suspected: that he had never intended to bargain over the occupied territories. Instead, he announced, his strategy was to drag out the negotiations on Palestinian self-rule for another ten years. His remarks were published in the Israeli daily *Maariv*. "I would have conducted the autonomy negotiations for ten years," he said, "and in the meantime we would have reached half a million souls in Judea and Samaria." Shamir went on to say that while he knew that the majority of Israelis did not support his call for a Greater Israel, he believed that "it could have been attained over time." Shamir's blunt admission sent shock waves through the Likud establishment, whose major leaders claimed that the newspaper had "put words in his mouth." But no one was that surprised by the admission—it was one of the reasons that Likud was defeated.

In Washington, the Bush administration greeted Rabin's election with barely concealed jubilation and, in a series of meetings with prominent Jewish leaders, attempted to repair relations with the American Jewish community that had been damaged during the administration's fight with Shamir. Secretary of State Baker welcomed the news of Rabin's election by announcing that the stalled peace talks should be reconvened "just as soon as it is conveniently possible" and privately hinted that now that Rabin was prime minister, his search for peace and his political standing would be reinforced by a quick infusion of the $10 billion in loan guarantees that had been denied Shamir.

Rabin wanted to make a clean break with the past: Within days of the election, he cut subsidies for settlers, announced that he was ending construction in all but those settlements needed to ensure Israeli security, and pledged to accelerate Israel's negotiations with the Palestinians. Rabin's address to the Israeli parliament, on July 13, when his government took office, reemphasized this commitment to peace, an improvement of relations with the United States, and the battle against unemployment. The speech went out over Israeli TV, and into the occupied territories, where it was closely watched. He presented his government—a broad coalition of parties from the right and left who agreed with his policies—and named Shimon Peres as his foreign minister.

The most dramatic moment in the speech came when Rabin spoke directly to the Palestinian population of the West Bank and Gaza. "And you, Palestinians in the territories," he said, to the hushed chamber, "who live in the wretched poverty of Gaza and Khan Yunis, in the refugee camps of Hebron and Shechem; you who have never known a single day of freedom and joy in your lives—listen to us, if only this once. We offer you the fairest and most viable proposal from our standpoint today—autonomy—self-government—with all its advantages and limitations. You will not get everything you want. Perhaps neither will we. So once and for all, take your destiny in your hands. Don't lose this opportunity that may never return."

Within weeks, Rabin welcomed Secretary of State Baker to Israel with a promise to reinvigorate the peace process. Baker was delighted by the Israeli government's new policies. "It's a pleasure to be going to Israel under circumstances in which I anticipate that we will not be met with the opening of new settlements . . . something that I think can only inspire trust and confidence," he said before the five-nation tour of the region. Privately, Baker was visibly relieved that the pressures he had faced in dealing with Yitzhak Shamir had suddenly evaporated. "The Israel-U.S. relationship is back on track," a Baker aide confidently predicted.

Rabin's election threw the large, politically active Jewish community in the United States into disarray. After years of nearly open support for the Likud party, a number of conservative American Jewish organizations found themselves in a difficult situation: Their long-term alliance with the Israeli right put their relations with the new Rabin government in jeopardy. This was especially true of the powerful American-Israel Public Affairs Committee, the highest-profile Likud supporter of any American Jewish group. AIPAC had stood behind Shamir in his fight for the $10-billion loan guarantee and then editorialized on his behalf in the months that followed. AIPAC and other Jewish groups were widely resented for this by Rabin and his top Labor party strategists.

In the days following the election, the Labor government took its revenge: An editorial in *Davar,* a Labor-supported Israeli newspaper, called for the resignation of Tom Dine, AIPAC's executive director, while *Ha'aretz,* an influential liberal daily, called for the resignation of Malcolm Hoenlein, the executive director of the powerful Conference of Presidents of Major American Jewish Organizations. Both Dine and Hoenlein were considered "pro-Likud" Shamir partisans. The editorials reflected the view common among Rabin liberals that American Jewish leaders were meddling in Israeli affairs and that key officials in the American Jewish community had actually set out to ensure the new prime minister's defeat.

The criticism of Dine, Hoenlein, and others was brutally frank and went to the heart of the relationship between Israel and the American Jewish community. "American Jews sometimes think that they know what is better for Israel than Israelis," one Rabin assistant said in defending the *Davar* editorial, "but what is really at issue for them is not Israel, but money. They have spent so long selling Israel as a nation under attack that the prospect that peace might break out scares the hell out of them. Let's be real honest about this: every time that we're threatened they end up padding their pockets."

Officials at AIPAC, the Presidents' Conference, and other conservative Jewish organizations had heard this type of criticism before, but never from officials at the top of the Israeli government. They rushed to heal the breach in their relations with Rabin as best they could, and took solace from official Israeli government pronouncements on the unbreakable alliance between Israel and its supporters. "Prime Minister Rabin counts on the support that Israel receives from the American Jewish community," a Labor spokesman intoned in the wake of the election, "and will build on that long and valuable relationship."

Privately, however, Rabin was infuriated by AIPAC's pro-Shamir lobbying. As far as he was concerned, American Jews were interfering in Israel's internal affairs. So after issuing the standard slogans about Israel's ties with the American Jewish community, his aides quickly discarded the traditional potboiler praise for AIPAC and its allies. "If there is such a thing as being more Israeli than an Israeli, then AIPAC has done it," a Rabin spokesman said in a not-for-attribution interview six weeks after the election. "He [Rabin] will set the foreign policy of this government and will deal directly with the [Bush] administration. No one else will set the policy. The government of Israel resides in Jerusalem, and not in some lobbyist's office in Washington."

Rabin himself made this startlingly clear during his first post-election visit to the United States, in August. During a private meeting with AIPAC leaders, Rabin attacked them for souring Israel's relations with the American government. "You've aroused too much antagonism, you keep too many enemies for yourself and your record is poor," he said. "We decided in a democratic way what are our priorities. It's we, the Israelis, that will decide about it." This litany was received in stunned disbelief. During the meeting, he reiterated the promises he had made to Israel's voters: an end to settlement activity and the conclusion of an agreement with the Palestinians. There was more to come.

After meeting George Bush at the President's vacation home in Maine, Rabin met another group of American Jewish leaders in New York, where his message was repeated. After a warm welcome, Rabin directed his criticisms at Shoshana Cardin, the chairwoman of the Conference of Presidents, but it was meant for each of the more than one hundred Jewish leaders in the room. A leading businessman who attended the meeting described Rabin as "livid," and "enraged" by the actions of "American Jews who confuse support for one political party in Israel with support for Israel itself."

The new prime minister also made it clear that he did not come to the meeting to seek approval for his programs from American Jews. "He told us that he did not need our permission to act as a prime minister," an American Jewish leader later summarized. "That was pretty much the gist of it." Rabin ended his remarks by saying that Israel could stand on its own. Jewish leaders reacted with surprise at Rabin's outpouring. "It was a real shocker," one of them confirmed. "I can understand his sensitivity, but to say that we damaged Israel. Really, it's too much."

David Harris, the executive vice president of the American Jewish Committee, believed that Rabin's remarks symbolized a fundamental shift in Israel's relationship with American Jews. "The American Jewish community certainly saw itself as an important actor in the ebb and flow of U.S.-Israel relations," he told *Washington Jewish Week,* "nurturing its strength, moving it along, advancing it in consultation both in Washington and Jerusalem. Prime Minister Rabin has given a very clear signal he sees things differently." Other Jewish leaders were not as evenhanded; a prominent fund-raiser for Israel felt betrayed. "Rabin simply does not understand what we do for Israel," he said. "When Israel needed us we were there and we always will be. When Rabin needs us, he will be back."

That sentiment seemed to dominate the thinking of conservative American Jewish organizations. In an August 21 editorial, the American Jewish newspaper *Forward* confidently predicted that Rabin would continue to act independently of Jewish fund-raising and support organizations until the point where "Mr. Rabin starts getting asked to make concessions he doesn't want to make." At that point, the newspaper predicted, "Mr. Rabin will begin to see the value of [organizations like AIPAC] and like-minded partisans with the stomach for the kind of fights that go on in Washington."

The director of the American Jewish Congress, Henry Seigman, on the other hand, explained the rift between Rabin and Israel's supporters as the natural result of twelve years of Likud rule and Yitzhak Shamir's inflexible position on the peace process. As a result of these policies, he told one reporter, American Jews had come to view any form of compromise with disdain—even if it *was* put forward by an Israeli. "I must tell you that when they hear that kind of message, the vast majority of mainstream leaders, the folks representing the traditional Jewish organizations, the religious organizations, the Zionist organizations, sit there in a state of shock. They don't know what to do with it."

In other words, AIPAC and other Jewish organizations in the United States were having a difficult time acclimating themselves to the new Israeli political reality—a fact that AIPAC officials, for one, firmly denied. "When the Labor Party was elected this organization turned on a dime," Raphael Danziger, AIPAC's director of information and research said. That defense did not impress Israel's Labor party stalwarts, who said that they did not want American Jews to shift their position. "They're not supposed to turn on a dime," one said. "They're supposed to be non-partisan supporters of Israel, not of the Likud. If AIPAC were doing its job it would not have had to turn on a dime."

Rabin's basic mistrust of the pro-Likud slant of many of the American Jewish community's major political organizations, however, signified only a small part of the deepening problems between Israel and its most ardent supporters in the United

States. As Rabin was meeting with the leaders of AIPAC, an Israeli publishing house was readying the final proofs of journalist Matti Golan's book on Israeli-American relations, which was entitled *With Friends Like You: What Israelis Really Think About American Jews*. Golan's book was a bitter indictment of American Jews who gave money to Israel, and fought for it in Washington, but who would not make the ultimate sacrifice of living and working in Israel itself. Golan's book hit a nerve in the American Jewish community, but it spoke for many Israelis. "You want a Jewish state?" Golan asked his fictional American Jewish counterpart. "Then please be so kind as to stand guard over it yourself. I've been doing it for dozens of years. Now it's your turn. Let's switch lives. You come here, serve in the army, worry about the Intifada, deal with the Orthodox, and shell out 50 percent of your income in taxes, and I'll live in America, send you money, and visit you now and then, and criticize."

Whether intended or not, Matti Golan's words reflected Rabin's own frustration over the American Jewish community's inability to understand that Israel's voters had put him in office to deliver peace. Israeli election figures confirmed that view: The vote that put Rabin over the top came from the Israeli political heartland—the city and suburbs of Tel Aviv, where most of Israel's most sophisticated and educated voters live. For them, the two issues of the economy were inextricably bound.

For hundreds of thousands of Israelis, Rabin knew, economic growth was tied to political stability. Without that stability, he feared, the Israeli people would tire of the endless political battles and abandon the Zionist dream of a Jewish state. They would vote with their feet—as thousands of them already had. Rabin had obliquely hinted at this fear in his July 13 speech in the Knesset. "We want the new immigrants and our sons and daughters to find work, a livelihood, and a future in this country," he said, and added, somberly, "We don't want Israel's main export to be our children." In many ways, it was this fact—that thousands of Israelis had left their homeland over the last forty years, and thousands more might—that was the greatest crisis that the new prime minister faced.

*   *   *

It is a six-hour flight from most of Europe to Tel Aviv, but
for many of the world's Jews who live outside of Israel the
journey marks one of the greatest moments of their lives. The
passengers line up at the gates of Paris, Frankfurt, or Madrid
for the direct flights that head out over Italy and then over the
eastern Mediterranean. The flights from Paris and Frankfurt,
for instance, take passengers directly over Mont Blanc and later
over the Dalmatian coast—where Bosnians and Serbs contend
for the remains of Yugoslavia. The airliners are always packed
and here and there, if you watch closely, you can see a plainclothes Israeli security officer smiling and talking to some of the
passengers. This is standard practice for the Israeli government—which is always on guard against terrorist intruders—
and is a security measure that is tolerated by the governments
of France, Germany, and Spain.

Flights to Israel mark great occasions for the devout, who
pray in the back of the plane, or for American and European
Jews who are on their way to Israel for the first time and talk
excitedly about their visit. It is not at all unusual to be aboard an
aircraft filled with passengers who, on their first sight of the
coast of Israel, will break into prolonged applause, which is
repeated on landing. In most cases, however, non-Jewish travelers are poorly informed about the situation in Israel and especially in the occupied territories—as was the case when a
group of Masons from Hamburg on their way to the Old City
of Jerusalem to measure out the foundation of Solomon's ancient temple in mid-1988 were surprised to learn that there
were troubles in the Holy Land. They had heard of the intifada, of course, but they did not think it would have any effect
on their travel plans. They believed that the troubles—which
had been in the headlines of all the papers—were far removed
from Jerusalem, as if they were restricted to a remote part of
the Arab world.

That would have come as a distinct shock to another group of
travelers: The two dozen or so unfailingly handsome, elderly
British men in their crisp gray suits and handlebar mustaches

who were traveling to Jerusalem for a reunion of the Palestine
Police—the British soldiers who tried to maintain order during
the British Empire's retreat from the Mandate after World War
II. The former policemen were on their way to the National
Palace Hotel in East Jerusalem for banquets, receptions, and
special memorial services to honor those who had fallen during
the series of Arab and Jewish revolts that were aimed at the
British occupiers and each other. The English were divided on
who exactly had started all the trouble; some blamed the Israelis
and some the Arabs. Still, the reunion was a special occasion,
since it gave them a chance to relive a unique time in the life of
the Empire, when they were young and had come to love the
land that would eventually be Israel.

Things had changed by 1993, when Yitzhak Rabin was still in
his first half-year as Israeli prime minister and the intifada was
in its fifth year and still causing problems. The Madrid Conference had come and gone and the long and seemingly endless
peace negotiations in Washington were deadlocked. Europe
was cold and rainy and the European airliners transporting
their passengers to the Holy Land were stacked up in a thin
no-fly zone over Bosnia. It was during such a flight that a
woman in her mid-sixties, smiling and nodding, came back into
the smoking section of an Air France flight to Ben-Gurion to
enjoy a rare cigarette. She commented that she had tried to give
up the habit, but had only succeeded in cutting her intake to
half a pack each day. As she sat in an empty seat in the back of
the aircraft, the darkening sky began closing in on all sides.
After a moment, she stared straight ahead, turned to smile
again and then, with water welling up in her eyes, she took out
a handkerchief to dab self-consciously at the tears that were
suddenly streaming down her face. She smiled slightly, then
shook her head, and turned away.

"Is there anything wrong?"

"Oh no, it's nothing," she said.

"Are you sure you're all right?"

"Yes," she said. "I'm just a little sad."

"Is there some way that I can help?"

"Oh no, no, thank you," she said, and then decided to share her grief. "I am returning to Tel Aviv to close up my home," she said, "which I have had for many, many years. So it is a sad time for me."

The woman then began her short tale. She said that her name was Alya and that she had come to Israel from Europe after the war, as a Holocaust survivor, to begin a new life. She met her husband in Israel (he was also a survivor of the death camps) and they had made a happy life together. He was a professional and they had lived well and raised a family. But he had died several years before, the victim of a heart attack, after many years of hard work. She wasn't alone, however—she had her son and her daughter-in-law and their two young children, both girls, who had come to live with her on the outskirts of Tel Aviv, in one of the city's upper-working-class suburbs. It had been a difficult life, even after the horror of the Holocaust.

The woman related her story in short, choppy, matter-of-fact sentences. She said that she had lived a simple life, but it was clear that she had not. Her son served in the Israeli military and fought in its wars and they were proud to be part of the effort to build a new nation, she said. Everyone knew that there would be sacrifices and they were willing to put up with them—at least for a short time. But Israel was a very difficult place to live and there was no sign that it would ever change. "I thought it would change for a time after the peace treaty with Egypt," she said, "but that did not seem to change anything." Her husband provided a good living, but their money did not seem to go very far. The situation worsened in the 1980s. "It was just becoming more and more difficult to stay there," she said. In late 1991, she decided to move to France along with her son and his family.

"I don't want to move, I don't want to leave Israel," she said, "but I really do not have any choice. My son is well-educated and he has a beautiful and intelligent wife. I have dreamed of Israel all my life and I have always wanted to have Israel as my home. And it is my home. It is the only home that I have ever had and the only one that I have ever felt comfortable in. I am a Jew, I wanted to live with Jews. I had a very good life there and I met my husband in Israel and we were both there from the beginning. In 1948, you cannot imagine how difficult it was and what a challenge. But I cannot do it anymore and my son cannot do it anymore. My son works all the time and most of his money is taken up with the necessities of life. There is just no other way and so we made the decision, together."

Later, she expanded on the problems she had had in Israel. "The taxes are very high in Israel and everything is expensive," she said. "We just cannot seem to get ahead. We are under constant pressure. How much can you sacrifice before you become tired? How many years can you go on and on before you need some peace? We thought that it would come by now but it has not come. I cannot bear to think that we will have to fight again and make even more sacrifices." She dried her tears and lit another cigarette. "I hope no one is sitting here," she said.

Alya might well have been a symbol of Israeli history. She had lived through it all—the War of Independence, the Suez Crisis, the Six Day War and the Yom Kipper War of 1973, the Lebanon invasion, and the intifada. She had seen Israel grow from a nation of 1.5 million people to nearly 4 or 5 million and had endured the hardships of Israel's early years—when sacrifice and simplicity were the hallmarks of the Zionist tradition. When she had arrived in Israel, it was not even a state and she had lived and worked with her husband through the terms of every Israeli prime minister, from Ben-Gurion to Meir to Rabin and Begin and finally, now, back to Rabin. Through all of those years, she had never once considered leaving Israel. But in 1991 she finally made the decision. She would leave behind a nation that had built itself and leave behind, also, the modest home her family had built and the grave of her husband, whom, she said, was buried outside of Tel Aviv. The fact that she would even consider leaving obviously sparked a deep emotional trauma.

"It feels strange to talk like this about the country that you love," she went on to say, "but after all these years I have to admit now that life somewhere else would be better." Suddenly, she was apologizing, explaining the decision to herself. "So last year my son went to Paris and looked for work and he got a very good job. So we moved. I have just come from Paris and we have an apartment, not much really, but it is quiet and calm and there is a chance for a good life there. It is just not that way in Israel. There are very few jobs and the pay is not that good and we want to work for something. To not have to struggle all the time. You have to understand, I love Israel, more than I have loved anywhere because I am a Jew and I love the Jewish culture. But I cannot take living there anymore. It is just too difficult. So I am going back to sell the home that my husband and I lived in for forty years and I am getting out. Do you think that that is such a terrible thing?"

Most people who visit Israel have ties to the country. They are American or European Jews who are visiting relatives who live there. But beginning in the mid-1980s, and for many years thereafter, at least some of the traffic was going the other way. Large numbers of Israelis, like Alya, were abandoning the dream of Israel to live in Western Europe and the United States. People who leave Israel are called *yordim*, which means "those who go down," a pejorative term that implies that those who participate in such a *yerida*—or "descent"—are abandoning their true spiritual home. Alya was a *yordim*, and while she was obviously despondent over her decision, she also was convinced that she had little choice.

Most Israelis are no longer embarrassed that a large percentage of their population, perhaps one fifth of the total of those who have immigrated to Israel since 1948, have decided to leave—the pressures of living in Israel are too common and the enticements of life in the West are too great: 500,000 Jews have left Israel since its founding and 20,000 leave each year. The number will reach 800,000 by the end of the century. Ten percent of those are doctors, lawyers, technicians, and scientists—the cream of Israeli society. And most of them, like Alya and her well-educated son, have come from Tel Aviv and its closest communities. This is Israel's silent crisis, and one of the reasons that Yitzhak Rabin won the Israeli election in June of 1992.

Golan touched on this silent crisis in *With Friends Like You,* and explained why Israelis have changed their minds about leaving Israel. They do not fear the stigma of being a *yordim.* "The very fact that they're in America and not in Israel is considered a success," he wrote. "Because in America they're not called to reserve duty, their children don't have to serve in the army, they don't have to give half their earnings to income tax, their daily routine doesn't include the PLO, settlements, and other existential problems. . . . We can't carry the burden any longer by ourselves. We're not willing to carry it any longer by ourselves."

The problem of emigration, of *yerida,* faced Israel for many years, but it seemed to grow worse in the late 1980s and early 1990s. The Shamir government had siphoned off millions of dollars to subsidize settlements in the occupied territories that could have been used to provide services to Israeli citizens in Israel itself. Then, faced with the prospect of a deep economic crisis, Shamir attempted to win $10 billion in loan guarantees from the United States. Hundreds of thousands of new immigrants placed an additional burden on the economy and while thousands of these new Israelis found jobs and acclimated themselves to a new life, thousands of others became dependent on government handouts. By mid-1992, Israeli industrial growth had stagnated, jobs dried up, and unemployment increased.

It is easy to exaggerate the crisis: While unemployment, slow growth, and the constant pressure of being under seige had a debilitating impact on Israeli society, the nation was not coming apart at the seams. There was no mass abandonment of Israel in the late 1980s. No one in Israel was ready to concede that the Zionist dream was over. Far from it. But enough people were leaving the country to cause concern. It was as if Israel was being engulfed by a prolonged period of self-doubt.

It was Rabin's task to infuse this suddenly questioning society with a new self-confidence. The suddenness of his postelection actions in freezing the settlements and then, during a trip to Washington, gaining approval of the $10 billion in loan guarantees (which, in the wake of his settlements decision, became suddenly available) helped to stem the tide of pessimism that gripped Israel during the last months of the Shamir government. But he had little time to act on his other promises, especially when it came to fulfilling his pledge to settle matters in the occupied territories within the next six to twelve months. But he tried.

One of Rabin's first actions was to appoint Itamar Rabinovich as ambassador to the United States and the new negotiator with the Syrians in Washington. After a series of high-level meetings in Jerusalem, Rabin instructed his negotiating team to present a revised set of peace proposals to their Arab counterparts. When round six of the talks convened in Washington at the end of August, he said, he wanted to be sure to set a new tone for the negotiations. Rabin instructed Rabinovich to tell the Syrians that Israel was serious about peace and that it agreed to the principle of exchanging "land for peace." That, in itself, would send a new message to Syria, since it marked the outright abandonment of Yitzhak Shamir's "peace for peace" proposal—which had gotten nowhere. Rabin also directed Rabinovich to accept the principle of a withdrawal from the Golan Heights, but without specifying just how far the Israeli government intended to withdraw.

The most important new proposal, however, would be presented to the Palestinian delegation. Rabin approved a draft proposal on a new Palestinian Interim Self-Government Agreement, or PISGA, which provided for the election of administrative councils responsible for most areas of governance in the territories. But most important of all, Rabin said, was the new tone that would be set in the negotiations. Israeli diplomats were no longer to treat their Arab counterparts to a repetition of endless Israeli grievances, or demand the impossible—a straight peace-for-peace proposal that had no hope of success. The talks were to be formal, but cordial, and Israeli negotiators were to listen to the positions put forward by the other side. Nothing would be rejected out of hand.

Rabin confirmed this change in tone to his top aides, saying that he hoped it would set a new precedent for the Washington talks. If the Palestinians began to negotiate on the model of self-government that he proposed, with municipal elections and a Palestinian police force that could take control of parts of the territories, then an agreement might not be as far away as he had thought when he became prime minister. The Palestinians would also be pleased that the new government would hold back nothing, and was willing to hear their ideas on a model of self-government that would be acceptable to both sides. Above all, he said, the new Israeli government had to make it absolutely clear that it did not want to continue the occupation. It wanted to withdraw and leave the running of Palestinian affairs in the hands of Palestinians.

Rabin made it clear that he would never gamble with Israel's security and that the months ahead would contain many obstacles. But a start had to be made. The search for peace had to begin, and everything had to be put on the table. In the end, he said, there was only one thing that could not be negotiated— and that was Israel's capital.

CHAPTER SIX
JERUSALEM

Jerusalem is more fundamental to the beliefs of Christians and Jews than any other city in the world. It is the third most revered city for Muslims and the destination of pilgrims from all three religions. The city contains some of the most sacred and historic buildings and sites in the world—the Church of the Holy Sepulchre, the Dome of the Rock, the archaeological outline of the Temple of Solomon, the Garden of Gethsemane, and the Wailing Wall. As the ancient capital of David, Jerusalem is the religious, cultural, and political center of world Judaism.

It is a cliché to declare Jerusalem an international crossroads, but it is. During the day the streets of the Old City are crowded with Arab traders from the West Bank, Franciscan monks from Western Europe, Christian Copts from Egypt, Muslim pilgrims from Africa, and young Israelis making their way to religious classes. In West Jerusalem, crowds of Israelis shop along Ben Yehuda Street, or commute to work in the banks and office buildings nearby. The Israeli government has its headquarters in the western part of the city and camera crews and reporters crowd the modern steel-and-glass Jerusalem hotels covering the latest debate in the Knesset or a press conference outside the prime minister's residence.

After sunset, however, Jerusalem is one of the quietest cities in the world: Outside of the half-dozen bars, restaurants, and a mall-like walkway dominated by ice cream parlors, the rest of the western part of the city seems almost deserted. Even in the summer, the shops close early in West Jerusalem. In East Jerusalem, Arab elders stand watch outside the entrances to the mosques and young Israelis guard the streets leading to the Wailing Wall with automatic rifles. In some few places, Palestinian restaurants remain open behind closed doors, but the practice—especially during periods of heightened political tension—is frowned on.

While Israelis claim that Jerusalem is "one city," everywhere you turn it seems to be two. The lines of Jerusalem are drawn by concrete, culture, custom, and language and by the political differences that separate Israelis from Palestinians. It is as if there is a wall through the center of the city that separates west from east, and Israelis from Palestinians—just as there once was, before the 1967 war. The foundations of this wall (the former "Green Line") can still be seen, near the American consulate, along the eastern side of Yafo Street, and running in a straight line just west of the King David Hotel.

The western part of Jerusalem is dominated by Israeli culture. Impressive marble-and-glass hotels dominate West Jerusalem's skyline, and a business, banking, and cultural district thrives on the wide avenues near the Israeli parliament. In the late afternoon, the restaurants on Ben Yehuda are filled with customers and groups of young people. Some of the shops sell T-shirts that show an Israeli fighter streaking through the clear blue sky, and underneath, the words DON'T WORRY, AMERICA, WE'RE COMING. The young soldiers in the streets carry automatic rifles.

There is a practiced method to the soldierly look; the adolescent girls and boys wear green fatigues and sling their rifles over their right shoulders so that they hang nearly to the ground. They wear no caps or hats of any kind and never swagger—no one with an automatic weapon would ever need to be so arrogant. Part of the affectation comes from a practiced lack of fear; in Jerusalem, carrying a rifle is as much a part of growing up to a young Israeli as a high school prom is to an American adolescent.

Up Ben Yehuda Street, there are clothing stores and newsstands before the turnoff into Yafo Street, which is crowded and filled with buses. The sidewalks are shoulder to shoulder with Israelis hurrying to and from work, and during the late-afternoon rush hour the streets are packed with cars. On Fridays, just before the Jewish Sabbath, Yafo is nearly impassable. Down Yafo to the south, the street moves into a shallow valley where the crowds thin out and beyond it, up a long hill, is the King David Hotel and the road to Bethlehem.

In the slight hollow of Yafo Street, it is possible to cross over the torn-away wall between the two Jerusalems and enter a barren no-man's-land. Two blocks past Yafo Street, there is a car-rental dealership, with its sign written in Arabic. The streets here are deserted and there are few houses. Where once there was a border, there are now wide gardens and blinking traffic lights. It is possible to see the wall of the Old City shimmering in the distance. One hundred yards beyond this is East Jerusalem.

One hundred fifty thousand Palestinians live in East Jerusalem. The majority of them could rub shoulders nearly every day with Israelis two blocks distant if they chose to, but many of them do not. During the day, literally hundreds of private traders display their wares on the steps of the Damascus Gate to the Old City. While Israeli soldiers constantly patrol the streets, most Palestinians simply ignore them. Hostile stares sometimes greet Israeli jeeps, or the rare paddy wagon, or a four-man foot patrol, but there are few confrontations.

The lights have gone out in East Jerusalem every night since the beginning of the intifada; the restaurants and shops close, the newsstands are dark, and the streets are empty. Late at night, it is possible to get a meal at the Philadelphia restaurant if you know the right person and knock on the right door, or you can sit at the rooftop restaurant of the National Palace

Hotel and look out over the dark city to the lights of Mount Scopus in the distance. At sunset, the muezzin's lilting call to prayer can be heard rising above the Arab neighborhoods. By dark, the streets are deserted.

Is Jerusalem one city or two? The question poses problems for both Israelis and Palestinians; for those who insist that Jerusalem must be united and for those who say that it already is. And it is a problem for journalists who decide to take a room at one of the many hotels in East Jerusalem that cater to tourist groups from America. The hotels are clean and inexpensive, but staying in them presents real difficulties. Foreign journalists, in particular, are often judged on where they stay in Jerusalem and closely questioned on who they know when they try to arrange interviews with Israeli officials.

The truth is that if a journalist mentions that he or she is staying in a hotel in "East Jerusalem," they are very unlikely to get an appointment with an Israeli official. There is no East Jerusalem, you are politely told, there is only Jerusalem. Click. But if the journalist somehow overcomes this obstacle, he is soon faced with another. It would be all right to stay in East Jerusalem, except for the fact that many of the hotels in East Jerusalem are owned by Palestinians. There is a great deal of sensitivity on this point.

"Where are you staying?"

"In East Jerusalem."

"There is no East Jerusalem."

"I'm sorry, I mean in eastern Jerusalem."

"Where in eastern Jerusalem?"

"Near the Knesset."

"This is a small city, everything is near the Knesset."

"I am staying in the Arab district."

"You mean East Jerusalem."

"I thought it was all one city."

Silence. "It is."

But it isn't. If it were, then those questions would never be asked. If Jerusalem were really one city, under the rule of one government, and answering to one political system with one culture, then Israel would have no reason to worry about its security. If Jerusalem were really one city, then Palestinians in the eastern part of Jerusalem would not say that they were under occupation and Israelis in the western part of Jerusalem would never have to live in fear. If Jerusalem were really one city, then Israelis would not worry that a newly formed Palestinian state—complete with a Palestinian army—would pose a threat to Israel, as they say that it does.

Jerusalem is not a beautiful city in the everyday sense of the word and has very little in common with Paris or Rome. But visiting Jerusalem is an overpowering experience. Outside of its known attractions—like the history that floods the senses during a walk through its ancient neighborhoods—there is one other salient fact that makes Jerusalem so important. Located in the middle of a long ridge that separates the Jordan Valley on the east from the Mediterranean on the west, Jerusalem is the strategic linchpin of the lands of the former Mandate. Jerusalem's location was one of the major reasons why the city was settled in the first place.

All you have to do to understand the importance of Jerusalem is leave it. The city falls off onto an escarpment in the west, where a modern six-lane highway carves a series of hairpin turns on a sheer and dizzying descent to the sea—some thirty miles away. When the road levels off onto the coastal plain after the precipitous drop, the traveler is only twenty miles from the outskirts of Tel Aviv. It does not take a military genius to see that Jerusalem guards the highway to the Israeli heartland. That someday Israel might lose control of this highway, as it nearly did during the War of Independence, remains one of the Jewish state's greatest nightmares.

The Israeli parliament is unpretentiously located on the top of a small, seemingly out-of-the-way hill in the government district of West Jerusalem, but it seems to dominate the city's skyline. Built in 1966, the Knesset is perhaps the best-known institution of Israeli democracy—open, austere, enigmatic, but somehow impressive. It has an air of permanence. In front of the entrance facing west to Ruppin Street is an imposing sixteen-foot-high menorah, which was designed and cast in bronze by sculptor Benno Elkan. The Knesset is the center of the Israeli government, with the ministries of finance, interior, and the prime minister's office just down the street.

It is a long walk up the hill from Ruppin Street to the iron gates of the building, which are closed to all without passes. The building is heavily guarded. It is possible to take a tour, of course, but the guides are expertly trained and all visitors are closely questioned. Cameras are not normally allowed in the building—even during the tours—and passports are routinely checked and double-checked. The polite but professional security guards are proud of their record; since the building was dedicated nearly thirty years ago, there have been few ugly incidents on the grounds and none at all in the great hall where the parliament meets in session.

A huge portrait of Theodor Herzl dominates the entrance hall, and the upper foyer is decorated with a breathtaking triple tapestry designed by Marc Chagall. Chagall's work seems to be everywhere in evidence in Jerusalem, but he is at his most impressive in the Knesset. The modern art fits well with the building's architecture, showing a triumphant, albeit tasteful, depiction of the three epic pillars of Jewish history: the creation, exodus, and return. The hand of God working through his Chosen People is implied in each of the works.

Knesset member Ze'ev Benyamin "Benny" Begin's office is below all of this, down a long stairway and through a warren of hallways at the far end of the building. The office is nearly impossible to find, but the aides, staffers, and occasional parliamentary members are helpful, if suspicious. Begin himself has given detailed directions by telephone on how to find his cubicle because he knows how easy it is to get lost, but his instructions are useless. The Knesset is spacious on the inside with wide hallways and large windows, but the building seems overly crowded with Spartan offices. The bevy of aides, assistants, secretaries, and press people that seem to dominate

Washington's congressional community would be considered a luxury by Knesset members.

Begin's office is a sparse single room the size of a large closet and may well be the smallest office in the Knesset. The modest surroundings are surprising because Begin is one of the rising young leader of the Likud party as well as the son of Menachem Begin, arguably the most legendary and controversial leader in Israeli history. Like Yitzhak Shamir, who followed him as prime minister, Begin was a Polish-born Jew who emigrated to Palestine before World War II, where he became the head of the Irgun Zvai Leumi—"the Irgun"—which waged a bloody underground war against the British during the period of the Mandate. The British printed wanted posters with his name and picture and circulated them throughout Palestine.

Begin is credited with masterminding the July 1946 terrorist bombing of the offices of the British military headquarters in Jerusalem's King David Hotel. The bombing was praised by his allies, condemned by his opponents, and, later, lionized for American consumption in the movie *Exodus,* which showed an entire wing of the hotel dramatically collapsing in a huge cloud of dust. Despite this later sheen of respectability, however, the incident brought an outpouring of protest from most of the Jewish population. The incident resulted in the deaths of ninety-one people, including a number of Jews. The British wrapped the dead in cloaks on the street in front of the hotel and began a manhunt for the perpetrators, but Begin got away.

Begin came out of hiding in 1948 to lead the Knesset opposition to David Ben-Gurion. Begin was unimpressed by Ben-Gurion's reputation and attacked him at almost every opportunity. He first accused him of giving up the Jewish people's ancient right to Eretz Yisra'el and openly advocated what amounted to a near insurrection against Ben-Gurion's government when it opened negotiations on reparations with the German government. "This will be a battle of life and death . . ." Begin declared. "Today the Jewish Premier is about to announce that he will go to Germany to receive money, that he will sell the honor of the Jewish people for monetary gain . . .

There is not one German who did not murder our parents."

Ben-Gurion turned Begin into a near pariah in Israeli parliamentary politics and refused to identify him by name or even look at him during Knesset debates. In the middle of one particularly memorable session during the debate over German reparations, Ben-Gurion continually referred to Begin as "the member sitting next to Dr. Bader" and accused him of cowardice during the War of Independence. When Begin responded by saying that Ben-Gurion was visiting the brothels of Paris while he, Begin, was busy killing British soldiers, the prime minister shouted, "Do not interrupt me, you still do not have a Cheka and a Gestapo."

Begin was infuriated by these slights and carried out a campaign of personal slander unrivaled in Israeli political history. His ugly assaults on Ben-Gurion's government earned him a reputation for political nastiness. Begin was branded as a right-wing Zionist ideologue and showed so poorly in his competition with the beloved first prime minister that he was loathed by most of the Israeli electorate, openly reviled by Ben-Gurion's political allies, and branded as a troublemaker whose views of democracy remained in doubt. Ben-Gurion's stature, on the other hand, only increased.

No one in Israel in the 1950s or 1960s would have believed that Menachem Begin would become prime minister, and yet, in 1977, Begin's Likud party ended the Labor coalition's hold on the Israeli government. Begin campaigned as a fighter, democrat, and honest family man. He attracted voters using the political touchstone of Zionism and the memory of the Holocaust. He preached that Jews could not be safe anywhere, not even in their own state. Israel needed to be a nation of fighters. After years of rule under successive Labor governments, that was a compelling message.

Begin's reign at the head of the Israeli government began with great promise—and an apparent contradiction of his own hard-line political philosophy. After only six months as the head of the Israeli government, he welcomed Egyptian President Anwar Sadat to Jerusalem and then, in 1978, he signed the

Camp David Accords that returned the Sinai to Egyptian control. But after Camp David, he refused to make the same overtures to the Palestinians. In 1982, Begin launched a massive ground, air, and sea assault on Lebanon with the purpose of driving the Palestine Liberation Organization from the country. The offensive soon bogged down into an embarrassing and costly war of attrition, which brought hundreds of thousands of Israelis into the streets in protest. At its end, Begin was a shattered man.

The tragedy of Lebanon destroyed Menachem Begin's political career. In his last year as prime minister, he turned to his son Benny for advice, and after he retired his son became his chief political adviser. But there was little advice to give. At the end of a contentious political career, Begin retreated into his own solitary world—he refused to comment on public matters and harbored a deep bitterness against senior Israeli officers, whom he blamed for involving the Israeli army in the costly and controversial debacle in Lebanon. The death of his wife was the last of Begin's tragedies. He was emotionally distraught and began to live the life of a recluse. He appeared furtively from time to time from behind his door, an unshaven and confused man. He died in 1992.

In spite of Menachem Begin's controversial political career and the mixed feelings he inspires, his son remains his most ardent defender and the inheritor of conservative, nationalist Zionism—and he is a political force to be reckoned with. Benny Begin is a geologist by training and the proud father of a large and patriotic family who promotes the Begin legacy as the great hope for the future of Israel. Like his father, Benny Begin is the unrepentant defender of Greater Israel. When he answers reporters' questions about his own plans, he is as curt and outspoken. "I will be prime minister of Israel," he says, "and my policies will be the policies of Menachem Begin."

As an experienced politician, Begin has taken some of the edge off of his father's old hatreds. He is modest, articulate, thoughtful, and rarely raises his voice. But this sense of balance

is quickly dampened by any suggestion that compromise or
retreat might be the one way to ensure Israel's future. At such
moments, he is as volcanic as his prime minister-father ever
was. Explosive invectives seem to run in the family. The issue of
Jerusalem, or, rather, the fact that it is not an issue, is central to
his thinking.

What is so central to Begin's message is his view of the vulnerability of the Israeli state—which is keenly felt by every Israeli citizen, regardless of their political affiliation. So while
Begin makes his stand at the opposite end of the political spec-
trum from Yitzhak Rabin, his thinking reflects the views of a
large number of Israelis. In the wake of the PLO-Israeli accord
of 1993, it is easy to dismiss the political position of someone
like Benny Begin as "radical" or outside the Israeli mainstream.
But just the opposite is true. Every politician in Israel must take
into account the nation's security fears—all of which revolve
around the question of geography. And at the center of that
concern is Jerusalem.

"I know that you have been to talk to Faisal Husseini," he
says. "Did he tell you that he is a liar, a thief, a cheat and a
crook? That he's a bandit? Or did he talk about 'special sovereignty'—or 'limited autonomy'?" Begin is seated in his office, a
pen in one hand, his eyes boring in on his questioner. "Husseini
has many friends here, you know," he says and he gestures
expansively with his right hand, indicating the floors of the
Knesset above his office. "We tolerate them in our midst, but
they are idiots and fools." He laughs and shrugs his shoulders.
"You can walk from here to Husseini's office, you know. That
ought to tell you something.

"I have a completely different view of peace and what it
means for Israel than many others in this building," he says.
"What has happened in Madrid and what is happening now in
Washington is not about peace; it is about placing Israel at risk.
So we must talk about these facts. This is a good story because
it is what every Israeli has in mind when people start talking
about land for peace. You hear this phrase quite a bit now, as

if land did not mean a thing, as if the land of Israel did not mean a thing. But that is a myth. Really.

"I want to give you some facts," Begin continues. "Here they are and you can take my word for it—they are correct. But just in case, I have erred on the side of what you call peace. Never mind." He pauses then and leans forward in his chair, gesturing, as his father did, with the tips of the fingers of his right hand squeezed together, as if he is holding a single, obvious truth for all to see. "My story is about security, about the survival of my country, Israel. That is all I care about. Everyone else uses words like stability, free trade, and the like. I am only interested in the survival of Israel. Anyone who says that is not this nation's top priority is lying. So there are only a few things that you need to know to be able to talk about peace.

"Israel is a nation with five million people—just five million. And that number is charitable because in fact there are 800,000 Palestinian Arabs who are citizens here, so really we have about four million Israeli Jews who can defend the country. But let us say for the sake of argument that there are five million Israelis. Even so, many of the five million are old. They are the survivors of the Holocaust or their children and are among the first people who settled this land and most of them are well past middle age. So in order to determine if we can defend ourselves you need to cut that number in half—to get to the number of men and women who might possibly be able to defend Israel. We have 2.5 million people who can enlist in the armed forces and of that number maybe sixty percent, at the most, are fit to serve. That's a good percentage and a very liberal number. So we are now down to 1.4 million people. But of course we don't have 1.4 million people in our military, we can't afford it. People have to work.

"So the numbers tell the story of Israel. At present we can only afford a small standing army and a large ready reserve—where everyone of age can serve for a limited period. Even so, our need for protection is a strain on our economy. Never mind that though. Let's just say that we have a standing army of about 250,000 men and women—and that number is very high. But we have tanks, an air force and a navy. They are very well trained. But still the numbers are small, especially in comparison to the armies of our enemies. The Syrian Army alone is three times our size and I am not counting Jordan. We have huge armies facing us, enemies on every border and in Samaria and Judea we have a restive population that is attacking us each and every day." Begin stops for a moment and raises his eyebrows. He is marshaling his arguments.

"What these numbers mean is that in time of war we will have to mobilize all our reserves—all of them. Everyone who can even hold a rifle will have to defend the country. And we must mobilize men and women and put the country into a state of total war. This is not happening in some foreign land, it is right on our borders. When we mobilize everyone it means very simply that we must shut down our economy, close our stores, strip our government bare and transport people to the battlefield as fast as we can. Even so, even in the best of circumstances, it will take us two days to do this. Something like 48 to 56 hours.

"It will take us 48 to 56 hours at a minimum to mobilize our military," he emphasizes. "What that means is that 250,000 men and women of our standing army will have to fight and survive for two days until they are reinforced against three or four times their number." Begin smiles wryly and his next words are emphasized as he leans forward in his chair, as if he is making an unusual admission. "I will tell you a secret," he says, shaking his head. "*We cannot do it.* We cannot mobilize our population, arm our young people and transport them to the battlefield in two days, and expect to survive as a nation. We cannot do it. We have barely done it in the past and the situation is much worse now."

Begin talks about the fears of Israelis that resulted from the Gulf War and his own reactions to the fact that missiles fired from Iraq landed in Tel Aviv. He admits that there has been "a psychological change" in how Israel views its own security, but he castigates Israel's political leadership for their reaction to the Iraqi attacks. "The missiles frightened people, made them doubt," he says, "but the reaction was mishandled. Israel has always been attacked and has always been in danger, but that has been true of Jews through all time. We should have told our people the truth. And the truth is that occupying land means something. All of the experts after the Gulf War argued that the fact that long-range missiles landed on Israel proved that occupying land means nothing. But that is a lie. That is the biggest lie that has come out of the Gulf War and the Israeli people should never have believed it. The truth is that land buys time—which is what we need.

"When the next war comes—and the word is 'when' not 'if'— there are only two ways, and no more, that Israel and its people will have a chance for survival. The first chance we have at surviving is to attack our enemies before they have an opportunity to launch their war. We have done that in the past and while it is much less politically acceptable to do it now, I think that under some circumstances we would be forced to do it— and we would do it gladly if we had to. Our second chance at survival is to create a series of security zones to make certain that when we are attacked we fight our enemy on our terms and not on theirs. Very simply that means that we must hold on to the West Bank, Gaza and the Golan Heights—the so-called Occupied Territories. If we give them up, if we retreat from Judea, Samaria and the Golan then the armies of our enemies are just eight miles from Tel Aviv *at the start* of their offensive.

"And that is unthinkable.

"So this is our nightmare—that in the name of peace we will cede our only security, which is land, and that we will wake up one morning to find a well-armed and vengeful Palestinian brigade in downtown Tel Aviv. Do you know what a well-armed Palestinian brigade could do in downtown Tel Aviv? I will put it to you bluntly: There are many of my colleagues in this building who are willing to take this gamble—who are willing to trade land for peace. But I am not one of them. Judea and Samaria are Israel's land, our ancient homeland. Promised to us. In the name of trusting our enemies many, many of my colleagues are willing to part with Judea and Samaria, but I am not. I cannot part with it. If we in Israel agree to part with Judea and Samaria it will become a Palestinian state, and I know that a Palestinian state is a dagger aimed at the heart of Israel.

"You know, I call this scenario a nightmare for a reason. For if I am wrong in my beliefs then this admittedly difficult, brutal and often violent occupation in Judea and Samaria will continue into the far future. And in many ways it is a terrible psychological price for us to pay. I agree, it is very bad. It is exhausting, but if those Israelis who want to trade land for peace are wrong then we as a nation cease to exist. I like my gamble much better. We continue to offend the world's people, we gather the criticism of even our close friends and maybe we even appear to be oppressors. This is the price we pay for surviving as a nation. But it is better than the other gamble, which is that someday we will be fighting at the sea wall in Tel Aviv.

"It is very easy to sit in America and write about the peace process and have your articles appear in the newspapers," Begin concluded, "because really it is not happening to you. It is easy to say 'we must push Israel to sign a peace agreement with its enemies because this will ensure stability,' but it is not your land and your future that is being bargained with. This is not diplomatic history. People live here in Israel, just one dozen miles from their bitter enemies. From here you can walk for fifteen minutes and you will be in the company of people who have vowed to destroy the Jewish State. So make no mistake, when Americans discuss peace in the Middle East they are discussing the prospect of our national annihilation. They are discussing extermination. We are not a nation of victims. We were not given this land out of pity, we fought for it by force of arms and we won it. I say that we have put our heads in the ovens already once in this century and we will not do it again. Ever."

Yitzhak Rabin was elected on a platform that included coming to a swift agreement on Palestinian autonomy. The agreement would not settle the final status of the territories, but

Rabin believed that it would begin the long process of resolving the one-hundred-year dispute between Palestinians and Jews. But in spite of this promise, and his personal desires, Rabin knew that he had to take into account the views of Begin. In many respects, they were not much different from his own. While he promised a change from the policies that had guided Yitzhak Shamir, he, in fact, adopted many of his positions. During the campaign, he had even issued three uncompromising positions that looked a lot like the views held by Shamir: no to a Palestinian state, no to a return to Israel's 1967 borders, and a united Jerusalem "under Israeli sovereignty."

In the months that followed his election, Rabin's last point became an increasingly volatile issue in the Washington talks; Jerusalem was a subject that simply would not go away. The first round of negotiations following Rabin's elections, which were convened on August 24, began auspiciously. There was a new tone in the exchanges, and a new seriousness on the part of the Israeli negotiating team. While Rabin retained Elyakim Rubinstein as the chief negotiator on the Palestinian track, there was a perceptible change in his attitude and tone. "It is not the same person," a Palestinian delegate said. "It is clear that he has new instructions."

After hailing the "change in tone" among the Israeli delegation (and the "realization that it must deal with a changed situation," in the words of Haidar Abdul Shafi), the Palestinians got down to business. They said that they wanted to discuss the arrangements for self-rule in the occupied West Bank, Gaza, and East Jerusalem. Rubinstein was pleased by the statement: Negotiations on Palestinian self-government would now become serious. But, as he made clear, any proposals on a Palestinian self-governing authority could not include Jerusalem. That had to wait for the negotiations on the final settlement of the territories. During the third session of the round, Rubinstein added that Jerusalem was "indivisible." It was not a subject for negotiations.

It was suddenly clear to the Palestinian team that nothing had really changed at all—at least so far as Jerusalem was concerned. The Israelis simply did not accept that any part of Jerusalem was an occupied territory. Since all of Jerusalem was taken over during the Six Day War in 1967, Israel had annexed it, expanded its boundaries, and ringed it with settlements. The Palestinian delegation continued to mention that the subject of Jerusalem had to be considered now—as part of the interim arrangements. It was part of the occupied territories. It had been taken over in 1967. Rubinstein did not agree. The issue of Jerusalem was not on the table. By the middle of the sixth round, Palestinian negotiators were telling reporters that the "change in tone" did not mark a change in positions and the talks were nearing a stalemate.

"The question of Jerusalem's status is not an issue for the Israeli delegation," Palestinian delegate Saeb Erakat confirmed. "So when Israel talks about the occupied territories, they not only call them 'disputed territories,' they say that the land that they are talking about does not contain Jerusalem. In fact, to be more precise, they do not even *say* that they are refusing to talk about Jerusalem, because there is nothing to talk about. None of their proposals contain the word." Erakat was disgusted. "This new Rabin team is the same as the old Likud team. The only difference now is that they smile."

Eventually, the impasse over the status of Jerusalem intruded into every aspect of the Israeli-Palestinian negotiations. Both sides had difficulty, for instance, discussing the status of Israeli settlements in the occupied territories. Palestinian negotiators wanted the settlements removed. That was not acceptable to the Israeli negotiators, who wanted to deal with the issue during future talks. But even if Israel had agreed to discuss the issue, it was clear that they would not discuss the status of those being built in Jerusalem. All new settlements within the environs of Jerusalem were not, by Israel's definition, on occupied territory.

This was also true when it came to negotiating the form of an interim self-governing authority. The Palestinians and Israelis clashed over how large a Palestinian "authority" should be: The Israelis proposed a fifteen-member "administrative council," while the Palestinians pressed for a "legislative assembly." The term "legislative assembly" bothered the Israelis, since it seemed to suggest that the Palestinians were in the process of forming a state—which Rabin opposed. But even if the two sides *had* been able to agree on the mechanics of self-government, there was still a question of whether such a council (or assembly) could include Palestinians who lived in East Jerusalem. The Israeli answer was Rabin's—why would a Palestinian council contain members from an Israeli city?

The question of Jerusalem did not consume the Israeli and Palestinian delegates in each and every discussion, but it remained a clear obstacle to progress during substantive meetings between the two sides. As a result of these problems, the Palestinian delegation soon began to talk differently about the "changed tone" of the Rabin government. The breaking point came on just before the end of the sixth round of negotiations, on September 18, when Hanan Ashrawi accused the Israelis of refusing to discuss exchanging land for peace. "You have to define territoriality," Ashrawi argued, "even if [the Israelis] want to make us garbage collectors; you have to define the area where you collect your own garbage, and where you dispose of your garbage."

The Rabin government had a different view of the bilateral talks. Israel wanted to negotiate a step-by-step process of turning over the daily lives of Palestinians to a Palestinian governing council. According to the Israeli scenario, the Palestinian governing authority would slowly be given more and more responsibility over more and more territory. Ways to deal with the stickier problems of Israeli settlers and Palestinian refugees—and the status of Jerusalem—would be postponed until the discussion on the permanent status of the territories, which was three years down the road.

There were aspects of Rabin's proposals that improved on the attitudes and positions brought to the table by the Shamir government, but they were still not acceptable to the Palestinians. Any discussion of an interim agreement that did not include the status of Israeli settlements, Palestinian refugees, and Jerusalem, the Palestinians believed, would not meet the stip-

ulations set out in UN Resolutions 242 and 338. Nor, the Palestinian delegation claimed, were the Israelis negotiating
according to the rules—they were completely ignoring the
terms of reference set out in the formula presented by James
Baker in Madrid. The optimism that had greeted the election
of Yitzhak Rabin had disappeared by the end of the sixth
round. The talks were deadlocked. While there had been some
minimal progress on a number of fronts, it was obvious that
both sides were still arguing about the rules of the game.

The sixth round of the Washington negotiations concluded
on September 24, one month after they had begun. Little had
been accomplished: The Palestinian delegation continued to
claim that the Israelis were not negotiating on the basis of the
UN resolutions or the Madrid terms of reference, while the
Israeli delegation said that the Palestinians were too busy talking about principles to engage in any substantive discussions.

"The problem here is real simple," an Israeli official said.
"The fact is that the Palestinian delegation just can't make a
deal. They keep wanting to create a Palestinian state. That's not
going to happen."

The most telling evidence of an Israeli-Palestinian stalemate,
however, came near the end of the seventh round of the bilateral talks. Near the end of October, just days before the American elections, Palestinian delegation head Haidar Abdul Shafi
confronted Rubinstein on the lack of progress in the talks.
Showing visible signs of strain, Abdul Shafi icily asked Rubinstein if the Israeli delegation had any intention of talking about
"the important issues." Rubinstein responded that the most important issue was Palestinian autonomy. Abdul Shafi did not
disagree, but he pointed out that UN Resolutions 242 and 338
and the Madrid terms of reference compelled Rubinstein and
his team to "discuss the whole range of issues affecting the
lands conquered by the Israelis during the 1967 war, including
East Jerusalem." Rubinstein nodded his head. The Palestinian
negotiators, he said, should "feel free" to discuss whatever they
wanted. But, he added firmly, "the Israeli position on Jerusalem will not change."

*   *   *

Bill Clinton was elected President of the United States on
Tuesday, November 3, 1992—in the middle of the seventh
round of bilateral talks between Israel and its Arab neighbors.
The Arab-Israeli conflict had played almost no role at all in the
American elections, which were dominated by domestic issues.
Clinton was elected on traditional pocketbook issues, and he
made it clear in the immediate aftermath of the national vote
that he would focus on problems close to home, like the economy and health care. Foreign policy concerns would not be a
top priority, a view that was confirmed when the President-elect
announced that he would leave international issues in the hands
of Warren Christopher, his nominee for secretary of state, and
Anthony Lake, his new national security adviser.

When Clinton announced his new Middle East team, Arab
delegates were pleased that he maintained much of the continuity of the previous administration. Clinton said that he would
keep Edward Djerejian as the State Department's assistant secretary of state for Near East affairs. Djerejian had served as
United States ambassador to Syria and played a key role in
convincing Hafez al-Assad to talk with the Israelis. At the same
time, he was viewed as "evenhanded," "willing to listen," and "a
pragmatist" by Arab diplomats. That he was labeled a State
Department "Arabist" by some pro-Israeli lobbyists in the
United States was seen as a definite plus.

Clinton also decided to keep one of James Baker's key aides,
Dennis Ross, on his Middle East team, though he shifted him
from the position of director of the policy planning staff at the
State Department to special adviser to Christopher on the peace
negotiations. The appointment came as a distinct surprise to
Ross, who planned to leave government to head the Washington Institute on Near East Policy. More than any other Washington official—with the exception of Baker—Ross was
instrumental in the negotiations that led to the Madrid Conference and he was noted for his steady, reasoned, and
nonideological positions. Clinton further reinforced his belief
in the continuity of the peace process by keeping many of Bak-

er's Middle East experts in place at the State Department, including Daniel Kurtzer, who stayed on as Djerejian's deputy, and Aaron Miller, a key member of Ross's policy planning staff.

But another of Clinton's appointments was met with skepticism by many Arab delegates. Clinton's appointment of Martin Indyk, the executive director of the Washington Institute, as a special assistant at the White House in charge of the Middle East, seemed to confirm that the new President would come down on the side of Israel in any dispute in the peace talks. Indyk, an Australian-born Middle East specialist, had a reputation for being an outspoken supporter of Israel. The appointment also raised hackles in the close-knit world of Washington's Middle East community. Despite his service at the Washington Institute, Indyk was viewed by some as a "carpetbagger." The Clinton administration rushed through his United States citizenship at the last minute to make his appointment more palatable.

But what raised the most questions was Indyk's stint with AIPAC, where he served as a research specialist. Indyk's appointment in such a sensitive and important position was especially surprising, considering Yitzhak Rabin's troubles with the pro-Israel (and, he apparently thought, pro-Likud) lobbying group. Although he was articulate, opinionated, and clearly well-versed on the Arab-Israeli conflict, many Arab-Americans nonetheless doubted that Indyk could make the transformation from being an advocate for Israel to evenhanded presidential assistant.

These worries were dampened somewhat by senior advisers to the President-elect. Clinton was interested in continuity, they said, and wanted to reinforce the beginnings made by Bush and Baker. Warren Christopher would be handling foreign policy issues while the President concentrated on domestic issues. Even the most pessimistic Arab delegates to the Washington talks were convinced that Clinton's primary concern with the American economy would mean that there would be less money —and hence less support—for Israel. Whether that would, in turn, result in getting the stalled negotiations started up again was yet to be seen, but at least the new administration's commitment to following the course set out in Madrid meant that there would not be any revolutionary changes in American policy.

In Gaza, Haidar Abdul Shafi reflected on the change of administrations by emphasizing Clinton's strengths. He pointedly dismissed private worries that Indyk's appointment—and Clinton's very public support for Israel—spelled a change in directions in American policy. "I know that people are very worried that the election of Clinton is bad news for the Arab delegations," Abdul Shafi confirmed, "but I do not share that belief. I have met with the President-elect and I think that he is very honest. And to tell you the truth, I don't think that he is as pro-Israeli as many people believe. He too has his doubts. If the Rabin government continues to stall on these negotiations, I think that Mr. Clinton will act."

Seated in his home in Gaza, Abdul Shafi reflected on the change in administrations and the prospects for progress in the bilateral talks. In 1988, he had predicted an agreement on the Palestinian question by 1993. But now he was not so sure. "I think that the new president will attempt to move the talks along just as President Bush did," he said. "I don't think that we can expect any major intervention. The big fear now is that the talks will stall altogether. And they have. The Israeli position has not really changed." But would the talks collapse? "No, not yet, I don't think we are at that point," Abdul Shafi said. "But we must guard against the unpredictable. The situation of the people in the territories is very bad, they want progress. If things blow up here [in the West Bank or Gaza] then I think that that could jeopardize what is going on in Washington."

On December 15, 1992, the mutilated body of Sergeant Major Nissim Toledano, a twenty-nine-year-old Israeli border policeman who had been kidnapped by Palestinian religious fundamentalists, was discovered by the side of a dirt road near a small Palestinian village not far from East Jerusalem. Toledano's kidnapers had first announced that they would release their captive in exchange for Ahmed Yassin, the founder of Hamas, who was serving a fifteen-year sentence in an Israeli jail, but when it became clear that Yassin would not be released, Toledano was stabbed and strangled. The murder shook Israel and threatened to undermine the Rabin government, which looked helpless in the face of the rising tide of Palestinian violence.

Just after Toledano's body was found, Israel's Tsomet party called for the deportation of twelve hundred Palestinians identified with the Hamas movement, and a crackdown on suspected Hamas supporters of the fundamentalist organization in the occupied territories. Even the left-wing Meretz bloc, whose leaders were part of Rabin's cabinet, were enraged by the crime and pressed the prime minister for "an iron-fisted war" against the religious group. Pressed to act quickly, Rabin promised through a spokesman that the fundamentalist movement and its leaders would be "hit as hard as possible."

But it was the opposition Likud party that exerted the most pressure on the government. Likud spokesmen excoriated the prime minister for not heading off the wave of violence sweeping through the occupied territories and called on Rabin to pull Israel out of the Washington talks. But Rabin was not willing to take that step. "We have but one way," he told reporters in an impromptu news conference in Jerusalem, "[and] it is divided in two: efforts to reach peace and [a] war to annihilate terrorism. We have no intention of withdrawing from the talks being conducted in Washington."

In his six months as Israel's prime minister, Yitzhak Rabin had faced many crises—but none had been as explosive as the one that was ignited by the Toledano incident. The border policeman's murder seemed purposely designed to push the government to the limit of its political abilities: While the prime minister had made a personal commitment to negotiating peace with Israel's Arab neighbors, he knew that he could not continue them so long as Israeli citizens lived in fear. Rabin was caught in a political squeeze: If he suspended the talks in Washington, he would be condemned as an opponent of peace, but if he did not act tough, the promise to maintain Israeli security would be questioned. In either case, his government would be endangered.

The Toledano incident also had a crippling impact on the Arab community, where Palestinian leaders feared that the murder would lead to a new round of escalating violence between gun-toting Israeli settlers and well-armed Palestinian radicals. There could only be one result from such a confrontation—IDF soldiers would have to step in to prevent an all-out war between Palestinians and Israeli settlers. Considering their own fears, it seemed unlikely that they would willingly protect the Palestinians from their fellow Israeli citizens. They might decide to look the other way.

The Toledano killing was the most recent signal that relations between Israelis and Palestinians were deteriorating. In the week prior to the kidnapping, three Israeli soldiers were killed in the Gaza Strip, four were wounded in a gun battle near Jenin, seven Palestinians were injured in street fights with Israeli soldiers, and twelve cars were burned in Jerusalem. The incidents were timed to coincide with the fifth anniversary of intifada's beginning; the increasing tension between Israelis and Palestinians was proof that the current situation was worse than anything experienced in the territories since December 1987. Open conflict between Israeli soldiers and Palestinian radicals seemed imminent.

The Toledano murder, however, actually boosted the standing of Hamas in the Palestinian community, and even among well-known Arab moderates. While few Palestinians applauded Hamas's actions, the incident symbolized the growing power of the fundamentalist movement and highlighted the increasing vulnerability of the PLO. The public mood was unmistakable: Frustrated by the lack of progress in the Washington negotiations privately, the organization was credited with standing up to the Israelis—which is more than could be said for the PLO. "Hamas keeps its promises—it is willing to fight an all-out war against Israel to liberate all of Palestine," a young Palestinian man said just one week after the Toledano killing. "Everyone knows that the PLO gave up on that goal long ago."

The profound effect of the Toledano incident was everywhere in evidence in the West Bank and Gaza Strip—and in Israel. It was the most prominent symbol of the crisis, and frustration, that gripped both societies. Israelis began to feel vulnerable in a way that they rarely had before: While Israel itself was not under a wartime alert, individual citizens felt besieged. No one was safe, but no one could clearly identify the enemy. The murderers of Toledano could be anywhere on the West Bank or in Gaza. Or they could be in Haifa, Nazareth, or Tel Aviv. Individual Israelis began to draw comparisons between their plight and that of the Jewish community of pre-Holocaust Germany, where unseen, murderous forces were not only close to home, but were right next door. The border policeman's murder was a brutal reminder that no Jew was safe anywhere—not even in Israel.

Large numbers of Palestinians harbored similar fears. The Toledano murder rekindled anxieties that Israel would finally impose its threat to annex the West Bank lands of "Judea" and "Samaria" and transfer the Palestinians to Jordan. The fear of a mass expulsion was especially prominent among older Palestinians in the West Bank's twenty-two refugee camps, where over 110,000 Palestinians and their descendants had been forced into exile after 1948. The anxiety was heightened by reports that Israeli police units were on the move in the West Bank and Gaza and that travel to Israel, where many Palestinians had jobs, was being curbed.

Less than twenty-four hours after Toledano's body was found, Prime Minister Rabin ordered the expulsion of over four hundred Hamas activists to Lebanon. The Palestinians were given fifty dollars, a blanket, jackets, and a small amount of food. "We saw a need to take action against the body which leads in terror and the war against the peace negotiations," Rabin said. The prime minister added that the decision was made upon the advice of the Israeli attorney-general and did not violate international law.

Just hours later, the first in a rising crescendo of violent incidents was set off in the West Bank and Gaza. Rabin's action seemed to confirm the worst fears of the Palestinian community: It was confirmation that the Israeli government was acting on a secret policy designed to deport the Palestinian people one at a time. The deportations were followed by the wholesale arrest of sixteen hundred Palestinian activists. The occupied territories were being slowly stripped of their most important leaders.

In Washington, the eighth round of the bilateral talks ended on a rancorous note. Haidar Abdul Shafi predicted that the Israeli action would deal a "death blow" to the peace process and he vowed that the Palestinians would not return to Washington until the crisis was ended. To emphasize their objection, the Palestinians and the other Arab delegations boycotted the last day of the talks. There was no time set for reconvening the negotiations.

The deportations set off riots in the Gaza Strip, where six Palestinians were shot in a single day near the Khan Younis refugee camp. Palestinian spokesperson Hanan Ashrawi called the Israeli action "a massacre" and she criticized left-wing Israeli cabinet members for standing behind Rabin's decision. Demonstrations, rioting, strikes, and attacks on Israeli soldiers escalated and schools and businesses shut down in protest over the expulsions. The disturbances were particularly bloody in the Gaza Strip, where ten Palestinians were killed during the last week of December.

For many Palestinian delegates, the deportations were the latest in a series of provocative Israeli actions designed to undercut the delegation's credibility in the territories, and many vowed that the end of the current round of negotiations marked the end of the search for peace. During a meeting with American officials, the Palestinians presented their case in stark terms: If Rabin's action was not condemned and the United

Nations did not take steps to enforce sanctions against Israel, the peace process would collapse. The Palestinian delegates were adamant: They would not return to Washington.

In Tunis, however, Yasser Arafat and his senior advisers did not agree; in the immediate aftermath of Rabin's expulsion order the PLO issued a halfhearted condemnation of the action and then explicitly stated that the Palestinian delegation would be returning to Washington. "I see no reason why we should not continue to search for peace," a PLO spokesman said, without explicitly stating whether the delegation would return to the talks. "We will have to see about the rest."

The day after the Palestinians boycotted the last session of discussions in Washington, Haidar Abdul Shafi flew to Tunis to talk to Arafat. He was infuriated by the PLO's lukewarm condemnation of the expulsions and its refusal to bluntly back a full boycott of all future talks. "Arafat has lost touch," Abdul Shafi told a fellow delegate on the last day of the talks. "He clearly does not know what effect this will have." Abdul Shafi had to make his point to Arafat directly and in the bluntest terms possible: His tepid response to the expulsions was a disaster for the delegation, did not reflect their views, and could actually spark an intra-Palestinian war in the territories.

In actuality, such a war was already taking place, and had been under way since the previous July, when Hamas and PLO cadres fought each other in a series of street battles in the Gaza Strip. Since then, Arafat had steadfastly refused to deal with Hamas leaders on any level, and had monitored the street battles in the Gaza Strip from a special operations room, which had direct links into the refugee camps he had set up in Tunis. Eventually, the two groups agreed to a truce, which was mediated by Abdul Shafi, and a National Reconciliation Committee that he established, in his home in Gaza. Tempers eventually cooled, but a simmering hatred between the PLO and Hamas continued just below the surface. Abdul Shafi was now clearly afraid that Arafat's almost public dismissal of the expulsions could result in another blowup, and a possible civil war.

Abdul Shafi arrived in Tunis on the afternoon of December

19, drove to Arafat's villa, and did not emerge until the next day. It was nearly impossible to obtain information on what was said, but it was clear what was decided. "The PLO strongly condemns the expulsions, which are inhumane, violate international law, and cannot be allowed to stand," a Tunis spokesman said in a telephone interview two days later. The decision had been made to support the Hamas deportees.

The deportation of the Hamas activists struck Faisal Husseini like a thunderbolt. The talks in Washington had not been going as well as expected by either the Israelis or Palestinians, but Rabin's expulsion order ruined whatever chance there was of even minor progress. The reaction in Tunis was even more astonishing and left Husseini and his colleagues in East Jerusalem sputtering in helpless rage: It was easy for Arafat to act like a judicious statesman, but he did not have to live in the occupied territories. His belated condemnation of the deportations eroded Fatah's support in the territories and fueled the violence that followed the expulsions.

Conditions in the territories deteriorated in mid-January 1993, when the Rabin government imposed a harsh curfew and cut off large segments of the West Bank and Gaza from Israel. Husseini was becoming more disheartened by the worsening situation and was more agitated than many of his friends had ever seen him. He spent his days in his office at the New Orient House in East Jerusalem (what one Israeli member of the Knesset bitingly called "the de facto government of Palestine in the territories") attempting to keep up with the fluid situation. The hallways around him were abuzz with activity, but he rarely looked up from his papers, spoke impatiently, waved off aides and secretaries, shouted into telephones, and ran both of his hands through his thinning gray hair during interviews—as if he were about to explode. During interviews with journalists three weeks after the Rabin order, his voice still quivered and snapped in frustration, and he had a difficult time keeping his temper.

"I fear that Mr. Rabin has made a terrible miscalculation,"

Husseini said. "He thought that he could easily divide the Palestinian community in the territories, but he has been proved wrong. He thought that he could divide the leadership in the territories from the leadership in Tunis, but he has been proved wrong. Instead of dividing the Palestinian people he has provided a rallying point for them, and now he must find a way to broker a peace that moves beyond the current crisis. I am telling you that the United States must help him in this in the only way that they can—by making Israel obey international law, by making sure that the United Nations acts consistent with its own mandate."

Husseini angrily dismissed a question about the political pressure that might have caused Rabin to expel the 415 Hamas activists. "We have political pressures here too, in this building," he said. "We have political pressures in the territories, among our own people. There is political pressure from other nations. We have had forty years of political pressure. This is not simply a deportation of Hamas activists; this is the expulsion of Palestinians. They have ties to us, we know these people. This places enormous pressure on us so that now we cannot and we must not return to the talks. So Mr. Rabin, to save himself some political trouble may have caused the gravest political trouble."

Husseini was silent, then nodded his head and leaned forward. "I am telling you this. Mr. Rabin must deal with the situation that is. We must negotiate peace now and it must succeed, but we will not do so until the deportees return to their homes."

Husseini rose from his chair and extended his hand. "They will come to arrest me, they have done that before and they have put me in jail," he said. "But if the Israelis do not now make a move for peace, if they do not resolve this crisis, then I will oppose them and fight them. I cannot make peace with them. But I am a realist, I am a realist. I know that they can come here and they can sit at this table and sign a piece of paper with some Palestinian. But if they do not resolve this crisis then when they come here they will not find me. They can sign the paper with someone else. There are Palestinians who would do that. But I won't be here. I will be out there." Husseini thrust his finger over his left shoulder. "I will be out there somewhere in the hills fighting them. But I cannot allow the division of my people."

Hanan Ashrawi sat in the hallway outside of Husseini's office, leafing through the papers in her briefcase. She smiled, then turned serious, reviewing her notes. She was at her best during the deportation crisis, trying to parse the anger felt by Husseini and others into the discourse of everyday life. But instead of saying "How would you like it if it happened to you," she used other words, the product of the language she had been trained with in the American educational system. It was precise, measured, even-tempered, certain, and very effective. It had the tone of moral authority.

"I will not indulge in recriminations every time an Israeli dies because of violence in the occupied territories, because they do not deplore it every time it happens to us. The truth of our violence with Israel and of their violence with *us* is that violence distorts the moral fabric of the occupied and the occupier equally."

Sari Nusseibeh's cubicle was down the hallway from Husseini's. One of the most controversial and captivating figures of the Palestinian national movement, Nusseibeh was fiery, temperamental, scholarly, and (like Husseini) the intellectual heir of an aristocratic family. He carried that imperial imprimatur with him—he had been accused of being haughty, theoretical, and impractical, but Nusseibeh was, and remains, one of the Palestinian movement's great pragmatists; while other Palestinians crowded into the conference halls of Madrid, he stayed in Jerusalem and created some two hundred political committees to make independence a fact, regardless of what might later be negotiated in Washington.

"If you are going to have a two-state solution, a Palestinian state living alongside an Israeli state, then you have to start planning. No one is going to do it for you," he said at the time. Nusseibeh is surrounded by books, and ideas have been the motive force in his life. He does not enjoy talking to journalists, but he motions to a chair anyway, shrugs his shoulder, and waits for the expected question on the deportations. "I am not a politician," he says.

Educated at Oxford and Harvard, where he took his Ph.D. in philosophy, he leans back in his chair, smiles, and rattles off the names of his professors—who are among the great luminaries in modern academia. "W.V.O. Quine. Have you read him? He was my teacher," he says. This is a disguise; for while Nusseibeh is a scholar, he strikes everyone who meets him as the consummate revolutionary theorist, and he talks like one. There is an uncanny similarity between Nusseibeh and the late American author Jerzy Kosinski, who played Gregori Zinoviev in the movie *Reds*. Kosinski captured the understated revolutionary zeal of Zinoviev perfectly; he was a studied, romantic, hard-nosed pragmatist, and a man of very few words. But there are differences. Zinoviev's religion was historical determinism; for Nusseibeh there is no law to history but the certainty of change. He is a studied, romantic, hard-nosed pragmatist—and his words come like shells fired from a rifle.

"When you weigh all the dynamics versus the obstacles, surely you think that the obstacles will be overcome," he says. "But having said that I must admit that there is no inevitability in history. There is only the fact of the process—that Israelis and Palestinians are now walking down one path together. I must have faith that we will finish this journey together and I feel that we cannot diverge from this path that we have taken. We walk it together into an uncertain future. The deportations have created a crisis now, though, and a negative public mood. Perhaps we will have to stop this journey because our people will demand it. That is what we are trying to find out. But . . ." Nusseibeh stops, hesitating, and brings his hands up in defeat. "Why are you asking me these things? The Palestinian revolution is not being made in this building, but out there, among Palestinians."

CHAPTER SEVEN
BETHLEHEM

A cracked and crumbling two-lane highway runs south along the arid escarpments from Jerusalem to Bethlehem through some of the most ancient and sacred land in the world. Small villages and simple Palestinian homes surrounded by occasional olive groves dot the landscape, and the roads are sometimes blocked by small herds of goats or sheep, or by an Israeli military checkpoint. Jesus and his disciples preached here, and here, sixty years after Pontius Pilate ruled, the ill-fated Jewish Rebellion against Rome recruited its most radical and dedicated adherents. More than six hundred years later, with the Jewish population dispersed, the armies of the Prophet came, claimed the land, and converted thousands of the inhabitants to the banners of Islam. Since that time, the West Bank has been the one place in the world were Jews, Christians, and Muslims have lived together. Today the much traveled road from Jerusalem to Bethlehem is the main street of Palestine.

The highway south from Jerusalem is crowded with taxis, called sharecabs, which ply their trade through the occupied territories. The taxis, usually older models of Mercedes-Benz station wagons, are an inexpensive means of travel. They transport their travelers to anywhere on the West Bank or even across Israel into Gaza, so long as there are enough people in the cab to make it profitable for a driver. A traveler in the occupied territories can find dozens of sharecabs in a parking lot set aside for the purpose near the northwest gate of the Old City of Jerusalem, or at the taxi stands in any large West Bank city. Sharetaxis are organized by destination and only leave when there are enough people available to make the trip to Nablus—or Jenin, or Ramallah, or Hebron—or anywhere else. It is a surprisingly efficient and inexpensive system.

Palestinian drivers enjoy seeing Americans and testing their English on them, and it is possible to get an unofficial tour for the asking—or even if one is not requested. A Palestinian share-cab is probably the best place in the Middle East to learn Arabic, hear the latest rumor, or be interrogated about the United States. Political lectures are also free, and occasionally there are orations on Islam. Since the rise of Hamas, the nature of religion is one of the most popular topics in the West Bank.

That was the case on a cold, windy, and rainy day in mid-January of 1993, when the Hamas deportations were still in the headlines. "I have been praying about what it means to be a good Muslim," a driver on his way to Bethlehem said in Arabic. He reached out his hand to take the money from the passengers, passed from person to person, from back to front. "I have come to some conclusions."

The seven passengers in the sharecab listened with rude disinterest to the driver's announcement and continued to look at the cold, rain-soaked land they passed. But the driver was not insulted; he had a captive audience, and throughout the trip he directed his words at the Palestinian journalist seated next to him. He began his discourse on the road south from Jerusalem, paused for a breath as the highway climbed a short distance past a group of concrete homes, and quoted liberally from the Koran on the road that ran past Bethlehem. He interrupted his lecture to navigate the wide, puddle-filled road that curved suddenly to the west, past Bethlehem, then continued his sermon as the road climbed south.

The Palestinian journalist listened to the driver with feigned interest and nodded in agreement in the appropriate places. The driver spoke in Arabic and after the trip was ended, the journalist tried to remember everything that he said. His talk went something like this: "God wants us to be good Muslims or he would not have sent the Prophet—praised be his name— among us to show us his way. So, just as it is necessary to be a good Muslim, we must also be good Palestinians. After having given it much thought, I believe that to be a good Palestinian we must realize that the religious struggle is a political struggle and our political struggle is religious. They are one and the same thing. As the Prophet (blessed be his name) spread his faith, so we must spread our national dream. That is what I think." In the midst of this, the driver paused to collect his thoughts. A man was waving through the rain on the road ahead.

The cab pulled over to pick the man up and everyone in the cab was forced to make room. The traditional greetings were exchanged in Arabic. In the back of the cab, a woman was seated with her young son, whose face was streaked with tears. The woman was holding a plastic bag filled with bread; she was coming back from the market and her son, it seemed, had somehow misbehaved and been disciplined. After a mile or so, the woman began to fall asleep and could be heard breathing heavily in the back of the cab. The young boy was embarrassed that his mother had fallen asleep and looked around the cab to see if anyone had noticed. No one paid any attention and the driver continued his talk.

"The call to prayer is a way of reminding us every day that we are Muslims," the driver said. "We must put politics and religion together this way: As we are called to prayer as Muslims we are also called to remember our special place as Palestinians. The Prophet—blessed be his name—reminds us that we have a special place and a responsibility that is both political and religious. This is one of the things that makes Muslims different from other people. To say that we are good Muslims does not mean that we are just devout. We also have political duties. These political duties are very important now, in this crisis."

The cab pulled over to the side of the road just after the turnoff to Bethlehem, outside the gate to the Dheisheh refugee camp. Sealed off from the highway by a high fence, Dheisheh was built back from the road and against a large hill to house refugees from the former Mandate. A second fence had replaced the first—as in Jebalya—which was bulldozed. It lay in jagged disuse near the highway, as an obstacle course for those who wanted to visit. Several paths led to the camp's single entrance. Someone had cut a hole in the fence about thirty yards from the gate, but the Israelis had patched it. The fence was topped by barbed wire.

Dheisheh was awash with a cold January rain that came down the mountain in wide rivulets between the flat-roofed concrete houses. The refugee camp did not have sidewalks, or gutters, or paved roads, so that walking from house to house along the steep hill was treacherous. The houses were built next to each other, and although the camp was crowded, it was nearly silent in the January rain. People stayed indoors during the winter, though one group of Palestinian children continued to play in their shirtsleeves in a muddy street. Up one alley on the side of the hill was the home of camp director Hosein Shaheen. The door opened into a large room with chairs and sofas and a single table—a greeting room for guests that can be found in any traditional Palestinian home. Shaheen appeared, smiled, and greeted his guests, and said that he was honored by their presence. He sent a small boy to notify the neighbors. Welcoming visitors from America is a community event.

"The camps here were temporarily established in 1949 as a result of the Arab-Israeli war but now they are permanent, as you can plainly see for yourself," Shaheen says. Shaheen is a physically imposing man and the head of a large and extended household. He is a man of great stature in the camp and is called on to mediate disputes, manage the camp's clinic and school, and make certain that the distribution of food and clothing is equitable. "The United Nations is taking care of everyone in the camp," he says, "but I am responsible for them. This is not a good life, but the United Nations works hard here and there are some extra services that have been added. It is crowded here and some of the families are cold in the winter."

He recites the camp litany. "There are 1,650 families here, 8,000 people in all. We have a health care clinic, a vaccination program, our own sanitation unit, and we have started a physiotherapy unit since the beginning of the intifada to take care of those who are badly injured," he says. "The young men come into the camp from the streets with broken or shattered arms and legs and we repair them. We send the worst cases on to Bethlehem or Jerusalem. We have a new community center that has been donated by the Japanese government. Some officials came here from Japan and asked us what we needed and we told them. They gave us the community center. We are grateful for this help. More than 1,900 boys and girls receive their preparatory education here, then they go to school in Bethlehem. My own children go there every day. Individual residents here received packets from their friends in America or in Europe."

Shaheen paints a grim picture of camp life. "Things have been very bad here since the intifada. There are many confrontations all the time and they have increased since the deportations," he says. "There is a settlement near here and the settlers are armed. There have been shootings. Our people are living under conditions that are very bad. The camp has been under many curfews and all of its entrances have been sealed except for one." Shaheen says that he has been changed by the unremitting tension of the Israeli occupation. "I will not live to see the day that I want to see," he says. "In the beginning, at the start of the intifada, I had a lot of hope. We were reviving our society. I thought that we might win our independence, or at least force the Israelis out. But that was five years ago and things have gotten worse."

The Palestinian journalist, who has known Shaheen for many years, relates that there is some fear that the residents and settlers will someday come to open conflict. There was one shooting, where a father of a large family was killed when a settler fired into the camp, he says.

Shaheen's father, an elderly man, comes into the room to listen. His son translates what he has said so far and then continues. "Palestinians fled what is now Israel," he says. "My own family came here from a small village called Artuf, which now has a different name. It is southwest of Jerusalem in Israel. I remember it as a young boy and I am teaching my children about it. My father had a farm in Artuf and his father before him and his father before him. It goes back many generations. It was our land and it was near our village and the Jews came and chased us out. That was in 1948. We came here to Dheisheh and we have been here ever since. Now we are afraid that the Israelis will chase us out again. This time we will never come back. That is our worry."

"I believe in the peace negotiations and I think that there must be peace negotiations," Shaheen says, "but there are many others who disagree. There is a great level of frustration in the camp and among the Palestinians. We are very weak, and we are negotiating from a position of weakness, so I am not an optimist. While I approve of the peace talks I do not really think that they will lead anywhere. I do not trust the Israelis. We have to learn: Zionism will give nothing to the Palestinians. Even now, the Israelis are planning to put us out of this place."

Shaheen's daughter walks in from school, swinging her knapsack, smiles at the guests, and disappears. Other men come from the neighborhood to meet Shaheen's American visitors. They walk across the room from the front door and stand stiffly, hands extended. A woman appears from the kitchen, counts the arriving guests, shakes her head, and departs quickly to make more coffee. She brings the coffee (Turkish, thick, dark, and strong) in on a tray, places it on a table in the center of the room, and leaves. But the daughter returns to listen to the discussion and exchanges a greeting with her father and grandfather.

The Israeli occupation has played havoc with Palestinian family life. In many refugee homes, women have taken on added tasks because of the occupation and their work is unending and backbreaking: Women do the cooking, cleaning, and raise the children, but many women of Dheisheh are also given the task of searching out enough food to put on the table at night. The United Nations provides food and clothing for the most destitute, but both always seem to be in short supply. "There is not enough," Shaheen confirms. "There never seems to be enough. There is always a problem with food, clothing, medicine, the necessities of life. Some families need blankets."

The traditional practice of raising large families has placed an additional strain on Palestinian women. While Hosein Shaheen is responsible for passing out parcels to the camp, his wife is responsible for making the same equitable arrangements in their home.

At first glance, the women of Dheisheh seem to fit the easy stereotypes that Westerners have of women in the Muslim world: as intimidated, cloistered, silent, acquiescing appendages to a largely male-dominated society. It is not that simple. The high literacy rate among the Palestinian population and the premium put on education applies to men and women alike. In addition, the example set by politically sophisticated, well-educated, and literate middle-class women has had a profound effect on women in more traditional families. Everyone has a stake in the outcome of the Israeli-Palestinian struggle and Palestinian women have been very active in political organizing.

In the midst of Shaheen's talk, his wife returns to the room and stands in the doorway. She nods a greeting and speaks in Arabic. "She says that there is a lot of talk here," Shaheen says, "and that it is enough to say that the Israelis have made a terrible mistake and that we are united as a nation." In this sense, Palestinian women fit the stereotype. When there are visitors in the home, the men traditionally engage in the political discussions. The coffee is prepared by the women for the men, and served by the oldest son (the same is not true for Palestinian Christian homes, where the traditions of Islam have not been felt). But since the intifada, Palestinian women have been emerging from the kitchen to participate in political debates. Hosein is translating.

"She wants to know whether what she has heard is true—that there are some very religious Jews who think that Israel should not exist because their messiah has not come." Everyone in the room nods. It is true. There are some very Orthodox Israelis who believe this. Some of them have come to Washington to pass out press releases. Israel can only be formed, they believe, when the messiah comes. The woman nods. "She wants to know," Shaheen says, "whether Rabin will deport them too?"

Yitzhak Rabin's order to deport over four hundred Hamas activists placed the question of religious fundamentalism on the Palestinian national agenda. Suddenly, the Palestinians were being forced to choose the kind of society they wanted to live in. Rabin believed that the choice came down to one between a fundamentalist and a secular state. The leadership in the territories thought differently. They believed that their choice was between an open society and a closed one. Given that reality, they had little choice but to listen to the voice of the Palestinian street—which condemned the deportations. This was not what Rabin had intended; he wanted to end attacks on Israelis by Palestinians and show that he could be as tough in maintaining Israeli security as his political competitors. Instead, he united the Palestinian community in a way that it never had been before.

"It is certain that Mr. Rabin miscalculated the effect of the deportations on us," Haidar Abdul Shafi said after he returned from his late December meeting with Yasser Arafat in Tunis. "I do not believe that he thought that the Palestinian community would speak with such a loud, single voice. We are united in our stand against these expulsions. We must point out again and again that this is a violation of international law and that this illegal action cannot be allowed to stand." Everywhere in the West Bank and Gaza in January of 1993, there was talk of American hypocrisy. "Clearly what the Israelis have done goes against the agreements of many nations. Why is it so important

for Saddam Hussein to obey international law," Hosein Shaheen asked, "and not Yitzhak Rabin?"

That Rabin might be caught between contending political
forces (pushed by one side for an accommodation with the
Palestinians, and by the other for increased security) made little
difference to Shaheen, or to the Palestinian leadership in East
Jerusalem. For both, the reality was that for every Israeli political action there was an equal and opposite Palestinian reaction. The tougher that Rabin became, the more difficult it was
for the Palestinian leadership to continue negotiating with
him—and the more difficult it became for people like Shaheen
to support the peace talks. The Palestinian leadership was
caught in much the same political trap as the Israeli prime
minister; everyone wanted peace, but no one wanted to give in
to the Israelis. As Rabin's popularity soared in the wake of the
deportations, therefore, the PLO's plummeted in the West
Bank and Gaza.

The expulsion of the four hundred-plus Hamas activists was
the greatest challenge Palestinian society had faced during its
twenty years of occupation by Israel: They were now being
forced to sort out their own long-standing political problems.
For many Palestinians, the deportations sparked mixed feelings. The overwhelming majority of Palestinians condemned
Rabin's expulsion order, but many of them also questioned
Hamas's long-term political goals. "What can they offer, really?"
an East Jerusalem resident asked. "Do they have a plan, or do
they want to fight Israel forever? Do they think that they can
really win? That they can continue this battle forever? I think
that they are deluding themselves." A young Fatah activist,
speaking on a Ramallah street, was even more outspoken. "The
worst thing about the deportations is that it does just the opposite of what Rabin thought it would do," he said. "Now everyone is sympathetic with Hamas. That is very distasteful."

The Hamas deportations threw the PLO into a quandary.
After Yasser Arafat's mid-December political fumble, Fatah organizers in the West Bank hurried to patch up relations with
their Hamas counterparts. But even as they did so, Hamas

leaders who had not been deported continued to emphasize the PLO's inability to bring pressure to bear on Israel to resolve the crisis. "The Tunis leaders should not listen to leftist, Zionist, perhaps American, spokesmen who tell them that this is a blow to the Moslem fundamentalists which opens the door to the implementation of a peaceful settlement in the region," Hamas official Ibrahim Ghosheh told *Mideast Mirror* in a postdeportation interview. "Israel does not differentiate between one Palestinian and another. If the PLO does not endorse Hamas's cause now, its turn will come in the future."

Hamas leader Ibrahim Yazoorie, one of the few fundamentalist leaders not to be nabbed in the roundup, agreed. "Yasser Arafat is pulling the strings of the delegation in the peace conference," he said, "but what good is that? Since the peace negotiations have begun the situation in the territories has gone from bad to worse. The PLO leadership is clearly not the leadership of the Palestinian people."

In the weeks following Rabin's expulsion order, a large number of Palestinians began to suspect that the PLO had approved of his deportation plan beforehand. According to a widely circulated rumor, Rabin had sent a secret envoy to speak with Yasser Arafat in Tunis. The messenger wanted to know whether Arafat would oppose the temporary deportation of religious fundamentalists. Arafat answered that the PLO would not oppose such an action and assured Rabin's envoy that the PLO would recommend that Husseini, Abdul Shafi, Ashrawi, and the other Palestinian delegates return to the peace talks.

The story was not true, but the fact that it was repeated and widely believed showed just how weak the PLO had become. The rumor gained credence among large numbers of Palestinians because of Arafat's unwillingness to condemn the deportations immediately following Rabin's announcement: It seemed to confirm that the PLO was playing a double game. It was no secret to any Palestinian that the deportation of Hamas activists benefited Arafat, and Fatah, the PLO's mainline political organization. With Hamas leaders out of the way, Fatah could rebuild its battered political networks.

The Fatah-aligned leadership in the territories understood the damage the story could cause and let it be known that it was Haidar Abdul Shafi who persuaded the reluctant Arafat to shift his strategy. Within four days of the expulsions, the PLO condemned Rabin, announced that the Palestinian delegation would not be returning to Washington, called on the United Nations to impose sanctions on Israel, and ordered its Fatah organization in the occupied territories to form a united front with Hamas in opposing the Israeli occupation. Arafat even took the extraordinary step of inviting Hamas leaders to negotiate their participation in the Palestine National Council.

It was too late. Like the poker player who inadvertently shows his hand before the last bet, Arafat exposed his own weakness, thereby confirming what Israeli political leaders had long suspected—the PLO's organization in the West Bank and Gaza Strip was losing ground to the better-organized and better-financed Hamas cadres. But how strong was Hamas, and could it count on the full support of the Palestinian people in the West Bank and Gaza? In many ways, this was the most important question facing the Israeli government in the wake of the deportations.

Any hope for reaching an agreement on Palestinian autonomy rested almost solely on the ability of the Israeli government to negotiate with Palestinian moderates in the occupied territories—and not with the PLO. Unfortunately, however, the moderates of the territories were isolated. They simply did not command the broad-based support of a large number of Palestinians in the West Bank and Gaza. If they could be strengthened, however, then the Rabin government could negotiate a credible agreement with them that would have a good chance of succeeding after an Israeli withdrawal. One of the ways to strengthen them was to neutralize the growing power of the Hamas fundamentalist movement.

Once again, however, the view from East Jerusalem was much different. For Faisal Husseini and other senior Palestinian moderates in the territories, the expulsions became a test of their belief in what they had termed the "indivisibility" of the Palestinian people. The Palestinians would succeed or fail together, Husseini had often said, and he intended to stand by that principle. But the answer that Husseini gave to Rabin's challenge was not dictated by the leaders in East Jerusalem; it came instead from the territories, from people like Hosein Shaheen, and his father, at the Dheisheh refugee camp.

"The PLO is weak, yes it is true," Shaheen's father said in Arabic, "and it is true that the Palestinian people are in a weak position, but we are not weak people." The elder Shaheen, with his vivid memories of Artuf, stabbed the air with his index finger: "I am not Hamas, I can never be Hamas. But Hamas can never stop being Palestinians. So Mr. Rabin has made a terrible mistake: Maybe someday these religious men will stop being so devout, that is possible, but they will never stop being Palestinians."

Later, the younger Shaheen stood in the doorway and thanked his guests for coming. Outside the rain came down in torrents, washing off the steep hill and into the camp. It took only a moment to hail a sharecab to Bethlehem. The driver no longer gave his oration about religion or what it meant to be a Muslim. And no one talked endlessly, as Palestinians did just after the deportations, about what it meant to be a Palestinian. As the elder Shaheen had put it, it was now evident that being a member of Hamas was just one part of being a Palestinian. Hamas was a fact of life.

But what did they want?

"An Islamic state."

Dr. Ali Jirbawi, the leading Palestinian authority on Hamas and an American-educated professor of political science at Bir Zeit University, was as taken aback by the question as he was by the simplicity of the answer. "Hamas leaders believe, very simply, that this society should be an Islamic society," he says. "But we should not be fooled by what this means. Americans always think of Iran, and the mullahs. That is not the case here. Hamas is different; it is a very politically sophisticated organization and has always been able to transform itself to meet existing conditions. Its leaders are very astute. It's not that Hamas compromises on its principles—it doesn't. But it knows which battles to fight and when to fight them."

Hamas—an acronym for the Islamic Resistance Movement (the Harakat al-Muqawama al-Islamiyya, in Arabic)—was organized in Gaza at the beginning of the intifada by clerics who traced their roots to the Society of Muslim Brothers founded in Cairo in 1928. Originally established to reform individual morality, the Cairo group became a well-organized political movement that actively opposed Western influence in the Arab world. Branches of the brotherhood took root in Syria (where it was violently suppressed by Hafez al-Assad) and in Jordan, where it became a conservative counterpoint to King Hussein's campaign to create a Western-style democracy.

After its founding, the Muslim brotherhood underwent a divisive controversy on the question of whether reform of the individual must precede an Islamic revolution, or whether political action could be carried out without the spiritual transformation of the Arab people. The argument was resolved in Egypt in the 1930s, when radical elements took over the brotherhood's leadership and committed the organization to a violent confrontation with the West and secularism. They did not end their efforts to reach individual Muslims, but political organizing now became as important as their social program. In Jordan, however, the brotherhood's conservative leaders maintained their hold on the organization and preserved its reformist, moderate, and nonconfrontational character. The brotherhood's influence among Palestinians reflected these divergent views. The Gaza brotherhood maintained close ties to Egypt, while the West Bank brotherhood was more influenced by events in Jordan. The two views inside the Palestinian brotherhood became a function of geography.

After the partition of Palestine, Gaza's clerics believed that their former homes in Israel could only be "liberated" by strict adherence to Muslim religious principles and by a violent war with the Israeli occupier. This unyielding stance struck a chord with students at Gaza's Islamic University where, in December 1987, a campaign was under way to eliminate pornography,

drugs, and other "corrupt Western influences." The intifada
caught this movement in mid-stride. When the intifada began,
Gaza clerics organized Hamas by adding a political component
to the brotherhood's student-based, anti-Western social program. Within weeks of its founding, the new organization grew
into one of the most influential political movements in the Gaza
Strip.

Hamas's Gaza leaders knew that in order to be successful,
however, they had to influence a larger portion of the Palestinian population. In February 1988, therefore, they decided to
infiltrate the West Bank through student and professor exchanges. Within a few months, Hamas had a political infrastructure in place in Nablus, Jenin, Ramallah, and Hebron.
Using this infrastructure as a base, Hamas was soon strong
enough to vie for power with the PLO-controlled intifada strike
committees. By the summer of 1988, Hamas cells in the West
Bank were so strong that they survived a series of violent confrontations with PLO leaders over strike policies. Their survival
brought them new respect and recognition from the intifada's
command structure, which was charged with running the day-
to-day activities of the intifada.

At the same time that Hamas was gaining influence with
intifada commanders, however, it was being torn apart by a
serious inner dispute between the organization's radical Gaza
founders and the group of Jordan-influenced West Bankers.
The West Bank clerics claimed that the Gazans were subverting
the brotherhood's basic tenet: It was simply impossible to have
an Islamic revolution without first creating devout Muslims. A
political revolution, they argued, could only take place after a
religious awakening. The Gazans, on the other hand, maintained that the revolution was *already* under way and that devout Muslims were being continually strengthened by it.

Inevitably, perhaps, the viewpoint of Hamas's Gaza-based
clerics was adopted as the organization's program. The victory
was due, in large part, to the fear among the Hamas leadership
that unless they continued to participate in the intifada, they
would lose strength to other fundamentalist groups, like Is-

lamic Jihad. No one, not even the West Bank clerics, wanted that to happen. As a result, by the early summer of 1988, the brotherhood's moderate West Bank leaders had agreed to support the program put together by Hamas's Gaza founders. "It was a coup really, that took place when the younger generation forced their way into the old camp," Jirbawi says now. "The [West Bank] Brotherhood agreed to support Hamas in order to regain the allegiance of young Muslims. Under the formula Hamas would become the political branch of the Brotherhood. The coup gave the Gaza leaders a lot of options."

Nearing the end of its first year, Hamas had made extraordinary progress in building a grass-roots organization and had proved to be a serious competitor with the PLO for the leadership of the intifada in the streets of the West Bank and Gaza. But in late 1988, Hamas faced yet another crisis; this one was far more critical to the organization's future than any other earlier dispute. The organization's early attraction to young Palestinians, its leaders discovered, was being slowly eroded by fears over its commitment to creation of an Islamic state. The West Bank's community of Christians (nearly 20 percent of the total Palestinian population) feared Hamas's call for Islamic dominance. In addition, Palestinian women (a large portion of whom made up the West Bank's professional class) resented Hamas's implicit disregard of women's rights.

Fears about Hamas's domestic program sparked a number of verbal attacks on the organization by leading Palestinian businessmen, scholars, and political organizers; the organization began to lose its force. The crisis plunged Hamas's leadership into an acrimonious debate over the best way to respond to the challenge issued by Palestinian secularists. Not surprisingly, the group of Gaza hard-liners argued heatedly that any softening of Hamas's message would be fatal to the organization's cause. The group of West Bank pragmatists, however, contended that any unwillingness to compromise with secular forces meant the movement would be isolated and eventually strangled. Finally, facing a destructive split, the two sides agreed to a mutually uncomfortable compromise: Hamas would retain its Islamic character, but it would recognize the political realities of Palestinian life.

The formula was made public in the organization's charter, which was widely circulated in the occupied territories in October 1988. The first article of the charter reaffirmed Hamas's commitment to Islam's "guidelines," from which it "derives its thinking, interpretations and views about existence, life and humanity . . ." The charter confirmed the organization's call for the establishment of an Islamic state, but subsequent articles took note of the political realities of Palestinian society. Hamas guaranteed religious toleration to Christians and Jews "under the shadow of Islam" and recognized the central role played by women as "guides" and "educators" in the "war of liberation" against Israel.

"Hamas has learned; they know how *not* to intimidate Christians, secularists, women; they are very aware and they are extremely organized and sophisticated," Jirbawi explained. "They want to establish an Islamic state, but that does not mean the end of secular life. They have learned their lesson. As a result of that, they are a powerful force in some segments of Palestinian society. They are being listened to and, in many respects, they are the symbol of Palestinian resistance. So while the majority of Palestinians in the territories do not agree with their program, they admire their anti-Israeli actions."

The Hamas leadership also worked to end its confrontation with mainstream PLO groups. The street battles with Arafat's Fatah regulars were becoming costly and alienating the fundamentalist group from large numbers of Palestinians who admired the Tunis leadership. In its charter, therefore, Hamas acknowledged the central role played by the PLO. "The PLO is among the closest to Hamas, for it constitutes a father, a brother, a relative, a friend," the Hamas charter said. "Can a Muslim turn away from his father, his brother, his relative, or his friend? Our homeland is one, our calamity is one, our destiny is one and our enemy is common to both of us."

The charter is what gave Hamas its reputation as a cagey and potent force in the occupied territories: Its bow to the role of women, Christians, and the PLO compromised nothing, but it allowed the organization to survive and grow. In the meantime, it continued to organize its political programs and it developed a strategy of high-profile attacks on Israelis that it knew would gain the support of Palestinians from every walk of life. By 1989, Hamas's unyielding political stance began to define the most radical actions of the intifada.

Ironically, the Israeli reaction to the rise of Hamas was, in large part, influenced by its fear of the power of the PLO. Israel believed that the Tunis leadership formed the basis of resistance and the only real Palestinian threat to Israel. Because of that, the Israeli government was slow to react to Hamas's growth and, for a number of years, did not take the fundamentalist movement seriously. Even when Hamas cadres became a force to be reckoned with on the streets of the West Bank and Gaza, Israel's security services focused their attention on Fatah and other PLO groups. Hamas's growth went forward largely unimpeded.

When the Palestinian leadership decided to participate in the peace process, Hamas condemned them, and the cease-fire that had characterized Hamas-PLO relations since 1989 began to break down. Coupled with its inability to provide funding for social service programs in the West Bank and Gaza, the PLO began to lose strength, and more and more Palestinians turned to Hamas for leadership. "There is no split between Hamas and the PLO," Hamas leader Ibrahim Yazoorie claims. "We are both looking for the end of occupation. But in fact, the Palestinian leadership is not accepted by many, many Palestinians. They have compromised too much."

That view is not unique to the Hamas leadership. Like most secular Palestinians, Ali Jirbawi has come to admire Hamas's unwillingness to compromise with Israel. "I am a secularist, but I have a true spot in my heart for Hamas," he says. "That feeling, I think, defines our dilemma, the dilemma we are facing as Palestinians. There is a basic contradiction between our political stance today in resisting the occupation, versus the social program of Hamas. Now the national resistance comes first. So the social clash between secularists and Islamists has been postponed until the occupation is finished. It is then, I think, that we will be faced with the ultimate question about who we are—about our national identity."

Six miles south of Bethlehem is the small Palestinian village of Za'tara, which was built by the Ta'mari tribe during the 1960s. The most famous of the sons of Za'tara is Salah Ta'mari, who left his village to study English literature at Ain Shams University in Cairo. The 1967 war interrupted his studies. Ta'mari left Cairo for Jordan, where he moved into a command position in the newly formed units of Palestinian freedom fighters, the *fedayeen*. He became one of the PLO's most successful commanders. Today Ta'mari is one of Yasser Arafat's closest and most valued associates.

Ta'mari is known throughout the Palestinian diaspora as "the hero of Karameh," a battle named for a small Jordanian town near the border with Israel. The fighting took place on March 21, 1968, during a cross-border raid launched by Israeli forces to destroy Fatah units based in Jordan. When the first column of tanks appeared, Ta'mari rallied his fighters and deployed them on the outskirts of the Jordanian village.

Ta'mari was outnumbered and outgunned, but he had absolute faith in his fighters. The results were predictable; the Israeli units routed the Palestinian defenders. But in the valley beyond, Ta'mari rallied his forces and they held their positions against repeated assaults for several hours. Surprised by such tenacity, the Israelis withdrew, leaving twenty-eight dead and four tanks on the Karameh battlefield.

Karameh was a turning point for Fatah. Yasser Arafat's movement became a rallying point for thousands of Palestinians, who flocked to Amman, where the funeral for the martyrs of Karameh was held. Ta'mari trained hundreds of the new recruits in Jordan and later in Lebanon, where he served as a leading Palestinian commander in Sidon. When Israel invaded Lebanon in 1982, Ta'mari was captured and incarcerated at

Ansar prison in southern Lebanon. But he continued to organize Palestinian resistance to Israel.

"I will be the last one to leave this prison," he told Ansar's commander, "and I will take the key." Ta'mari organized hunger strikes, political discussions, informers, and protests, and planned an uprising and breakout. When the commander called on him to end his political activities, he refused. "You are in charge of maintaining order," Ta'mari told him, "and I am in charge of maintaining disorder." In late 1982, Ta'mari led the Ansar uprising. The strike did not make international news, but it became a legendary moment in the history of the Palestinian community. Later, the methods used in Ansar were adopted by the strike committees of the intifada.

During his prison stay, Ta'mari struck up a friendship with Aharon Barnea, a noted Israeli reporter. Barnea later wrote about the relationship in *My Enemy, My Friend,* an influential book for those who wanted to end the Israeli-Palestinian conflict. Finally, in 1983, Ta'mari was released in a prisoner exchange. True to his promise, he was the last one out of the camp. "Get the key," he told a group of Israeli soldiers. After they had retrieved it, he put it in his pocket. Later, he made his way to the United States, where he organized a Palestinian youth group and raised money for trips to the West Bank and Gaza for interested Americans.

While in America, Ta'mari focused his efforts on ways to strengthen Palestinian nationalism. It was the same question that faced the Palestinian leadership, and every resident of the occupied territories. "Every time we face the Israelis in peace or in war, in negotiations or even across a cup of coffee," he says, "there is an engagement, a meeting with the enemy." Defining a Palestinian identity or, as he says, "finding out just how tough we really are, and whether we can truly survive"—has consumed the last ten years of his life. Such thinking has made Ta'mari one of the few genuine political theorists in the Palestinian movement.

Tall and thin, Ta'mari is thoughtful, intellectual, deliberate, and a puzzle for his more politically motivated colleagues in Tunis, who are preoccupied with the minutiae of running a liberation movement. It is precisely this ability to step back, "to be able to think," however, that propelled him into the upper ranks of Fatah and made him so valuable to Yasser Arafat. Ta'mari is also appreciated because of his detailed knowledge of Israel and Israelis. "Salah knows them very well," a colleague says. "He understands them. When we need to know what they are thinking we ask him. He can climb inside their heads."

In the midst of the deportation crisis, Ta'mari's advice, and his hours of reflection on the question of Palestinian nationalism, became especially valuable to Arafat, who was pressed on every side to call an end to the bilateral talks. Ta'mari argued the opposite point of view. "If we walk out of the negotiations now because there are human rights violations," he told Arafat in one telephone conversation, "then why did we go in the first place? There were human rights violations during the Madrid Conference. We did not quit then. We are negotiating with our enemy. Did we really expect them to treat us well?"

As the deportation decision forced Palestinians in the territories to debate their future, it propelled Ta'mari to focus his thinking on the unthinkable: that the Palestinian nation might not survive many more such catastrophes. "The Hamas deportations are a symbol of our continuing crisis as a people," he said at the time, "because they recall what happened to us in 1948. That is why the Palestinian people feel so deeply about it. I too feel this way. Our identity is slipping away and I cannot find a way to stop it. We have to find something to bind us or we will disappear."

"I have studied Zionism for twenty years," he says, "and I think I understand the worries of the early Zionists. Their problem was that they could foresee the possible death of Judaism in Europe, the slow and inevitable washing away of Jewish culture. Pogroms and prejudice were a historical and very real worry, but so was assimilation. Zionism could solve both problems. It could remove the Jews from Europe and salvage them as a distinct and unique people. So the early Zionists built an ideology based on the unique nature of Judaism and tied it to the idea of a state. We have not done that."

Not ironically, Ta'mari's thinking seems a strange parallel to the views of early Zionism and, for a time, he even thought of convening a congress in Basel—"in the same hall where Herzl founded Zionism"—to define the new national identity. "Being a Palestinian," Ta'mari argues, "must become almost like a religion for us, a Palestinian-ism." Such a "Palestinian-ism" would work toward the fulfillment of a Palestinian homeland in the same way that Zionism worked for the establishment of a Jewish state. The call of the Palestinian to prayer will not be issued from the mosque, but according to the principles of a new political theology.

Ta'mari was not thinking in a vacuum. During his years in Washington, he joined with groups of Israelis and Palestinians in relaxed atmospheres, in dinners and lunches, to talk about relations between the two communities. The gatherings seemed unplanned and unfocused, but inevitably the groups found that they shared a common political heritage. Zionism found its echo, perhaps not in the PLO, but certainly in the aspirations of the Palestinian national movement, which was undergoing many of the same stresses, failures—and successes. "In many ways we have learned from Zionism," a Palestinian associate of Ta'mari once reflected. "That is the great irony. Zionists claim that they have established a unique political doctrine that applies only to their people. But four decades of rubbing shoulders with them convinces me that that is not true."

But in January of 1993, it was still very much an open question as to whether the Palestinian national movement could succeed as Zionism had. "There is nothing inevitable in our struggle," Ta'mari said, "and there is no guarantee that simply because I believe that *we* are right and *they* are wrong we will somehow win in the end. I think that that is very much in doubt. Palestinians are beginning to disappear as a distinct identity. We have to save that identity: It will not happen by itself."

The deportation crisis deepened the crisis of Palestinian nationalism. After more than forty years of exile, it now seemed very possible that Palestinians would disappear as a distinct people—that, beset by crisis, financial ruin, and political incompetence, they would simply give up and disperse themselves throughout the world. From Dheisheh to Washington, Palestinians were desperately trying to find a way to salvage what they could; to stave off another "catastrophe."

It is six miles from Za'tara to the main north-south road through the West Bank and then another dozen miles north to Bethlehem. It is easy to understand why the national crisis that so concerned Ta'mari is an everyday reality for Palestinians. The drive to Bethlehem is a journey through the Palestinian version of Benny Begin's nightmare. Here the large homes of the Palestinian middle class are a silent testament to the crisis of Palestinian society. The large houses of Bethlehem are now boarded up and their residents have left, many of them for America. Like the Israeli woman on her trip back to Tel Aviv, many Palestinians have simply decided that they cannot go on.

The road to Bethlehem climbs past the homes and into the hills of the West Bank and then out along a precipitous ridge into the center of Bethlehem itself. Manger Square, a huge open area, dominates the center of the town. On one end of the square is the Church of the Nativity, built over a grotto identified in the sixth century as the location of the manger. The church is still a required stopping place for Christian pilgrims who make their way to the Holy Land from Europe and the United States.

There is probably no more emotional moment for Christians than the one that takes place in Bethlehem each Christmas Eve, when thousands gather to celebrate the birth of Jesus. A procession moves through the square and into the church. The crowd is preceded by a huge cross, and hymns boom out over the Palestinian landscape. Thousands of people come into the city, which has been the center of a Palestinian Christian enclave for hundreds of years. There is a synagogue in Bethlehem and, near the church, a mosque. Across the square is the may-

or's office and beyond it, Bethlehem spreads out into the sur-
rounding hills.

On the other side of the square past the church, a road leads
off to Beit Sahur, one of the many Christian villages that dot
this part of the West Bank. In 1990, Beit Sahur became a focal
point of the Palestinian intifada, when its Christian residents
decided to resist the Israeli occupation. The protest marked the
first attempt to apply the lessons of nonviolent civil disobedience to the Palestinian population. Taxes were withheld from
the Israeli authorities, Israeli goods were boycotted, and the
town began a wide-ranging program of self-sufficiency.

This was not the first time that the people of Beit Sahur had
attempted to defy the occupation authorities. Six years before
the beginning of the intifada, the teachers of the village went on
strike for higher pay and made demands for new and better
equipment for their school. The Israeli government acted
swiftly: They dismissed the teachers and closed the village
schools. Undeterred, the families of Beit Sahur invited Israelis
to visit them for the purpose of starting a dialogue on Israeli-
Palestinian relations. But the group broke up when a number
of its Palestinian members were jailed.

Jad Isaac (pronounced *ee-sock*), one of the Christian Palestinian leaders of the protests, has vivid and bitter memories of Beit
Sahur's experiment with civil disobedience. "Our village was
destroyed," he says. "The Israelis came in and took everything
that we owned; it was very thoroughly done." He shrugs his
shoulders. "I would not say that it was useless and everything
was lost," he says, "but military occupation can be very harsh. It
is not the same as working for civic change in America; there is
a conflict here between two different peoples. We are involved
in a national struggle and the Israelis are involved in theirs. It
is very different than working for equal rights. I think we
learned that."

Though he insists on keeping a low profile, Isaac is one of the
better-known Palestinian activists of the occupied territories.
He holds a Ph.D. in plant physiology (he used this knowledge
to help Beit Sahur during its protest by teaching the village how

to cultivate and irrigate its gardens) and he heads the Bethlehem-based Applied Research Institute, a modest, but effective operation that studies environmental problems in the occupied territories.

"We do everything here with a very limited budget," he says, "but we get along alright." He motions to a chair near his desk and brings out a space heater. "Everyone in America thinks the Middle East is a desert," he says, "so it must be hot all the time. They think there is no winter here. They should be here now."

On the wall of his office is a drawing that traces Isaac's family back to the seventeenth century. "That is the proof that we were here, when the Israelis arrived," he says, smiling. But the history of the Isaac family is also the history of its dispersion. "The Isaacs are spread out all over the world," he says. "We have relatives in Honduras, in South America, in Europe. We started here and one branch of the family is still here. We were the original settlers of this land. It would not surprise me if we were here two thousand years ago, at the time of Christ."

Tracing his family lineage is a hobby for Isaac, but his real work is with water. "We are facing a major environmental catastrophe in the West Bank and in Gaza," he says, "and the Israelis know it. But it is not just the Palestinians who are facing this crisis. The Palestinians will run out of water first, but the Israelis will run out of water, too. People do not want to believe this, of course, and they say that it is simply my opinion. But it is not an opinion, it is based on facts. Here is just one fact: Fifty percent of all the land in Israel is under irrigation. That is just a crazy policy. There is a huge aquifer under the Gaza Strip, the Gaza aquifer, and the Israelis have been pumping water out of it. That is alright, as long as they pump so that the aquifer can be replenished. But we have evidence that sea water is coming into the aquifer. So in a few years the water will be of no use."

The same holds true for the West Bank, Isaac says, where the water sources are beginning to dry up. Isaac remembers a day when his institute had to be closed for one week due to lack of water. "There are Israeli water pipes that run through Palestinian villages that have no water," he says. "The women walk miles in the morning with their jugs to the nearest well to get their water for the day. On the hills nearby the wells, they can see the swimming pools of the settlers. You don't believe me. We can go there now. This summer, this last summer, Dheisheh went without water for two months. People were suffering from dehydration."

Isaac pulls down a huge map of the West Bank that is on a roller behind his desk and points to it. "This is the Dead Sea," he says, pointing at the map. "But it is not the Dead Sea now because this map is out-of-date, and gets more out-of-date every day. Now the Dead Sea is really three different seas. It is the Dead *Seas*. The water has receded and there are new shorelines. You would think that since this is the Dead Sea that is not a problem, since the sea is dead. But it is a very great problem: It means that the Jordan River, which feeds the Dead Sea, is drying up. If you go to where the Jordan empties into the Dead Sea you will have to look very hard for the Jordan River. It is not there.

"The problem frankly is that we are a third world country, and that means that most of our water has to go to agriculture. One third of our GNP is in agriculture here on the West Bank. That means that we need every drop of water that we can get. If the people here cannot survive, we know that they will go elsewhere. The Israelis, on the other hand, can subsidize their water and they are doing so. Two thirds of all the water used by Israelis is subsidized by the Israeli government. They say to us, 'Well, you must learn how to conserve your water and use it where it is most needed.' They should know better. They have a designer's dream; they live in the fantasy world of the occupier." He says, "The truth is that they have converted their desert into a garden by turning our gardens into deserts." Isaac shifts in his chair, facing away from the map. "It is no wonder that we should make peace," he says, "because if we do not share the resources here, and conserve them, we are both finished."

Since the beginning of the peace talks, Isaac has traveled to Canada, the United States, and Europe to participate in discussions with Israel and the Arab states on water issues. The opening of a political dialogue with Israel, something that Isaac had worked for most of his life, has not made him optimistic. Like Shaheen and Ta'mari, Isaac believes that the Palestinian identity is slowly being subverted. He waves out the window toward the city of Bethlehem below.

"I will tell you a story about Bethlehem," he says. "This was a beautiful town and people came from all over the world to see this city. When you come into Bethlehem now, you are surrounded by the desert. But it is worse than that. If you have eyes in your head, then you have seen the houses of our town that have been boarded up. This so-called debate about the deportations. What is the debate? People are clamoring to get out of here. The Israelis are not worried about deporting us or expelling us—not really, because they know. They know that we are leaving by the thousands. We have lost our middle class. If you have been on the road into town you know that I am right; the Christians are gone from Bethlehem.

"There is a truth here that I think no one should miss," Isaac continues. "Though they try to ignore it. The truth is that at the beginning of the intifada the Israelis ignored Hamas because they did not take them seriously. But the other truth is that Hamas provided a good political counter to the PLO. The Israelis had a very good strategy. If the PLO and Hamas could fight, then both of them would become weaker. They did not think that Hamas would gain such strength. But it did."

Isaac is self-conscious about his speech, but he warms to the topic in much the same way that Benny Begin did when he talked about the Israeli nightmare. "The members of Hamas are Palestinians and my fellow countrymen, but the fact is that many Christians have left here because while these people are Palestinians, they are also Islamic fundamentalists. People are worried by that. The Palestinian Christian community is dying. There are many more people who would leave, believe me, but they cannot afford it, and those who can afford to leave have already left. And you know where they have gone? Do you know where they are?"

Isaac raises the large outline of his extended family tree behind him and shakes it. "I will tell you where they are—they are everywhere but in Palestine. This is our catastrophe. We are in danger of disappearing as a people.

"I think that the deportations have not had the effect that Rabin thought that they would. We would not have debated what kind of a nation we would be without Israel putting this issue before us, but now we are forced to face some very important issues. The question is, though, whether we really can afford the time it will take to resolve this debate. How can you debate what kind of a society you want when you are slowly disintegrating? Time is running out for us. There has to be peace very soon, very soon, or the community that is left here and in Gaza will disintegrate and it will be difficult for us to rebuild it. We are reaching that point."

Isaac moves through his offices turning over reports and papers, referring to research projects, and a coming meeting on the water issue. From the front of his office and down a long hill, the town of Bethlehem is silent. Since the beginning of the intifada, the tourist trade has fallen off. Still, some hearty souls come to walk through the Church of the Nativity, past the mosque across the street, and into the stores to buy mementos of their journey.

"When you go back to America," Isaac says, "I would like you to tell the American people one thing. Tell them that we are coming. Tell them that thousands of Palestinians are coming and they will live in Chicago, and Washington, and Los Angeles and Detroit. Tell them that the Palestinian Christians are coming to live among them and to go to church with them. And on every Sunday we will sing in those churches the same way that the Jews have sung for thousands of years. We will sing 'Next Year in Jerusalem.' It took the Jews two thousand years to gain their home, and it might take us ten thousand. But we will regain it. And we will not forget what was done to us."

CHAPTER EIGHT
TUNIS

While the number of violent confrontations between the Palestinian population and Israeli military units decreased at the end of January 1993, a series of incidents between Israeli settlers and Arabs led to increased tensions in the occupied territories one month later. Because the Rabin government seemed incapable of controlling the situation, Jewish settlers in the territories responded to the escalating violence by forming ad hoc defense committees that were much better armed than those established in the immediate aftermath of the first intifada incidents in Gaza, just a little more than five years earlier.

The first part of February was quiet, but by the twenty-fifth a series of attacks on Israeli citizens placed the security services on heightened alert. The situation grew worse in early March, when three Israeli citizens were murdered in the occupied territories and in Israel itself. New rioting broke out in the refugee camps, shots were fired at Israeli patrols, and an Israeli was knifed to death in downtown Tel Aviv. Israeli soldiers were popular targets. In a replay of the Toledano murder, a twenty-four-year old IDF soldier was kidnapped, shot at point-blank range, and his body dumped on the Tel Aviv-to-Jerusalem highway. Some of the incidents reached new heights of brutality—one Israeli was stoned to death in Gaza and another, an Israeli woman, was hacked to death after picking up Arab workers in the Gaza Strip. For a time it seemed that the deportation of some four hundred Hamas activists had not dampened Palestinian-Israeli violence, but only exacerbated it.

This new round of escalating violence forced the Israeli government to respond by reinforcing their troops in the most dangerous areas—more soldiers were sent into Gaza and Israeli Police Inspector Yaacov Terner told citizens that they should begin to arm themselves. "I don't suggest people go around with hunting guns," he said during an interview on Israeli radio, "but it is permissible during such a period as this that people carry their weapons on them." Terner soon learned, however, that it was a very short step from carrying weapons to using them. Israeli settlers began to take matters into their own hands. In March, rioting between Palestinians and settlers broke out in Gaza. Shots were fired from settlements into Palestinian crowds. By mid-month, the growing conflict was fueled by inflammatory statements from Rabin's own cabinet. "We know who the [Palestinian] murderers are and I hope that we can get them," Housing Minister Benyamin Ben-Eliezer said at the height of the crisis. "This is a war of attrition and whoever loses his nerve first will lose."

It almost seemed as if the outbreak of violence would lead to a general armed confrontation between the two communities: a *tawir wa tathwir*—in Arabic, a "deepening" of the battle and a "polarization" of the two communities. The situation worsened: Israeli policemen were soon busily investigating the deaths of three Arabs on three different days in early March—the apparent result of settler revenge. The execution-style murders threatened to turn the occupied territories into an urban war zone between competing gangs. There was a fear among Israel's left wing that the increased security measures and calls for the arming of Israeli citizens could lead to an uncontrolled situation. Education Minister Shalumit Aloni responded harshly to the dangers posed by armed citizens. "When I see these people rioting and waving a gun proudly in their hands, I very much fear what could happen," she said.

Yitzhak Rabin might well have agreed; he knew that beefing up security, recruiting new police officers, and passing out weapons was a dangerous, and very temporary, solution. It was a lesson he learned from the intifada; increased numbers of soldiers, new tactics, or even an all-out war against the Palestinian population in the territories would not stem the tide of violence, but only make it worse. Israel was being endangered by the fact of its occupation of the territories, and until that was ended, Rabin believed, Israeli citizens would remain threatened. March was the low point.

Ironically, Rabin was in Washington during the most critical and violent days of the month, just as he had been during the outbreak of the intifada. But the Israeli prime minister was dealing with a different situation from the one he had faced fifteen years earlier. When the intifada began, Rabin still hoped that Israel would be somehow able to pacify the occupied territories, or at least convince Palestinians to accept Israeli rule for the indefinite future, or until a settlement favorable to Israel could be worked out. It took him one month to realize that that would not happen. Having decided that Israelis could not live safely with the Palestinians "in our midst," Rabin had come to the conclusion that separating the two communities— actually sealing them off from one another—was the proper first step in turning over the territories to limited Palestinian rule. In late March and early April of 1993, he was finally in a position to see whether such a strategy would actually work.

The idea of segregating Israelis from Palestinians had a special appeal for the aging prime minister. Not only would it deny Palestinians access to Israel, it would convince the leadership of the territories that they had to take steps to control their own people. Rabin had no intention of withdrawing from the West Bank and Gaza without a negotiated settlement, but sealing them off could serve as a test run for limited Palestinian self-rule; the moderates grouped around Faisal Husseini at his think tank in East Jerusalem would now come face-to-face with the problems the Israelis had been attempting to resolve over the last five years, and they would have to begin thinking about how to maintain security in their own society. Debating Palestinian national identity would take a back seat to actually governing Palestinian society.

"Rabin has a very simple strategy," an Israeli political leader said at the time. "He is tired of all the sniping and criticism from both Israelis and Palestinians. He is ready to say very clearly, 'Okay, you don't like the way I'm handling things, you do it.' "

Rabin also had a personal stake in separating the two communities. He talked about this during his meeting with Bill Clinton, the new American President, at the White House on March 15. When Rabin and Clinton sat down for their two-hour discussion in the Oval Office, the Israeli prime minister purposely sidestepped a detailed discussion of his government's strategy for pursuing peace and instead embarked on an emotional explanation of his own commitment to resolve the Israeli-Arab feud. Rabin's Oval Office monologue was distinctly out of character for the soft-spoken, hard-edged, Israeli prime minister and his words took Clinton by surprise. As Rabin's subdued aides looked on in silence, the Israeli prime minister pointedly warned Clinton that the year ahead would be filled with surprises.

Rabin told Clinton that no one could predict the future, but that the opportunities for peace would not remain promising forever. He shook his head: The fact was that he was getting older, and while he was proud of his military career, he now found himself in a far different position. He was no longer a military man. As prime minister, Rabin added, he had to think differently about Israel's long-term security needs. Clinton listened in respectful silence. Rabin said that his youth as a developing Zionist in the small Jewish community of Tel Aviv had had a deep influence on his life. He had been able to see Israel being built by Jews, from its beginnings. But now, he said, that had changed. He wanted to make sure that, when he died, Israel would continue as a Jewish state.

Deeply affected by Rabin's personal reflections, Clinton pledged America's help and reasserted that traditional Israeli-United States ties, and America's commitment to the Jewish state, would not be weakened. But, choosing his words carefully, the President added that while the United States believed that the Washington talks held out the best prospects for success, the American government could not solve the Middle East problem if the Arabs and Israelis did not want to solve it for themselves. In a carefully phrased argument, Clinton implied that if the Washington bilateral talks broke down, the United States would not be able to expend the time and resources that it had in the past to bring the sides back together. Things had changed in America, Clinton said, just as they had in Israel.

Rabin was not surprised by this attitude. He had sensed America's weariness with the conflict and its need to turn inward to solve its own problems. That was, after all, what motivated his own dedication to the peace process. "We cannot waste any more time, you and I," he told Clinton at the end of their meeting. "This year is the time for peace—now is the moment."

When Rabin returned to Israel, he was greeted by a chorus of complaints about the security situation in the territories and the growing attacks on Israeli citizens. But instead of attempting to defuse these protests by announcing new security measures, he focused his attention on solving the economic problems of the West Bank and Gaza. He shared this view with the new American President: There was a direct link between economic health and national security. If the Palestinians in the territories could be given hope, and a better way of life, perhaps the violence would slowly end.

Rabin's arrival statement at Ben-Gurion Airport on March 19 symbolized this new thinking. "The international community should be more ready to invest in the territories and create jobs there," he told reporters, "thereby reducing the number of [Palestinians] coming over [to Israel]." The implication was that the less dependent Israel became on Palestinian workers, the safer Israeli society would become.

Rabin immediately started to put into place the first part of

his plan to make 1993 "the year of peace." After ordering
stepped-up security measures and increased monitoring of Palestinian workers, Rabin went on Israeli radio to announce a
new, fundamentally different program for dealing with the Palestinian threat to Israeli security. In a dramatic statement,
Rabin announced that he was barring Palestinian access to Israel. The territories would be sealed off indefinitely. This was
the first time that such an extensive program had been put in
place since Israel conquered the West Bank and Gaza, in 1967.
"There will be no Palestinians from the territories on the sovereign territory of Israel until further notice," he said. Rabin
knew that his policy was a hardship for Israeli businesses, which
depended on easy access to cheap Palestinian labor, but he
argued that his policy was necessary to save Israeli lives. The
next morning roadblocks were put up at the Erza checkpoint
between the Gaza Strip and Israel and two days later the Israeli
military sealed off all roads between Israel and the West Bank.

Few people would ever claim that Yitzhak Rabin was a deep
thinker, or one of the leading intellectual lights of Zionism. But
his April closure of the occupied territories can be viewed as
one of the most important events in the history of Zionism. For
the first time since the founding congress of the Zionist movement, in 1897, an Israeli leader had starkly drawn the boundaries of the Jewish state, and vowed to separate the Jewish
people from their enemies forever. For years, Israeli leftists in
the peace movement Yish Gavul (a Hebrew phrase that doubles
as a question: "Where is the border?") had been pushing Israeli
governments to define the state's national boundaries. That is
just what Rabin had done.

Most Israelis, however, responded to Rabin's actions as the
last gasp of a frustrated man and an admission that the IDF had
failed to provide adequately for the national security. Now, a
more accurate view is in order—especially in light of Rabin's
background as a native Israeli.

The key to Rabin's thinking lies in a number of well-
publicized statements he made after his dramatic announce-

ment closing the territories, when he toured Israel to explain his new policy. Rabin soon made it clear that, as far as he was concerned, Israel's dependence on Palestinian workers to carry out the menial jobs of the modern economy was at least as disturbing as the increased attacks on Israeli citizens. This was not the Israel that he remembered in 1948, he said, or even the fiercely self-sufficient and proudly independent yishuv community of the 1920s and 1930s. Palestinians were everywhere; they worked as busboys, drivers, cooks, janitors, carpenters, plumbers, and field hands.

While most Palestinians worked hard, long hours (tens of thousands of them arrived at Israeli-manned checkpoints at dawn and returned to their homes in the territories after dark), there was something fundamentally disturbing about the role they played in Israeli society: Because of Palestinian laborers, Rabin believed, Israeli workers had grown soft and spoiled. The unique and unfettered Jewish culture that Zionism's founders had dreamed of for Israel was beginning to disintegrate under the sheer weight of thousands of Arab workers, who brought their culture, values, and language into Israel. The Palestinians, Rabin knew, had to learn how to run their own society, but Israelis had just as important a task—they had to reclaim their birthright to the land of Israel.

"Now is the time when we can bring about substantial changes through separation," Rabin said in a speech on April 14, more than one week after the closing of the territories. "We must see to it that Palestinians do not swarm among us, so that the Jews begin to work and increase their ability to do so." This was the message of Rabin the sabra father-figure. He had worked hard all his life to provide a comfortable life-style for his children, but he now sternly disapproved of the indolent ways they had learned. There was nothing like a little hard work to make Israelis appreciate what his generation had labored so hard to create: Jews, he said, were never above hard work, they had simply forgotten how to do it. Now, with the closure of the territories, they could once again pick their own oranges and clean their own tables.

Rabin's defense of his actions was nothing less than a passionate plea for a Zionist renaissance. "It is inconceivable that out of 120,000 construction workers in the country, 70,000 are residents of the territories," Rabin said. "Once construction and farming signified the rooting and building of the Jewish people in Eretz Yisrael. We must not pass this [kind of work] on to foreign hands, to the Palestinians. We must not rely on the Palestinians. Let them stay there."

Corporate executives, farmers, and small business owners greeted Rabin's actions with skepticism bordering on outrage (the policy forced soldiers into the fields to help farmers harvest citrus), while Palestinian leaders condemned the policy for the hardship it visited on thousands of families in the occupied territories who made their living in Israel. (They also pointed out that the closing of the territories separated East Jerusalem from the rest of the West Bank, thereby dividing thousands of families.) Some Israeli commentators believed the prime minister had lost his senses and a number of Palestinian moderates viewed his actions as those of a former general who had not yet slaked his desire for harshness. But a few leaders in both communities began to slowly understand what Rabin was trying to do. "He has drawn the border," one of these Palestinian leaders said privately. "There is now, in fact, a Palestinian nation and an Israeli nation."

Shimon Peres traveled to Washington with the same message as Rabin and, in discussions with American Jewish leaders, defended the prime minister's actions. Israel must be built with Jewish hands, he said. In a series of interviews with the American press, he went even further in laying out the program of the Rabin government. When asked what he saw for Israel in fifty years, he did not repeat the well-worn phrases that had so often characterized Israeli government statements about security and safety. He turned instead to the mainstream vision of Zionism's founders. "Israel will be strong and self-sufficient," he said, "and it will be Jewish."

By the middle of April, the roles of Rabin and his foreign minister and political competitor, Shimon Peres, had been reversed. Rabin, the sometimes inarticulate, hands-on pragmatist, had become an idealist by calling on Israelis to build a new society in line with the vision of its founders. Peres, the dreamer, on the other hand, had now become a practical politician. During Peres's Washington visit, American officials began to hear a new formula for resolving the Israeli-Palestinian dispute. The closing of the occupied territories, Peres said, meant that there would be a "political divorce," between Jews and Arabs, that would be followed by an "economic marriage."

Peres's comment seemed an innocuous reflection of Israel's long-term policy and was virtually ignored by the American policy-making establishment. But the foreign minister was broadly and delicately hinting at what had been rumored in the press for months: Israeli and PLO officials were meeting secretly in Europe to hammer out an agreement that would begin to put an end to their one-hundred-year war. While the process did not get fully under way until after Rabin's Washington visit, in March 1993, it had its inception in the weeks immediately following the end of the Madrid Conference, when a group of well-known economists met to discuss the economic future of Israel, the occupied territories, and Jordan. The results of those meetings had an enormous impact on the thinking of Rabin, Peres, Arafat—and the group of Israeli and PLO officials who were beginning to discuss peace in Oslo, Norway.

But the story of the secret, behind-the-scenes negotiations in the Oslo channel (as it came to be called) does not begin in Norway, or in Tunis, or even in Jerusalem. Rather, the Oslo channel had its true beginnings in Cambridge, Massachusetts, in November 1991.

Several weeks after Arab and Israeli officials adjourned their meeting in Madrid, a team of well-known American economists brought together Israelis, Palestinians, Jordanians, Lebanese, Syrians, and Egyptians at Harvard University for a unique conference on the economic consequences of Middle East peace. The organizers of the unprecedented gathering were two highly respected American economic scholars, Leonard Hausman, the director of the Institute for Social and Economic Policy in the Middle East at Harvard University's John F. Kennedy School of Government, and Stanley Fischer, one of the nation's leading economic thinkers and a professor at the Massachusetts Institute of Technology. The rationale behind the unprecedented meeting had been developed through years of study by Hausman, Fischer, and their associates, who had spent a lifetime analyzing the economies of the Middle East.

The economic conference went well, and without all the political fireworks that its organizers feared might result. Hausman and Fischer were so pleased, in fact, that they decided to publish the proceedings in the form of a book, which they then released as *The Economics of Middle East Peace.* But prior to the book's release, the papers it contained found their way into the hands of leading political figures in the region. The results were intriguing. Many of the papers suggested that Israel, the Palestinians, and the Jordanians, in particular, might be able to resolve their political differences by forming an economic union. The formation of such a commonwealth would help to dampen the political passions that motivated the policies of Arab regimes and slowly integrate Israel into a newly emerging and powerful Middle Eastern economic bloc.

The two economists were surprised that the conference gained such widespread attention and sparked such broad international interest but, when the meeting was adjourned, Anna Karasik, Hausman's associate director, detected something lacking in the focus of the gathering. Karasik believed that while the conference provided a useful forum for an analysis of Middle East economies after a political settlement was finalized, it had failed to address some key aspects of the transition to peace in the occupied territories, Israel, and Jordan. All the long-range planning in the world was useless, Karasik argued, without a solid road map that would help Israelis and Palestinians, in particular, deal with the new economic realities of peace.

Karasik then suggested that a group of respected economists from Israel, the occupied territories, and Jordan be put together to outline a detailed plan for the economic transition that would come with the signing of a political agreement. She pointed out that this was something that no one else was doing.

Hausman and Fischer listened to her proposal with interest and thought it was a great idea. Over the next several weeks, the two professors and Karasik worked to assemble a list of economists from the Middle East who they thought might be willing to participate in the project. It was a fairly easy job: Fischer and Hausman knew virtually all of the most important scholars in the region and Karasik, a Hebrew University-educated management and human resources consultant, had well-formed ideas on how the meetings should work. On January 7, three months after the end of the Madrid Conference, the three met in Cairo with four economists—an Israeli, a Jordanian, a Palestinian, and an Egyptian observer—to talk about Karasik's idea. Over a period of just forty-eight hours, the group drew up a detailed plan and schedule of meetings, and agreed on a list of participants.

There was no assurance that the Fischer-Hausman-Karasik proposal would work—economists from each of the parties were suspicious of those from the others, and there were fears that once the group gathered at Harvard the meetings would degenerate into political squabbling. And there was uncertainty that some of the specific names that had shown up on the list of participants would actually come to the meetings, since some of them might be put in danger by being associated with such a project. At that time, it was still illegal for Israelis to meet with PLO officials (even if they were economists and only loosely associated with the organization), and some of the Palestinians and Jordanians were fearful about the reaction of students, colleagues, and leaders to their participation in the Fischer-Hausman-Karasik program. But after reviewing the problems involved, the three Americans and the four economists meeting in Cairo decided that it was worth a try, and set a start-up date for April of 1992.

*   *   *

It was only a coincidence that at about the same time that the three American economists were trying to imagine what the Middle East would look like if the Israelis and Palestinians concluded a peace agreement, Norwegian researcher Terje Roed Larsen, the director general of the Norwegian Institute for Applied Social Science (known by its Norwegian abbreviation as FAFO) was wondering the same thing. The forty-five-year-old Larsen had years of experience in the West Bank and Gaza as part of his institute's ongoing research program on the living conditions of the Palestinians in the occupied territories, and he was convinced that the peace process had to succeed if the people of the West Bank and Gaza had any hope of rising above their squalid conditions.

But what bothered Larsen the most was that the high hopes sparked by the Madrid Conference in October had virtually dissipated after only six months. By April 1992, the talks in Washington were at a standstill and it appeared that the Bush administration was too fearful of its own political survival to commit its prestige to their success. Meanwhile, the economic conditions of Palestinians in the West Bank and Gaza were slowly deteriorating—Larsen's own study of the situation, and his talks with Israelis and Palestinians, clearly showed that. In early April, Larsen decided to raise his concerns with a long-time Israeli acquaintance, Yossi Beilin, who was a Labor party insider, a member of the Knesset, and a respected, high-profile, and articulate member of the Israeli establishment.

Marshaling his huge data base of facts and figures, Larsen outlined his findings to Beilin in a short discussion during the second week of April. Beilin was intrigued but hardly surprised by Larsen's conclusions; he was well-versed in the problems of the West Bank and Gaza, but as a member of the opposition party there was little he could do to change the situation. Finally, at the end of the discussion, Larsen dropped a hint about his own views. He suggested that the political and economic situation in the territories would only worsen if the stalemate at the talks in Washington continued. There must be some other way to get the Israelis and Palestinians to talk together, perhaps by removing them from the glare of the international media spotlight, he said.

If Beilin took the hint, he did not say so, at least not right away. He agreed that the Washington talks were stalled, but no one should be surprised by that, especially given the policies of the Shamir government. In any event, he said, there was nothing he could do to support Larsen so long as the Labor party was not in power. Instead, he told Larsen to call on a professor that he knew from Haifa University by the name of Yair Hirschfeld. Maybe Hirschfeld can help you with your study, Beilin said. Before Larsen left, however, Beilin vaguely hinted that a new Israeli government might be interested in his proposal. Larsen should look up Yair Hirschfeld, he said, and keep him informed on his progress—if there was any.

Larsen did not take Beilin's advice; instead of meeting Hirschfeld, he returned to Norway to confer with the author of the FAFO study, Marianne Heiberg, who was not only an expert on Palestinian society and a respected scholar, but the wife of Norway's then-defense minister, Johan Jorgen Holst. In addition, Larsen's wife, Mona Juul, was a senior government official who served as a member of the foreign ministry's secretariat, a kind of inner cabinet. Larsen, Heiberg, and Juul—as well as Holst—were all close friends, had an abiding interest in the Middle East, and had connections with both Israelis and Palestinians. Larsen believed that this Norwegian group could provide a perfect forum for back-channel negotiations.

Larsen first went to Johan Jorgen Holst to discuss his proposal. Larsen and Holst had known each other for many years, but Larsen took nothing for granted. He outlined the deteriorating economic situation in the occupied territories and gave a detailed, and grim, description of the suffocating political atmosphere of the Shamir government in Jerusalem. Only after these introductory remarks did Larsen put forward his proposal for establishing a private back-channel link between Israeli government officials and Palestinian leaders. The PLO should be involved, he said. They were the only ones with the credibility to negotiate a settlement.

Holst took Larsen's proposal seriously, but told him that the climate in Israel was not yet ripe for the kind of face-to-face meetings that he was suggesting. Privately, however, Holst was very taken with Larsen's proposition; he believed that if Israel cooperated, Norway was in a good position to mediate the negotiations—it was trusted by both sides and was seen as a neutral intermediary with broad experience in the region. The Labor parties of Norway and Israel had developed an extensive relationship over the years, and Norway was considered one of Israel's most reliable European supporters. Norway also had ties to the PLO: During the Lebanese civil war, Norwegian troops served in the UNIFIL (the United Nations Forces in Lebanon) operation in southern Lebanon where Norwegian officials rubbed shoulders with PLO leaders on a daily basis. In addition, PLO officials were welcome in the Norwegian capital and were familiar figures in European diplomatic circles. FAFO researchers, including Larsen, had visited Tunis to seek assistance on their study of the occupied territories and Larsen had met personally with PLO officials on a number of occasions. It would not be difficult, therefore, for Holst to invite them to talks in Oslo.

Holst's hopes for an improved climate were realized a few weeks later when Israel voted the Labor party back into power after a fifteen-year absence. Larsen's contact in Jerusalem, Yossi Beilin, became Yitzhak Rabin's new deputy foreign minister. After waiting for the new Israeli government to get acclimated to its political surroundings, Larsen returned to Israel to see Beilin once again. He was hoping to confirm the Israeli government's support for opening an Oslo channel.

When Larsen returned to Israel for a second visit, he immediately scheduled another meeting with Beilin in the hopes of convincing him to use Norway as a back channel for discussions with the PLO. Beilin was ready: Since Larsen's first meeting he had been turning the idea over in his mind, but he wanted more details. Larsen began the meeting by again presenting some of the statistics he had gathered on the deteriorating economic situation in the occupied territories and added that the political situation mirrored these troubles. He then gave a short review of his own opinions on the Washington talks. Beilin agreed that the Washington talks were going nowhere, in large part because the Palestinian delegation was not in a position to strike a deal. Direct talks with the PLO were essential.

Larsen said that the best way to contact the PLO was through Oslo. But Beilin was wary. While such contacts might prove useful, he said, Israeli law still barred official contacts with PLO officials. Any such meetings would have to be arranged secretly, since the newly elected Rabin government could not be seen meeting with the PLO just months after taking office. Beilin therefore made the same recommendation to Larsen that he had made during their first meeting: The Norwegian professor should visit with Yair Hirschfeld at Haifa University.

That seemed like a strange suggestion; Hirschfeld was the quintessential absentminded professor and had no experience as a diplomat. In addition, he did not seem particularly well-suited to the role of unofficial go-between in a highly complex and tense negotiation. Hirschfeld seemed to be the kind of person who was continually searching for pens, papers, books, and notes that he left somewhere but could never quite find. While intensely intelligent, he could appear scattered and un-focused. Nor did he look the part of a globe-trotting deal-maker; instead, he appeared to be a native Israeli, a typical small-town farmer who stayed close to home. But Hirschfeld's seemingly disorganized personality masked a razor-sharp mind and a prodigious capacity for details. He was a highly respected historian whose scholarship was well known and respected. More than any other person in Israel perhaps, Hirschfeld un-derstood the historical and economic dynamics that might bring the Israeli and Palestinian communities together. And he knew how to keep a secret.

When Larsen met Hirschfeld in his home outside of Haifa, he was immediately impressed by his views of the peace process. Like Larsen, Hirschfeld believed that back-channel talks would allow Palestinian and Israeli officials to lay out positions in pri-vate that they would never dare propose in public. Larsen also learned that Hirschfeld had been active in organizing Israeli-Palestinian meetings on the peace process, using the cover of a number of dovish Israeli groups, since the early 1980s. Hirschfeld and Beilin had first met as participants in these dialogues and had struck up a friendship.

Because of his contacts among the left-wing political elite of Israel, Hirschfeld had also become a well-known and respected figure in the upper reaches of West Bank Palestinian society, where he met the top Palestinian leadership in the occupied territories. Coincidentally, just before being contacted by Larsen, Hirschfeld and his family had dinner in the Ramallah home of Hanan Ashrawi, the spokeswoman of the Palestinian delegation for the Washington talks.

Larsen learned that both Hirschfeld and Ashrawi were frustrated and worried by the lack of progress in Washington. But they were at a loss on how to break the impasse. With the American elections just over the horizon, they feared that there would be no movement in the bilateral negotiations for months. Over dinner, Ashrawi came up with a suggestion: While it was clearly too soon for the Palestinians and Israelis to negotiate a comprehensive agreement, they might be able to draft a joint declaration of principles that would guide their future negotiations. At the very least, she said, such a document could lay out where the two sides' viewpoints intersected and provide an idea of how to proceed. Hirschfeld agreed.

Hirschfeld explained Ashrawi's idea of a joint declaration of principles and convinced Larsen that it was the strategy with the best probability of success. By marrying Ashrawi's proposition with Larsen's back channel, it might be possible to actually negotiate some kind of breakthrough on the peace talks. Hirschfeld added that he would be happy to serve as the unofficial representative of the Israeli government, at least until the talks became serious. Larsen said that he would test these ideas with his contacts in Oslo and asked Hirschfeld if he had any objection to speaking directly with PLO officials about such a proposed declaration. Hirschfeld shook his head. "Not at all," he said.

When Larsen returned to Norway, he met with his contacts in the foreign ministry and then with Jorgen Holst to assess the Norwegian government's position on serving as a back channel. But few, if any, of these meetings could be called formal. Because of Larsen's personal relationship with Holst and Holst's wife, and FAFO's high profile in the Middle East, the discussions turned into brainstorming sessions on how best to conduct the talks. Holst emphasized that it was essential to keep the discussions secret because, as he later reflected, "secrecy [would allow] the participants to perform as real negotiators rather than mere spokesmen for opposing interests." Holding unrealistic positions merely for public consumption, he thought, was precisely what was happening in the Washington talks.

Holst was particularly enthusiastic about the prospects for the success of such back-channel negotiations because he trusted Rabin, Peres, and Israel's new Labor government. Perhaps more than any other diplomat in Europe, Holst understood the legacy that Rabin and Peres, who were both nearing the end of their careers, wanted to leave their grandchildren.

"Yitzhak Rabin and Shimon Peres came into office unencumbered by the stalemate which had developed through the dynamic of Likud policies and Arab reactions," he later reflected. "If they were to hand over to the next generation a different reality than that which shaped the first four decades of Israel's existence, they had to act. Hence, in addition to the geopolitical opening, there was a kind of biological compulsion." At the end of August, Holst gave Larsen permission to begin setting up the back channel.

On September 10, 1992, Larsen made another trip to Israel, but this time he was accompanied by the director general of the foreign ministry, Jan Egeland, the Norwegian government's second-ranking diplomat. Arriving at Ben-Gurion Airport on a warm, late-summer day, the two took a taxi to the Tel Aviv Hilton, where they met with Beilin and Hirschfeld. Egeland informed Beilin that the Norwegian government would be happy to mediate meetings between the PLO and Israel, if the Israeli government approved. Beilin said that he wanted the meetings to go forward but, he reiterated, they would have to be unofficial and conducted in the greatest secrecy: Talking with PLO officials was still a violation of Israeli law. Yair Hirschfeld, Beilin said, would be Norway's primary contact.

Holst, meanwhile, had contacted senior PLO officials in Tunis. In mid-September, the Norwegian foreign minister asked Yasser Arafat if he would send a representative to meet with an Israeli official at a yet-to-be-designated location. It was no surprise that Arafat gave his immediate approval, since Holst knew that the PLO leader had been angling for just such a back channel for months and had been exploring the possibility of secret talks with a number of European leaders. But Holst suggested that Arafat himself not be involved in the negotiations. Instead, he said, he should send someone who was familiar with economic issues.

Holst suggested that the PLO be represented by the head of its economics department, Ahmed Suleiman Krai, better known as Abu Alaa. Holst was familiar with Abu Alaa's economic work; several years before, the PLO official had circulated a paper in Europe that suggested the formation of a Middle East commonwealth could resolve many of the political problems facing Israelis and Palestinians. The paper had made its way into the hands of Labor party officials in Israel, where it was closely studied. Peres and Beilin, Holst knew, had been impressed by Abu Alaa's central theme, which mimicked their own views. Arafat agreed with Holst that the economist should meet with the Israelis. He trusted Abu Alaa's judgment and knew that the economist was an emerging power in the PLO. Over the last years, he had become closely aligned with the organization's pragmatists, which were led by Mahmoud Abbas—known as Abu Mazin—who was the head of the PLO's political department.

Three months later, on December 4, Yair Hirschfeld walked into the Gallery restaurant of the Forte Crest St. James Hotel in central London to have breakfast with Terje Larsen. After a short and jittery one-hour discussion, the two men shook hands in the lobby and Larsen left the hotel. Hirschfeld was nervous.

He paced the lobby while anxiously awaiting his contact—who was late. Finally, forty-five minutes after Larsen had left, and thirty minutes after Hirschfeld's contact was supposed to arrive, the small, white-haired Abu Alaa—a man who jealously guarded his anonymity and had never talked with reporters or even allowed his name to be mentioned in public—walked into the lobby of the hotel, spotted the thoroughly rattled Hirschfeld, and shook his hand in greeting. Hirschfeld nodded and wordlessly motioned to the hotel restaurant.

Over a tense cup of coffee the two agreed that the Washington talks were paralyzed and that a new opening was needed. The sixty-year-old Abu Alaa told Hirschfeld that he had Arafat's permission to explore the possibility of a back channel and he gave a detailed explanation of why the PLO wanted to reach an agreement with Israel. Abu Alaa's businesslike manner, his self-effacing, low-key attitude, and the conviction that rang in his words convinced Hirschfeld that Israel had a chance to reach an accommodation with the Palestinians.

Following a midafternoon telephone conference with Beilin, Hirschfeld took a nap, and then met Abu Alaa again, this time at London's swank Ritz Hotel, where the two hammered out the details of their next meeting. The two agreed that when they next met, in Norway, the best way to proceed would be to draft a declaration of principles. That would help to get their talks off the ground.

The Oslo talks held out hope as the first real channel for direct negotiations between the PLO and Israel. But there was no guarantee that simply because Israelis and Palestinians had decided to meet, a political accord would automatically be the result. If the Washington talks proved anything, it was just the opposite. Nor did Hirschfeld or Abu Alaa initially believe that their discussions would necessarily lead to a final, definitive agreement. That was not the purpose of their meeting: Instead, they both wanted to discover just how serious the other side was and to explore the possibility of coming to an agreement on a number of important points. Once a set of common principles had been established, the real negotiations could go forward.

The two men were also very different personalities. Hirsch-feld was expansive, talkative, and a fountain of ideas. He laughed hugely, argued pointedly, and immensely enjoyed the fact that he was carrying out a secret mission for his country. Hirschfeld had never guarded his privacy and, while he could keep a secret (and would be tried on this point on several occasions over the next eight months), he enjoyed sharing the story of his life as a young man growing up in Austria. During one trip to Israel when he was nine, he peered through the wall that separated Arabs and Jews in Jerusalem and then was pulled back by an Israeli soldier and disciplined for taking such a chance. (As it turns out, Hirschfeld's tale is nearly identical to one told to American reporters by Palestinian leader Sari Nusseibeh, who, as a child, regularly dared the cross hairs of Israeli soldiers by peering over his own wall to see the Israelis on the other side.) Now, more than thirty years later, Hirschfeld was being given the opportunity of scaling the psychological wall that existed between the Israeli government and the PLO.

Ahmed Suleiman Krai was very different. He would never think of giving a detailed description of his past to anyone. The result is that, to this day, very little is known about him or his career. "You can say that Abu Alaa has served with the organization in Tunis for many years," Anees Barghouti, a PLO official stationed in Washington, advised, "and you can say that he conducts himself very professionally, is educated as an economist, lived for a time in Saudi Arabia, is married, and has children that go to school in the United States. But that is all that you can say. He will not give an interview." While the details of Abu Alaa's past remain shrouded in mystery, his attitudes and beliefs began to emerge over the next year of intense negotiations. Where Hirschfeld was expansive, Abu Alaa remained soft-spoken. Where Hirschfeld would cajole and appear huffily frustrated, Abu Alaa would remain steely, silent, and cold. It took some time for both of them to be fully at ease with each other, though eventually they were. Hirschfeld slowly began to appreciate Abu Alaa's wry smile and dry humor.

While Hirschfeld and Abu Alaa were different in so many respects, they nevertheless shared a common belief in the need to reach an agreement to take advantage of the newly emerging world order. The international structure of the future, they both believed, would be based on economic interdependence and international trade. Both had conducted detailed studies of the history of their conflict and both were conversant with the factors that made negotiations like theirs successful. And while both knew that it might take the Arabs and Jews years, perhaps even decades, to resolve their social and political disagreements, there was no reason to believe that they could not cooperate in other, chiefly economic, spheres. Hirschfeld and Abu Alaa came together out of a shared sense of mutual self-interest in the economic prosperity of their peoples. They believed that the future of Israeli-Palestinian relations lay in their dedication to economic cooperation.

A large number of other experts were rapidly reaching the same conclusion. The hypothesis that a political agreement between Palestinians and Israelis would have to have economic cooperation as its centerpiece was advanced primarily by Hirschfeld and Holst, both of whom had long-standing connections with the European Economic Community—the EC—which provided a model for how former antagonists could make peace. (Holst, as a leading diplomat of a neighboring country, had worked closely with the EC, while Hirschfeld had done extensive research for the EC on the economies of Israel and the territories since the early 1980s.) The EC model seemed to fit well with the Israeli-Palestinian conflict: If the two sides could be persuaded to cooperate economically, a political solution would follow once the necessary incentives and favorable conditions had been established.

This strategy mirrored the thinking of Fischer, Hausman, and Karasik back in Cambridge as they put together a group of thirty-four leading Israeli, Palestinian, and Jordanian economists to investigate possibilities for economic cooperation among the three political units. The first two-day meeting of what came to be known as the the Harvard Group took place in April 1992, at about the same time that FAFO director Terje Larsen was first meeting with Yossi Beilin. Even with all the hard work that had gone into planning the meeting, however, Fischer remained uncertain that the concept of sharing ideas on the three economies would actually work.

"I was a little nervous," Fischer admits. "I thought there might be some problems. So I developed a rule very early on in this process, and the rule was that we would not ask the general questions. Because I found out that you really don't get anywhere when you ask those types of questions, like, Which one of your grandmothers started this thing? You stay away from those questions because they cause problems. But if you ask, How do you manage trade? or What are the implications of managing trade among three distinct political entities? then you start to get some answers and some agreement . . . [so] we decided to assume that somehow the peace process would work and that there would be a political settlement."

Once the rules were formulated and well understood, Fischer, Hausman, and Karasik began the work of dividing the thirty-four economists into six distinct working groups, each focusing on a specific economic problem: regional trade in agriculture, industry, and services; labor policies; economic authorities; fiscal policy; monetary and financial arrangements; and management of foreign aid. "There were some underlying principles to our program," Karasik says. "The first, and most important, was that none of the three parties could face the future alone—they had to do it together. It is true that the Israeli economy was doing fine, booming in fact, but Israeli economists knew that there was great potential in the Arab world, that they could open new markets, and that socially and politically there had to be some kind of economic cooperation in order to stabilize the political situation. So the question we had to answer was What kind of economic cooperation are we talking about?

The meetings of the Harvard Group took place at regular intervals during the following year in Cambridge, but between gatherings Fischer, Hausman, and Karasik studied the group's findings and attempted to give the study some unifying logic. The three were also faced with some delicate political problems. At one point, according to one of the participating economists, Hausman had to reassure members that their role in the workings of the group would be a closely held secret—at least until the final report was printed. Nevertheless, some of the economists showed visible anxieties about their participation in the Cambridge meetings, since they believed that their actions might be interpreted as acting against the interests of their own governments.

In one particular case, a Jordanian economist became so alarmed by the possibility that his participation would become public knowledge that Leonard Hausman himself, in one of his trips to the region, made a carefully choreographed approach to the Jordanian government to measure their reaction. He asked his contact whether the government would approve the participation of an unnamed economist in a hypothetical meeting on possible ties between the Jordanian and Israeli economies. The word came back from Crown Prince Hassan, the brother of the king himself, who said that Jordan would be very interested in such a study. The implication was clear: King Hussein had already somehow been informed of what was going on in Cambridge, and was very interested in hearing the results.

In another important case, a Palestinian economist was deeply concerned that PLO officials would frown on his participation and at one point he actually feared for his life. So Hausman advised him to contact Tunis directly to seek approval. After a few days, the Palestinian economist was not only informed that he should continue his deliberations in Cambridge, he was told that PLO Chairman Yasser Arafat knew about the meetings and was looking forward to reading the final report. In the meantime, Arafat let it be known that any interim findings should be passed on to him in Tunis for study.

That should have been a hint: While there were no official, direct links between the Harvard Group and the Oslo channel, there was an amazing amount of "cross-pollination" and "unofficial cooperation" between the two groups. In addition, there were ties between the Harvard Group and an assembly of Middle East diplomats put together in Madrid as part of the multilateral talks to study the economies of the region. This multilateral working group on economic development, as it was called, was assigned to prepare a detailed study on the occupied territories by the World Bank. By the beginning of 1993, there were close ties and a degree of close cooperation among all three entities: the Harvard Group, the World Bank, and the Israelis and Palestinians negotiating in Oslo.

Leonard Hausman, who is well versed on the Harvard Group's influence on the Oslo negotiations, draws a clear distinction among the different channels, but hints at a number of close connections among all three. "The economists involved in this process were keenly aware of and attuned to the nerve centers of their governments," Hausman says. "They knew what their political leaders were doing, and they believed that once they agreed on the economics among themselves, then they could get their governments to agree."

Some of the links between the Harvard Group and the Oslo channel were remarkably direct. A key member of the Harvard Group—Maher Suleiman El-Kurd—served with the PLO in Tunis as an economist and was the economic adviser to the Palestinian delegation to the bilateral talks in Washington. El-Kurd also served as a consultant to a number of internal committees of the PLO and was close to Arafat's chief negotiator in Oslo, Abu Alaa. Throughout the deliberations of the Harvard Group, El-Kurd kept Abu Alaa informed of its findings and even passed on drafts of some of the group's papers to the PLO economist. "Abu Alaa was constantly informed of and aware of what we were doing," Hausman confirms.

Several of the Israeli economists involved in the Harvard Group's study maintained direct links to the Israeli foreign ministry. Three of them had previously served in senior positions in the Israeli ministry of finance and were well known by leading figures of the ruling Labor party. There were also startling links between the Harvard Group and the World Bank, already deep into its own study. Three of the Israeli economists working at Harvard had at one time served as leading economists at the World Bank, and one of the Israeli members of the group, Michael Michaely, was serving as one of the World Bank's leading economists at the very time of the Harvard Group's deliberations.

But the most significant common denominator among the three groups was Fischer himself. Fischer, whose resumé reflects a mix of scholarly achievement with international influence—including a stint as the World Bank's chief economist on the Middle East—served as an unofficial liaison among the Harvard Group, the World Bank, and influential Middle East politicians. Fischer himself laughs at the characterization. "There were links, there is no doubt about that," he says, "but I don't know for certain whether our group's findings were used in Oslo, even though some of the language we used and what they ended up agreeing on is very, very similar. You have to understand, everyone who was familiar with this problem and studied it was thinking pretty much the same thing. On the other hand, if you were to ask me directly I would say that there is a fifty-to-one chance that as Abu Alaa and Professor Hirschfeld were sitting down in their final session, they had our group's study in front of them."

The ties may be even closer than that. The report of the Israeli finance ministry on the economics of the transition to self-rule in the occupied territories (used by Hirschfeld in Oslo) was written by members of the Harvard Group, and the series of papers on the same subject used by Abu Alaa was written by Palestinian members of the group. "There was a definite overlap among the three groups," says Palestinian economist Ghassan Khatib—who served with the Harvard Group and as an adviser to the Palestinian delegation in Washington. "Abu Alaa mainly used papers prepared by economists at the Washington talks, but the papers were prepared in light of what the Harvard Group was finding. There was a direct link. In addition, I will tell you that some people in Abu Alaa's group in Tunis

served on the Harvard Group. The economic annexes of the
final agreement could not have been written without the help of
the work done in Cambridge."

By the time that Hirschfeld and Abu Alaa met in Oslo for the
first time, the Harvard Group was launched on its all-important
economic study. In the months ahead, they would serve as an
unofficial "second channel" in the PLO-Israeli negotiations.

Pointing out that Israelis and Palestinians were interested in
establishing a new economic relationship does not, however,
explain why Arafat and Israeli officials would begin to search
for a way to bypass the talks going on in Washington. For years
the PLO had been Israel's intransigent enemy and for just as
long, Yitzhak Rabin and other Israeli politicians had vowed that
they would never deal with Yasser Arafat. Now, suddenly, in
January 1993, all of that changed. The explanation for the Oslo
channel can only be partly answered by referring to the promise held out by economic growth. A much more important part
of the explanation lies in the failure of the Washington talks
and in the mounting pressures on both Yasser Arafat and
Yitzhak Rabin to strike a deal while they still could.

Just as Abu Alaa and Yair Hirschfeld were preparing to sit
down for their first meeting in Oslo, the political situation in
Tunis took a turn for the worse. A crisis atmosphere pervaded
the PLO headquarters: The Washington negotiations were
stalled, the organization was under pressure from its constitu-
ents in the territories to show results, its coffers were nearly
dry, and the Fatah leadership in the West Bank and Gaza was
under attack by the increasingly popular and politically potent
Hamas fundamentalist movement. In addition, Yasser Arafat
himself was being criticized by the PLO power structure to
begin the transition to building a more democratic organization. That seemed more important now than at any time in the
past, especially in the aftermath of Arafat's initial support for
continuing the Washington talks even as some four hundred
Hamas activists were getting acclimated to a cold hillside in
Lebanon.

The situation in January also reflected an ironic shift in the relationship between the Tunis "outsiders" and the members of the Palestinian delegation—the "insiders." In the weeks following the Israeli elections, the Rabin government made a commitment to transform the negotiations in Washington by pressuring the Palestinian delegation to engage in an exchange of serious proposals that went beyond the discussions that had already taken place. The Rabin government's view was that it would be easier to deal with Husseini (not yet an official part of the Palestinian delegation), Ashrawi, and Abdul Shafi because they were more moderate than the radical hard-liners in Tunis. Rabin reasoned that he might be able to gain significant concessions from this group because they were closer to the action in the occupied territories, and they could see firsthand the terrible impact the Israeli occupation was having on the Palestinian community. They were a known quantity, Rabin thought—unlike Arafat's band of Tunis terrorists.

It did not take long for Rabin to determine that the official Palestinian delegation in Washington was not as moderate as he had first thought. In fact, the Palestinian "insiders" presented negotiating positions that were consistently more hard-line than those issued by the PLO leadership. This was puzzling: If the Palestinian delegation was taking its orders from Tunis, why did they continue to press their hard-line position? Rabin initially concluded that Arafat and his senior aides were engaged in a very coy game: The PLO was not moderate at all, Rabin concluded; they were setting up a kind of diplomatic honey trap in order to force Israel to bypass the Washington delegation. But once that had happened, Arafat and his cronies would revert to their real, hard-line, views.

The complexity of this delicate dance was not lost on either side. "It is difficult to know where anyone stands, or what is just posturing and what is a real position," an Israeli official said in early 1993. "If we are not careful, we will all end up outsmarting ourselves and there will be no progress at all." A Palestinian delegate had much the same reaction to the situation on the Israeli side. "Rabin always lets on that we can get a better deal

with him than with Netanyahu [the head of the Likud party],"
he said. "But every time a gun goes off in the territories, they
[the Labor party] have to prove to the Israeli people just how
tough they are—and Rabin looks just like Netanyahu, or
Shamir. The Labor Party is scared to death that they will lose a
vote of confidence [in the Knesset]. They have to realize that
you can't cure the patient if you are constantly taking his temperature."

Inevitably, perhaps, the dynamics of the negotiations in
Washington, and the continuing flurry of reports between
rounds, fueled internal disagreements inside each of the delegations. This was especially true for the Palestinian delegates,
who, since all pretense of their not having ties to the PLO had
been dropped, spent an inordinate amount of time shuttling
back and forth from Tunis for instructions. But each time they
returned to Washington, it seemed, their new hard-line negotiating positions were undercut by a moderately worded PLO
statement issued by Arafat or one of his assistants. At first, the
delegation put this down to a lack of coordination, but they
soon determined for themselves that Arafat and his senior aides
were using them as a foil to entice Israel into direct contacts
with PLO leaders.

What the official Palestinian delegation actually feared was
that, in their desire to remain financially solvent, the Tunis
leadership would move more quickly than they would to conclude an agreement with Israel that would reflect their own
positions, and not the desires of the residents of the occupied
territories. Put simply, they believed that the precarious financial position of the PLO made them vulnerable to political ex-
tortion. This is what ultimately caused the challenge to Arafat's
leadership that began in early 1993 and lasted well into August,
when the Oslo negotiators were beginning to finalize their declaration of principles.

There were a number of other factors that also had a significant impact on Arafat and the Palestinian delegation. One of
the PLO chief's biggest worries was that Israel would sign a
separate peace agreement with Syria. Rabin had even implied

that progress in the Syrian bilateral talks was his chief goal. Under normal circumstances, Arafat would have passed this statement off as a diplomatic ploy aimed at wringing concessions out of the Palestinians. But he simply could not afford to take that risk: An Israeli-Syrian agreement would place enormous pressures on the PLO to follow Syrian President Hafez al-Assad's lead, or face a settlement that would be unilaterally imposed by the Israeli government. Nor could he afford to assume that Syria was not engaged in a back-channel discussion with Israel of the kind that he was planning in Oslo.

Arafat decided to move first. In agreeing to send Abu Alaa to meet with an Israeli professor in Oslo, Arafat was hoping to cut through the complicated diplomatic game going on in Washington. There was only one way to determine whether Israel was serious about negotiating the establishment of an interim Palestinian self-governing authority in the territories, and that was to deal with Israel directly. While Rabin did not yet know of the Oslo discussions, he had come to the same conclusion. The only way to test whether the PLO could back their moderate statements with moderate proposals was to open a direct channel to Tunis.

"We always wanted a back channel in which talks could be held more candidly without any commitments, secret talks that would not be binding on anyone, in the hope of finding sentences, expressions, positions that could lead to a joint declaration of principles," Abu Mazin, the Fatah pragmatist, confirms. "We tried to do this from the moment that the Israeli government came to power." Yossi Beilin, one of Rabin's chief political appointments, echoes these words. "We came to the very simple realization that the PLO was the only one that could deliver on an agreement," he argues, "and we knew that we had to come to terms with that reality. They were the ones that we had to negotiate with."

CHAPTER NINE
OSLO

Accompanied by his trusted associate, researcher Ron Pundik, Yair Hirschfeld met Abu Alaa at the estate of the Borregard paper company in Sarpsborg, outside of Oslo. The two Israelis arrived by taxi so as not to draw attention to themselves. The remote site included all necessary amenities to ensure that everyone would be working and living in a relaxed atmosphere. This set a precedent for the fourteen subsequent meetings in the Oslo channel; Abu Alaa, Hirschfeld, and their small teams of assistants did everything they could to protect the secrecy of their talks, and their Norwegian hosts made certain that their environment remained informal. The delegates lived together, ate together, and took walks in the woods together. At one point over the next few months, the environment was so informal that Abu Alaa attended one meeting in his pajamas.

Abu Alaa and Hirschfeld were helped in their negotiations by a crack team of Norwegian assistants (all of them from FAFO) recruited for the job by Holst, his wife Marianne Heiberg, Larsen, and Mona Juul. The FAFO assistants were responsible for handling the endlessly convoluted travel arrangements, transcribing the meetings, typing the drafts of the agreement, and setting up living and eating arrangements.

Holst also played a key role in the negotiations—not simply by providing alternative negotiating proposals and working out the delicate language of the declaration of principles, but also by ensuring that neither Abu Alaa nor Hirschfeld allowed their basic disagreements to become so important that they shattered any possibility for a final accord. At key moments in the negotiations, Holst invited the principals to dine at his home, meet his family, and relax together. "The negotiations were informal in the sense that they did not involve all the paraphernalia of modern confidence diplomacy," Holst later explained. "An attempt was made to provide a setting conducive to human contact, conviviality, and solidarity of effort. Hence [the discussions] often took place in the countryside in small resorts rather than city hotels, providing opportunity for walks, joint leisure, and meals."

Holst also made sure that the meetings were kept a closely guarded secret, and that Abu Alaa and Hirschfeld were well protected. Plainclothes Norwegian security officers were posted in the woods of the Borregard estate. Holst also provided a cover story to help explain why the lights in the Borregard mansion burned late into the night. Two eccentric professors were engaged in a scholarly project on the Middle East, he said, and spent hours working on it and arguing over their research. You know how professors are.

The FAFO staff worked diligently to make sure that there were no accidental leaks about the meetings. Abu Alaa and Hirschfeld came to Norway over the next months by different routes, changing schedules and planes so that they would not be spotted together. Neither of them ever took a direct flight to Norway and, when they arrived, they rented cars or used taxis. Holst kept them away from crowded hotels. They were often isolated, so that they could concentrate on the issue at hand.

Even though the two negotiators liked each other, there was a certain amount of tension present in all of their gatherings. Abu Alaa did not want to appear as a supplicant and neither did Hirschfeld. So at the beginning of their talks, both men engaged in a short series of negotiating ploys designed to show diplomatic toughness. Hirschfeld led off the discussions by offering a number of economic proposals that would pave the way for a broad political accord. But while the two began to draw up a tentative agreement on that point, Abu Alaa said that it would be a mistake to postpone key political questions. Hirschfeld responded that while he could not speak officially for the Israeli government, he was willing to listen to any political proposal put forward by the PLO.

Abu Alaa said that the PLO believed that Israel should grant autonomy in the occupied territories immediately, or at least in a very short period following the end of official negotiations. The Palestinian leadership, he said, had to be able to present to the Palestinian people a credible autonomy agreement that promised immediate results. Hirschfeld repeated that he was not in a position to negotiate on such a delicate topic, but he promised to confer with officials in Israel. The two men then continued to work on the economic aspects of the agreement before their meetings were concluded.

After the first round of discussions, Hirschfeld returned to Israel to meet with Yossi Beilin and told the deputy foreign minister that he needed more detailed guidance. Abu Alaa, he said, wanted to deal immediately with a number of delicate political issues and was apparently getting pressure on this point from Tunis. What should he do? Hirschfeld's question put Beilin in a quandary. He knew Shimon Peres favored autonomy for Gaza, but Beilin did not want to approve the "Gaza-first" option without Peres's explicit approval. Since it was too early to tell whether the Oslo channel could lead to a serious agreement, and therefore too early to inform Peres or Rabin of the tentative talks, he instructed Hirschfeld to return to Oslo to see if Abu Alaa would make a more definitive proposal.

When Hirschfeld and Abu Alaa next met, however, the Palestinian did not immediately bring up the autonomy question. At the beginning of the second round of talks held at a resort outside of Oslo, therefore, the two men again focused on eco-

nomic issues. They made good progress in developing a number of cooperative economic arrangements and agreed on
language calling for the establishment of a regional development program for the West Bank, Gaza, and Israel. The result
was that by mid-February, Abu Alaa and Hirschfeld were fast
reaching agreement on a number of important fronts.

According to a source with direct knowledge of how this key
part of the declaration of principles was written, Hirschfeld
provided an early draft of the economic annexes based on his
own prior research and Abu Alaa used his sources to edit them.
The two men then participated in a detailed discussion of the
annexes' key provisions and then rewrote them. Both men were
aided in their work by a series of economic papers that had
been provided to them by the Israeli foreign ministry and Abu
Alaa's office in Tunis. A final draft of the economic accords was
then written, and laid aside as the stickier political questions
were addressed.

Between sessions, the two men got to know each other and
their hosts. The Norwegians made certain that the reality of
their environment forced them into a discussion of a range of
topics. They began to talk about their families and careers, a
sign that they were getting along. There was nowhere else to
go, and no one else for the two to talk with.

For Jorgen Holst, who continually monitored and served as a
friendly go-between in the discussions, the initial meetings between the two could not have gone better. While there had been
a few minor problems, both sides had made a good beginning
by focusing their attention on areas where agreement could be
reached quickly and without controversy. The exchange of positions was serious and substantive. Holst took a leaf from Stanley Fischer's book: He turned the discussions away from any
mention of the past—or of who was responsible for the one
hundred years of enmity between the two communities. "Much
discussion took place between the Norwegians and the parties
concerning long term perspectives and the transformation of
frames of reference," he said, using the language typical of a
professional diplomat. "We emphasized the need to focus on

shaping future history rather than negotiating agreement and judgement on past history. It was important [for us] to protect the future as much as possible against a return of history or its revenge."

At the end of the second round, Abu Alaa again insisted that the Israeli government begin to think about tackling the question of autonomy. In this regard, he said, the PLO believed that autonomy should be first granted in the Gaza Strip and that a large part of the West Bank should be added to give the Palestinian authorities a foothold in all of the occupied territories. Abu Alaa did not inform Hirschfeld that his proposal was the result of a position—called the Leopard Spot Plan—staked out over many months by Arafat and the small group of pragmatists at the PLO Tunis headquarters. Arafat and two of his associates—the pragmatists Abu Mazin and Yasser Abed-Rabbo—believed that Israel could grant autonomy to the Palestinians in Gaza and in selected towns in the West Bank. From there, the Palestinian self-governing authority could extend its government to the more remote Palestinian villages. "Gaza-plus," as it was called, reflected this design.

Hirschfeld said that he would take Abu Alaa's proposal to Yossi Beilin when he returned to Israel. Nothing could be done about it until it was studied at the highest levels. Beilin was pleased to learn of the progress in the talks, but when he heard about Abu Alaa's proposition from Hirschfeld, he knew that it was time to inform the Israeli foreign minister about the Oslo opening.

Beilin told Peres that the Oslo negotiations had begun to tackle the difficult problems between the PLO and Israel; there had been significant progress on writing a series of economic "annexes," or proposals, which laid out a broad program of cooperation between the Palestinian and Israeli communities. Beilin then told the foreign minister that Abu Alaa had suggested an agreement giving autonomy for Gaza first, plus a part of the West Bank. Peres was intrigued by this "Gaza-plus" option, and pleased with the opening. But he was especially gratified by Abu Alaa's Gaza proposal. Just two weeks before, Peres had asked the Egyptian foreign minister to tell the PLO that they should publicly propose an autonomy agreement on Gaza first, and he stipulated that the Egyptians not tell the PLO that the proposal had come from Peres himself. Peres waited for two weeks for the proposal to appear in the papers, but nothing happened. Now it seemed that his strategy had worked: He had fed the Gaza-first proposal back to himself through the PLO.

"Not everything was born in my head. I listened to a lot of people," Peres said after the conclusion of the negotiations. "One of my friends, a writer, warned me that the PLO had reached such a point of weakness that it would disappear from the map. I asked myself, what will happen after the PLO disappears? What will come in its place? To solve the problem, I went to Egypt. I convinced them to persuade the Palestinians to demand Gaza, and I intimated there was something else. I already went for the idea of Gaza thirteen years ago. For some time I showed coolness. That's how you have to conduct negotiations. What you propose to the other side—the moment you suggest it—it is nothing. If the other side demands it, it considers it an achievement."

Even given this elegant victory, Peres was skeptical that the Oslo meetings would lead to a final agreement. But he authorized Hirschfeld to continue the talks. At the end of the meeting, Peres instructed the Haifa University professor on a number of points. Specifically, he wanted to know whether Abu Alaa was in a position to actually negotiate for the PLO. In a matter of minutes, the foreign minister designed a test to answer that question and to determine just how influential Abu Alaa was. Since the Palestinian economist knew the intimate details of the PLO's position on a number of issues, Peres wanted Hirschfeld to suggest to him that the PLO drop its insistence that members of the Palestine National Council be included in multilateral meetings on economics and refugees. (Israel was embroiled in a public fight with the Palestinians on just this point, and it had become a matter of principle for both sides.) Israel simply did not want to negotiate with PNC members in the multilateral meetings. If the PLO's demand was dropped, Peres believed, then Israel could go forward with confidence. If not, then Peres would have to find another way to test the PLO's sincerity. In addition, Peres said, he wanted to ask Abu Alaa to make a more specific proposal on the question of Palestinian autonomy. Gaza was possible, he said, but Gaza and what? Hirschfeld returned to Oslo.

At the end of the third round of discussions, when the Norwegian team was writing what they hoped would be a final copy of the economic annexes of the agreement, Abu Alaa proposed adding Jericho to the Gaza-first option. The Palestinian negotiator told Hirschfeld that he had received specific instructions on this point from Yasser Arafat himself: Gaza by itself was not acceptable. The PLO represented all of the Palestinian people and their nation was indivisible. The Israelis had to add a part of the West Bank to the Gaza proposal.

In response to Hirschfeld's other suggestion, Abu Alaa announced that Tunis had agreed to drop its demand that members of the PNC be named as delegates to the multilateral talks. In exchange, the Palestinian economist added, the PLO wanted to take the talks in Norway to a higher level and engage senior officials from the Israeli government in detailed negotiations. When the parties returned to Oslo for the fourth round, Israeli officials who could strike a deal should be in attendance. Hirschfeld nodded his agreement: The Oslo talks were suddenly becoming very serious.

It was now clear that Abu Alaa was negotiating directly on behalf of Yasser Arafat. His agreement to drop the demand that PNC members attend the multilateral talks proved that point, as did his acceptance of what was now dubbed the "Gaza-plus" formula. But there were other key signs that the Palestinians were negotiating seriously and at the highest level. During the third round, Abu Alaa and his chief assistant, Hassan Asfour, would leave the meetings with Hirschfeld and go into an adjoining room, where they would place a phone call to Tunis. The conversations became longer and longer. Hirschfeld would wait patiently. "We saw their reaction when they came away from the phone," Ron Pundik said. "It was clear that the Old Man [Arafat] was part of the deal."

Hirschfeld and Beilin huddled again in Jerusalem in early April. The Israeli professor reiterated his belief that the Oslo channel held great promise for an eventual agreement between Israel and the PLO, but he added that much work needed to be done. He provided a copy of the economic annexes to the foreign minister and gave a detailed report on Abu Alaa's Jericho proposal. He said that Yasser Arafat insisted that high-level Israeli officials be involved in the next round of negotiations. Hirschfeld was nervous, but excited. Beilin went to Peres. The PLO is ready to get serious, he told the Israeli foreign minister, and he advocated upgrading the talks by including designated officials who had the authority to speak for the government and make a deal.

Peres was finally convinced. "The possibilities of contacts with the PLO are unlimited," he later said. "People talk and run to journalists. Headlines all the time. I came to the conclusion that the negotiations in Oslo were serious when I asked Ahmad Krai [Abu Alaa] through our people that the PLO drop the demand to introduce members of the Palestine National Council into the multilateral negotiations." When Abu Alaa agreed, Peres knew that the Oslo discussions could lead to a breakthrough: "Here we [had] found a reliable channel," the foreign minister said. Peres knew it was time to consult Rabin.

The prime minister was hardly surprised that there were back-channel discussions under way with the PLO, since he had guessed as much from hints dropped by Peres, but he was taken aback at the news that they had suddenly become so detailed: Other contacts had been made in the attempt to start a serious dialogue with the PLO, and every one of them had fallen through. Why would this one be any different? But the more Rabin studied Hirschfeld's draft proposal and listened to the arguments of Peres and Beilin, the more convinced he became that Oslo could be the breakthrough that he was searching for.

He questioned both men closely on the extent of the Oslo discussions and studied the draft economic accords that Hirschfeld had hammered out with Abu Alaa.

Rabin believed that if Oslo offered a better-than-even chance of success, it was worth pursuing. For him, it was the perfect channel: Negotiating with the earnest and well-connected Abu Alaa meant that Israel could talk with a legitimate and authoritative PLO leader who was untainted by the organization's more radical activities. In addition, Peres said that the Palestinian had passed an important first test—Abu Alaa had influence in Tunis. Furthermore, the Norwegians were credible intermediaries with deep experience in the region and a proven ability to keep a secret. Finally, Rabin was attracted to the PLO's willingness to undertake self-rule one step at a time, an approach he had been advocating for many years. When Rabin studied all the options, Oslo looked like the most promising. Besides, the Washington talks were going nowhere and, as a result, Rabin had come to the conclusion that the Palestinian delegation simply did not have the authority to negotiate seriously with their Israeli counterparts. The road to peace had to run through Tunis, he felt, but the road to Tunis went through Oslo.

In a few short minutes, the Israeli prime minister made a fateful decision. While Peres himself wanted to go to Oslo, the prime minister wanted to keep the talks below the ministerial level, to protect the secrecy of the contacts. He appointed Uri Savir, the foreign ministry's director general, to meet with Abu Alaa and assess the prospect for success in the back channel. Savir was told that his job was to finalize a declaration of principles. If he could do so to his, Rabin's, satisfaction, Rabin said, he would sign it. Rabin then instructed Peres and Beilin to continue to monitor the talks. He wanted to know, at each moment, whether they believed that PLO officials were negotiating in good faith.

Rabin then followed this up by instructing key foreign ministry officials to develop detailed and updated studies on the economics of a transition to self-rule for the territories—a topic that the foreign ministry had been investigating for some time.

Rabin liked the tenor of the economic annexes that had been agreed on so far, but he wanted to make sure they were absolutely right. In Tunis, PLO Chairman Yasser Arafat undertook similar steps. He upgraded the Abu Alaa mission and instructed his team to provide detailed analyses of the talks for his personal review. When he learned that Rabin would be adding substance to the Israeli side, he was very pleased. "When [the director of the Israeli foreign ministry] showed up, we felt that the Israelis were becoming more serious," Abu Mazin later acknowledged.

While Rabin was pleased with the pattern of the Oslo negotiations and the fact that progress could now be made with the Palestinians, he, like Peres, did not fully believe that the talks could succeed in bringing about a diplomatic breakthrough between Israel and the Palestinians. In spite of Peres's test of Abu Alaa, Rabin simply had no way of absolutely telling whether the PLO was negotiating in good faith. And even if Abu Alaa turned out to be a serious intermediary, Rabin did not want the Oslo channel to drag on forever, as it appeared that the Washington talks would. The PLO had to be given an incentive for moving quickly to a final agreement. Fortunately, Rabin had a ready-made way to put pressure on the PLO.

For months, Israeli officials had been complaining that the Palestinian delegation in Washington did not have the authority to conclude an agreement with Israel. Whenever it appeared that they were willing to compromise, they postponed further meetings to check with the PLO leadership in Tunis. Rabin, Peres, and other Israelis repeatedly complained about this problem to Secretary of State Warren Christopher. To help solve the problem, Rabin and Peres decided to suggest to Christopher that the Palestinians appoint Faisal Husseini as the official head of their delegation.

Husseini was widely respected in the Palestinian community, carried weight among moderates in the Israeli political establishment, and had won the trust of Peres during a series of secret meetings in East Jerusalem during the height of the deportation crisis. Israel's new ambassador to the United States, Itamar Rabinovich, succinctly summarized these views on the day that he took over the job as Israel's top diplomat in Washington. "We think that Faisal Husseini is a genuine Palestinian leader in the West Bank," he said, "and that he can instill authority and legitimacy into the Palestinian delegation and give the negotiations a much better prospect."

By insisting that Husseini be the chief intermediary with the Palestinian community, the Rabin government signaled its interest in moving the Washington talks to a more serious level. The Israeli government was even willing to overlook the fact that Husseini was from Jerusalem. Israel's insistence that no member of the Palestinian delegation come from the city was now quietly dropped and Israeli diplomats were instructed to pass over the point when reminded of it by journalists. Itamar Rabinovich apparently decided that the best thing to do was to joke lightly about Husseini's addition to the Palestinian team. "Well," he said, smiling, "he is a leading West Bank Palestinian who happens to have a residence in Jerusalem, yes, but I also understand that he has a new address now, in Ramallah."

Christopher's insistence that Husseini be included in the talks caught the delegation by surprise. On the one hand, most of the delegates welcomed Husseini's addition, but on the other hand they were upset that the Israeli government seemed to be once again dictating who should negotiate on their behalf. Haidar Abdul Shafi was already the Palestinian delegation's chief negotiator, they pointed out, and they did not want Faisal Husseini to replace him. "This was a very difficult situation for me," Husseini admitted at the time, "and very embarrassing." It was also embarrassing for Haidar Abdul Shafi, who suspected that the United States and Israel were colluding in some as yet unknown plan.

In fact, the Americans had nothing to do with it: It was all Israel's idea. The complaints that the Palestinians were dragging their feet in Washington came at a perfect time for Rabin, and for those Israelis involved in negotiating in the Oslo channel. In spite of the years of work that Israeli intelligence had spent studying the head of the PLO, the Israeli government had no clear idea on how to exploit Arafat's weaknesses in a diplomatic setting. Rabin was absolutely certain that if there was a deal between Israel and the Palestinians, Arafat would want it between Israel and him—and not someone from the Washington talks. And that meant that Husseini's official inclusion as a member of the delegation might be just enough to scare Arafat into hurrying the Oslo channel forward.

When the next round of meetings convened in Norway in early May, the Israelis came armed with a pile of proposals and studies—including the foreign ministry's recently updated economic review on the transition economy in the occupied territories. In addition to Savir, Yoel Zinger, an experienced lawyer close to Rabin, accompanied the delegation. Abu Alaa had also done his research; he came to Oslo with documents provided by his top economic assistants, some of whom worked on the Harvard Group. The Palestinian economist also brought along Taher Shash, the PLO's legal adviser, to help keep an eye on how the two teams actually worded the final declaration of principles. The Israelis and Palestinians spent much of the next few sessions reviewing and rewriting the economic annexes of the agreement, using Hirschfeld's own primary work on economic cooperation and his and Abu Alaa's previous document as a guide.

The appointment of Savir and Zinger had an immediate impact on the meetings. The two Israelis, in particular, had detailed instructions from Rabin and Peres on the draft agreement. They reviewed the work that had been done by Hirschfeld and Abu Alaa in the first negotiating sessions, then set about revising many of the document's finer points. The actual meetings between the Israeli and Palestinian teams became longer and more intense. The two sides were now involved in hammering out a detailed agreement that had to take into account the political views of Arafat and Rabin as well as the views of two very different communities. In addition, the Palestinian and Israeli teams were painfully aware that the final agreement had to be able to play to an international audience. All the *t*'s and *i*'s had to be crossed and dotted correctly.

After the fourth round of meetings in Oslo, other changes were made. Savir returned home from Norway worried that the talks had become too complex for just one senior official to handle. There were too many details to be worked out and, while he had extensive experience as a diplomat, he was not totally comfortable writing a final agreement with Israel's most intransigent enemy. We need a lawyer, a good one, Savir told Rabin back in Jerusalem. Rabin agreed and appointed Yoel Zinger, an Israeli lawyer who had played a key role in every Israeli agreement since the mid-1970s. The two returned together to Oslo.

Both Zinger and the newly upgraded Palestinian delegation to Oslo were astonished at what had taken place. But both sides knew that there was much yet to be done. While some of the earlier discussions between Abu Alaa and Hirschfeld proved important, they had not yet met the political requirements that were fundamental to Rabin's, or Arafat's, thinking. There were also aspects of the earlier draft declarations that were clearly not acceptable to one side or another. What happened over the next few months was essentially a cut-and-paste operation that added new substance to the document, while eliminating or clarifying ambiguous and controversial points.

"It is very difficult now to assess just how many drafts there were," a principal in the talks said. "There was a different substance to the drafts before and after Mr. Savir and Mr. Zinger joined [the talks]." This high-level source, who insisted on anonymity in exchange for an inside look at the Oslo talks, also said that Hirschfeld and Abu Alaa were "not negotiators, [they] were brainstormers. There is a big difference. . . . One is conducting an intellectual exercise, and the other is negotiating on behalf of governments." The addition of Savir, Zinger, and Shash changed the tenor of the talks and set them out along a new path.

Johan Jorgen Holst watched the process with admiration for the dedication of the two teams. When he later looked back on the talks in Oslo, he pointed to the May meetings as a key turning point. The back channel, he said, was beginning to take on a dynamic of its own. "The first phase [of the negotiations], which could be denoted the exploratory phase, lasted from January to April 1993 and involved three rounds of talks," he said. "The second phase involved authorized negotiations which went on from May through August through eleven rounds of negotiations. The negotiations were conducted in secrecy [which] permitted the participants to perform as real negotiators rather than mere spokesmen for opposing interests."

Even at this point, however, there was a degree of mistrust between the two teams. No one who met in Norway could quite bring themselves to believe that Israel was actually negotiating an agreement with the PLO, or that the phlegmatic and secretive Abu Alaa was conducting negotiations with Israeli officials. Jorgen Holst sensed these uneasy feelings. "A basic issue which hovered over the negotiations until the endgame was whether the parties were committed to cut consensus and make a choice in favor of agreement," he reflected. "To deliver on such commitments in a credible and persuasive manner added to the salience of the issue of mutual trust. From the point of view of both sides, the leadership of the other seemed to be unlikely peacemakers."

It took some time, but by mid-May the mutual suspicion that marked an upgrading of the Oslo discussions was slowly being replaced by a sense of ease as the Palestinian and Israeli teams got to know one another. The tension that had marred earlier meetings was replaced by joking, and sometimes long discussions about careers and families. Holst's efforts to provide a relaxed environment for the discussions were paying off; a sense of trust between the two sides was slowly being built. Holst reinforced the new sense of trust that had been built on both sides by inviting the chief negotiators to have dinner at his home. After the meal, Abu Alaa, the hard-nosed PLO official, got down on the floor of the living room to play with Edvard, Holst's four-year-old son.

At the same time that the Oslo negotiators were making relaxed progress, however, the Israeli leadership in Jerusalem and their counterparts in Tunis were starting to worry that their negotiators had become too friendly with one another. By mid-May, the atmosphere of the talks had unexpectedly shifted once again and the gamesmanship that marked the Washington bilateral negotiations was being transferred to the small meeting rooms of Oslo hotels and Norwegian resorts. One incident, in particular, reflects the negotiating style of the two teams, and gives some flavor of the give-and-take of the Oslo talks.

Noting that Abu Alaa and his team of negotiators were beginning to take on the characteristics of their comrades negotiating in Washington, the Israelis decided to play tough. In early June, Savir accused the Palestinian delegation of coming up with new demands. It had happened before. Just when Gaza was about to be approved, the Palestinians said that they needed Jericho. What would it be next? Every time we accept a demand, Uri Savir told Abu Alaa, you come up with a new one.

Abu Alaa was just as adamant. He wondered why the topic of Jericho was such a problem. Jericho was important as a symbol, he said. Uri Savir agreed that such a symbol was necessary, but how big should the symbol be? He answered his own question with a suggestion: Israel would withdraw from the "city" of Jericho. Abu Alaa objected: You should withdraw from the "*liwaa*" (province) of Jericho, he said. Savir responded that this was impossible, the "province" of Jericho led to the outskirts of Jerusalem. It was huge. Instead, Savir suggested that the two sides agree that Israel would withdraw from the "*qadaa*" (district) of Jericho. Abu Alaa would not give in: That is not enough, he said. Finally, Holst stepped in, suggesting that both sides agree that Israeli forces would withdraw from "the Jericho area." They could leave the details for later.

They agreed.

At key moments in the negotiations from the end of May to the end of August, Israeli officials in Jerusalem and their counterparts in Tunis attempted to pull back their teams for important consultations with the purpose of strengthening their negotiating position. The discussions lurched from point to point in marathon twenty-four- and thirty-six-hour negotiating sessions. But just when it seemed that both sides had reached an insurmountable obstacle, the Norwegians intervened to break through the impasse, "by communicating tempered and considerate assessments in writing to both sides," as Holst later said.

By early June of 1993, a new draft declaration of principles was being readied for review in Jerusalem and Tunis, but several major obstacles remained. According to PLO officials familiar with the talks, the Oslo channel "mirrored the bilateral talks" when it came to the problems of refugees and the status of Jerusalem. "After we tied Jericho to Gaza, we thought that we had overcome many of the procedural problems," said a PLO official, "but we knew that Jerusalem would be a real sticking point. So we saved it for last." In fact, however, the PLO never had any intention of dealing with the problem of Jerusalem at all—except, of course, as a purely rhetorical flourish.

By early June, it was clear that Yasser Arafat had turned the tables on Yitzhak Rabin—and on his own negotiators in Washington. During one of their many trips to Tunis, the Palestinian delegation to the Washington talks was informed that the PLO leadership had decided that the issue of Jerusalem was of paramount importance and that it should be emphasized in their discussions with Israel. There could be no progress on an autonomy agreement unless the issue of Jerusalem was solved, Arafat told the Palestinian delegation. But Arafat had his own agenda: He was signaling to Rabin that the only way to negotiate with the Palestinians was to negotiate directly with the PLO—in Oslo, not in Washington. When the official Palestinian delegation returned to the United States, the Jerusalem issue became a sticking point in their discussions with the Israelis, and the Washington talks stalled. The Israeli government now had no choice—they had to place their top priority on dealing with Abu Alaa and his team in Oslo. Rabin had lost his leverage.

Shimon Peres understood immediately what Arafat was doing. "The locals [those inside the territories] couldn't do anything," he said. "The moment Arafat told them to insist on the Jerusalem issue, the locals were erased." He then added: "What is there to understand here? Arafat finished them. Even before they weren't there. I know them. After all, I was also minister of defense. Those who conducted the negotiations [in Washington] represent in the best instance the Arab intelligentsia. There is a limit to what they can do." Peres admired Arafat's cleverness, but he was also amazed at how ruthless he could be and how he so willingly used the Palestinian delegation in Washington to fit his own personal agenda. Peres concluded that there was only one way to deal with such men. "Transfer them to Gaza," he told an Israeli newspaper in disgust.

That is just what the Israeli negotiators in Oslo were preparing to do. At the end of June, Yoel Zinger told Rabin that it was now likely that the Oslo negotiations could produce an agreement in a matter of weeks, with a Gaza-Jericho autonomy accord as its centerpiece. Zinger suggested that the prime minister and Peres work more closely with the group to draft the final language of the declaration. Rabin agreed. "Rabin was part of every word, every letter, every dot. He always knew what was going on," an independent high-level source who witnessed the talks says. "He was part of every line, of every letter. He knew everything at every step."

Seeing where the talks were headed, Rabin notified Egyptian Foreign Minister Amr Mousa of the progress that had been made in the Oslo channel. Johan Jorgen Holst, meanwhile, told American State Department official Daniel Kurtzer that the Palestinians and Israelis were discussing peace in Oslo, but he purposely left the details of the talks ambiguous. He said that a number of academics and scholars on both sides were holding general discussions and that they had not yet come to any conclusions. Kurtzer passed the information on to Warren Christopher, who ignored the report. From this point until the final agreement was initialed in August, Egyptian officials were the only nonprincipals who had detailed knowledge of the secret channel.

In addition to these moves, Rabin sent a number of Israeli

officials to meet with members of the PLO to assess the seriousness of their resolve. Lacking any direct contact with Yasser Arafat, Rabin was not about to conclude an agreement with Abu Alaa without finding out for himself whether Arafat was truly on board and how far he was willing to go. In one instance Nimrod Novick, an associate of Shimon Peres, had a meeting with Osama al-Baz, the chief foreign affairs adviser to Egyptian President Hosni Mubarak, who assured Novick that based on his own meetings with PLO officials, Arafat was fully engaged in the Oslo negotiations and had personally approved the changes in the draft declaration agreed to by Abu Alaa. In a separate meeting, Rabin dispatched Environment Minister Yossi Sarid on a separate trip to Cairo to meet with the PLO's representative there, Nabil Shaath. Rabin apparently gave Sarid explicit instructions, but without tipping information on the Oslo channel: Sarid was to question Shaath on Arafat's thinking on autonomy. Finally, Health Minister Haim Ramon was sent to meet with Dr. Ahmed Tibi, a confidant of Arafat, in Jerusalem for the same purpose. Both Sarid's and Ramon's reports reassured Rabin that the PLO was edging closer to a final declaration of principles on Israeli terms.

But while the Israelis looked forward to initialing a final agreement in the near future, PLO officials were much less optimistic. Abu Alaa reported to Arafat that the Israelis remained intransigent on a number of outstanding issues, including approval of full access between Gaza and the West Bank. In addition, Abu Alaa added, the Israeli negotiating team insisted that other outstanding issues—like the final disposition of the Israeli settlers—should be postponed until negotiations on the final status of the territories. They had given little ground.

Arafat was upset by the news: He knew he would have a much more difficult time convincing the Palestinian community of the worth of the Gaza-Jericho deal if the declaration of principles lacked strong language on the Palestinians' right to Jerusalem or, at the least, a promise that Jerusalem would be on the agenda when the Israelis and Palestinians moved past the Oslo accord to discuss a permanent settlement in the territories. But

Arafat was still worried that his insistence on explicit language on Jerusalem would ruin the chance for initialing a final agreement. He therefore instructed Abu Alaa to agree to defer negotiating the issue of the holy city and concentrate on a Gaza-Jericho corridor. The two Palestinian entities, he insisted, had to be linked. Arafat knew that any agreement that he signed would have to produce the hope of a united Palestinian state. Otherwise, he feared, his own leadership would be jeopardized and the accord would fall apart.

Arafat was right: He had faced a challenge to his leadership since January, but now his critics were becoming even more powerful. Evidence of this was made very clear to him by a strong challenge to his leadership that had been made by influential PLO leaders in mid-June.

In the midst of giving his full attention to what was happening in Oslo, Arafat was faced with the most serious threat to his leadership in thirty years. The controversy began during an early-morning meeting of the PLO's central committee in Tunis in mid-June. After opening the proceedings, committee members suggested that the question of Fatah's organizational structure be put on the agenda. The proposal took Arafat by surprise: Why should we do that? he asked. The answer came from Hani Hassan, Arafat's old nemesis and one of the organization's senior officials. Hassan had challenged Arafat's judgment during the Iraq crisis and had been one of his most constant critics; now, he attacked him again. Hassan said that he believed that Arafat was acting like a dictator, and that the PLO needed to debate ways to make the organization more democratic.

Arafat was infuriated by the suggestion. He said that the best way to discuss political reform was to open an investigation on Hassan himself. He charged the Fatah official with leaking PLO secrets to foreign governments and cooperating with the Hamas fundamentalist movement. The meeting degenerated from there, but it was soon clear that Arafat had overplayed his hand by criticizing Hassan. The PLO official had more allies on the

committee than he had guessed. "Why the suggestion of discussing Hani first?" Muhammed Ghoneim, the PLO's chief of
mobilization, asked. "Why don't we discuss you first?"

Arafat soon realized that he was facing a full-scale rebellion
that had been planned for weeks. Ghoneim's comment that the
committee investigate Arafat was seconded by Muhammed Jihad, the chief of military matters in the occupied territories,
and an official who had had to deal with a series of mounting
crises among Fatah units in the West Bank. He was in a position
to know that the PLO was quickly losing influence among the
population of the occupied territories and he was frustrated by
his inability to stem the anti-PLO tide. Jihad said that the committee should listen to Ghoneim, since he had important things
to say.

Before Arafat could interrupt, Ghoneim launched a broad
attack on the "corruption" and "poor management" of the PLO,
and he singled out Arafat's chief political advisers: Bassam Abu-
Sharif, Nizar Abu Ghazaleh (the head of the financially
strapped Palestine National Fund), and Fuad Shwaiki, Fatah's
chief financial officer and a colleague of Abu Alaa's. Arafat
listened in barely concealed contempt to his critics, who said
that the PLO chairman needed to allow a greater voice in the
organization from its other top officials. Otherwise, they said,
the PLO would be destroyed.

After this initial burst of dissent, Arafat's critics next turned
to the second item on the agenda. Hassan, Ghoneim, and Jihad
said that Arafat was making too many concessions to the Israelis
in the Washington talks and making too many decisions about
the peace process without keeping the other leaders in the organization informed of his moves. Arafat, his critics claimed,
had apparently met with Israeli officials in Egypt, but without
informing anyone of that fact. For a moment, it appeared that
Arafat's opponents had discovered the Oslo channel and were
attempting to sabotage the negotiations, but after a few moments it became clear that they had not. Arafat denied the
charge: He had never met with any Israeli official in Cairo—
which was true. After several hours of argument, the PLO

chairman adjourned the meeting. Nothing had been resolved.

Twenty-four hours later, Arafat launched his counterattack. The PLO chairman charged Hani Hassan with circulating anti-PLO leaflets in the occupied territories in an attempt to undermine the organization. But Arafat's claim had no effect. Hassan and his allies reasserted their view that Arafat had made unilateral decisions without support. They added that his unwillingness to consult with other Palestinian groups outside of the organization was costing the PLO badly needed support. PLO cadres were defecting in huge numbers in the West Bank and Gaza and the organization was in danger of "coming apart."

"We have very serious problems in the occupied territories, there is really no doubt about that," a PLO official said at the time. "There is always opposition to the peace process from fringe groups, but now that opposition has moved into the mainstream. Our Fatah groups are badly demoralized and we barely have a presence on the streets. We can no longer control a number of support groups in the territories, and this is hurting us. This whole thing could unravel."

Which is just what Arafat was worried about. The opposition arrayed against him was very formidable and even his threat to resign, which had always worked before, had no effect on his opponents: "Go ahead then, resign," Hassan said. "That's what we want." Faced with such withering criticism and on the verge of a major schism in the organization, Arafat finally agreed to a proposal that Hassan be appointed as the head of a new "national unity committee" to open a dialogue with those Palestinians disenchanted with the peace process. The opposition was mollified: It looked like Arafat's agreement marked the beginning of real democracy in the PLO.

Hassan's appointment to the new committee did not reconcile Arafat to his critics, but it allowed the PLO chairman enough time to continue concentrating on the Oslo channel. The critics were right: He was acting unilaterally. Only he, Abu Alaa, Hassan Asfour, Yassir Abed-Rabbo, Taher Shash, and senior PLO official Abu Mazin knew of the secret back-channel negotiations. No one else had been informed. Arafat had kept

the talks quiet because he knew that any leak on the Oslo opening would doom whatever chance they had of success. Ironically, Arafat was being just as stubborn and dictatorial in his
negotiations with the Israelis in 1993 as he was back in 1990,
when he supported Saddam Hussein. But this time, he was
actually engaged in negotiations with Israel over Palestinian
self-rule. He was not about to allow an internal PLO rebellion
ruin that unprecedented opportunity.

Just after the Tunis meeting, Arafat traveled to Amman to
attend a conference of senior PLO officials from the diaspora.
As in the Tunis meetings, he realized that he would be criticized
for acting unilaterally. There were also suspicions that he was
staking out a moderate position in the peace talks. His colleagues in Amman insisted that he discipline the delegation and
that Arafat himself take a tougher public line with Israel. Arafat struck back. In an uninterrupted nine-hour meeting, he
held firm to his moderate position. Without talking specifically
about the negotiations going on in Oslo, he told his colleagues
that the PLO must promote a moderate public negotiating
stance. That was the only way. There had to be an agreement.
He insisted on it.

Two days later, in Jerusalem, Yitzhak Rabin received a vid-
eotape of the session. He studied it closely, paying special attention to Arafat's position. He was relieved by what he saw:
Arafat wanted a deal with Israel.

At the same time that Arafat was fighting for his political life
in Tunis, the Harvard Group was wrapping up the final sessions of the six working groups and preparing their final report, which was to be issued at the end of June. "Securing Peace
in the Middle East: Project on Economic Transition" had taken
on a vast new importance—especially with the progress, at least
so far, in the Oslo talks. While no one in the group's meetings
had direct knowledge of the back-channel proceedings, their
work was being welcomed with increasing interest in Tunis,
Jerusalem, and Amman, and a number of their conclusions
were passed on to Israeli and Palestinian teams meeting in Oslo.

"Peres was very supportive of our work when we met with him," Anna Karasik later confirmed. "When the [Israeli foreign ministry] received the report and had time to look at it, it was obvious that they agreed with many of the points that we made." The report was also read with interest by high-level officials of the PLO, including Arafat himself, who received it in mid-July. The report was also presented in a full briefing to Crown Prince Hassan of Jordan, who then passed it on to his own working group, which was laying out the economic guidelines of an Israeli-Jordanian agreement. The work of the Harvard Group was obviously reaching the top levels of all three political entities.

"It is hard to say exactly what impact our report had on the final agreement," Stanley Fischer later added. "I can say that we must have had some impact because the group that we put together were very [much from the] establishment; these were top people, the top economists from Jordan, Israel, and the Palestinians. The emphasis in this report, and I think our main intellectual contribution, was that we had to have free trade. There had to be free trade between the three entities, between the Israelis, Jordanians, and Palestinians; otherwise none of this would work."

In fact, the Harvard Group's findings had a significant impact on the negotiations in Oslo. During the end of July and the beginning of August, the Oslo negotiators once again returned to the economic annexes of the now nearly complete declaration of principles with an eye toward including a number of proposals made by the Fischer-Hausman-Karasik group. Chief among these was the creation of "free trade zones," a hallmark of the Harvard Group's study and the only way that Fischer and his colleagues believed that the newly created Palestinian entity had a chance of prospering. Economists in the Israeli foreign ministry also had a hand in making sure that the final agreement included broad programs for Israeli-Palestinian economic cooperation.

But the success of the Harvard Group's efforts was due, in large measure, to its access to Israeli and Palestinian political leaders. "We went with the report to the Middle East. In July it was presented to Peres and he had a full briefing on our findings," Stanley Fischer says. "We discussed it with officials in the Israeli government at some length, and with the Jordanians, and we went to Tunis and presented it to the PLO. So while it is hard to gauge just what impact the report had, it is true that our ideas ended up in the declaration of principles."

Not surprisingly, the Harvard Group report was distinctively representative of the economic realities that would face the West Bank and Gaza during a period of political transition. Not only did it confirm the principle of free trade among Israel, Jordan, and a new Palestinian entity, it also endorsed an economic melding of the three political units in a way that had never before been articulated—the virtual creation of what one Arab paper later called "Israelistine." Specifically, the Harvard Group's report recommended the development of regional projects in the areas of tourist services, airport facilities, road and bridge facilities, and electric power.

In other words, what Fischer, Hausman, and Karasik—and their thirty-four colleagues—foresaw was the establishment of a Middle East commonwealth, an idea put forward by Hirschfeld, Abu Alaa, and Peres. This idea was one of the most prominent in their report, and it slowly began to be repeated by leaders in the region. Peres, in particular, was once again quoted as saying that he viewed the future Israeli-Palestinian relations as "a political divorce, but an economic marriage." The phrase had become very popular among Israeli officials and it was passed on to American economists. "Peres used the phrase with me about five or six times," Hausman confirms. The Harvard Group organizers told Peres that free trade across political lines had to occur sooner rather than later—despite opposition to the idea in segments of the Israeli government. "There was some immediate opposition to what we were saying in our report," Fischer confirms, "but we knew that there would be."

The Harvard Group's recommendations were controversial in some circles, but they were supported by senior officials in the Israeli government. "I think I have an even stronger vision of economic cooperation than do the people in the region who endorse it," Hausman says. "In order for there to be economic success there has to be completely free trade and completely open borders. What that means is that the Israeli market is going to have to open up to oranges grown in Jordan and in the Palestinian entity. And that means some short-term hardship. Israeli farmers are going to have to compete with cheaper citrus, for instance, but the short-term drawbacks are still necessary and very temporary."

Not surprisingly, the World Bank report, "Developing the Occupied Territories: An Investment in Peace," reached many of the same conclusions as the Harvard Group. After sending teams into the field in January and February, the bank produced a draft of their report that called for major investment in the infrastructure and economic authority of the territories, as well as providing relief to impoverished and underemployed Palestinians. It included an ambitious plan for funding the various projects, and not just in the transitional period. If successful, the plan would create a viable Palestinian economy intimately intertwined with Israel and Jordan.

Although the report was commissioned by the full multilateral working group on economic development—the same one that Shimon Peres had used to test the credibility of Abu Alaa—a World Bank official who requested anonymity confirmed that the early draft was made available in mid-July 1993 only to those parties who were directly affected by it—Israel, Jordan, and the Palestinians. This was apparently done at the insistence of the Israeli government. The recommendations of this report were then passed on to the principal negotiators in the Oslo channel. The final report, however, was not formally submitted to the full multilateral working group until November 1993.

The timing of the report's initial limited release was crucial, because it meant that Rabin, Peres, and Arafat had access to an authoritative version of a future Palestinian-Israeli-Jordanian economic union just as the Oslo talks were coming to a head. It was a vision that perfectly complemented the plans for economic cooperation that had been agreed on in Oslo and offered a detailed accounting of where the necessary funds would come from. Seeing this report by the world's leading financial institution could only have reassured the Oslo negotiators that their approach was the right one. And it reassured the Israeli government that the funds necessary to complete the broad economic program designed to rehabilitate the occupied territories would be forthcoming from international lending institutions.

By the end of July, the most important ideas of economic cooperation had already been well-established as part of the declaration of principles. The economic marriage might not have been fully consummated, but the planning for the wedding was well under way. Unfortunately, however, the planning for the political divorce was still not going very well.

Also, by the end of July, the secret talks in Oslo were nearing a breakdown: Abu Alaa and his Palestinian team would not budge on the major issues of political separation, including the status of refugees, the approval of a corridor between Gaza and Jericho, and the final disposition of Israeli settlements. While the details of this disagreement are not fully known, it is now clear that Israel and the PLO were nearing a major crisis that could destroy the months of negotiations that had already been completed. "July was a difficult month," a source who was a principal in the Oslo talks said.

The Palestinian negotiators were so frustrated by the impasse that, at one point near the end of July, Abu Alaa stormed out of a meeting with Uri Savir and threatened to break off the talks. The breakdown had no apparent effect on the Israeli position, but the Norwegian foreign minister was extremely worried that the months of work that had gone into drafting the declaration were about to be lost. The crisis tested Holst's abilities to the maximum as he attempted to mediate a resolution between the two sides. It was at this point that he proffered a number of proposals to help bridge the gaps in the two positions. At the same time that the two sides were inching toward an agreement, they were drawing back from some of their orig-

inal ideas—getting cold feet. It was almost as if they had difficulty putting the past behind them. They sensed that the
declaration of principles set Israelis and Palestinians adrift in
an unknown world.

"The talks were very trying, very trying," a Palestinian with
information on this critical period says. "There were no last-
minute compromises; rather, there was a general moving together that was built on a basis of months of trust." In essence,
the Israelis convinced their Palestinian counterparts that their
promise to deal with thorny problems like Jerusalem, refugees,
and Israeli settlements during future negotiations on the final
status of the territories was made "in good faith." In so doing,
they allayed the Palestinians' fears that the Israeli need to postpone a discussion of these problems was simply a negotiating
ploy.

Finally, after hours of conferring with PLO Chairman Arafat
by telephone, Abu Alaa returned to the talks and the mediation
of the Norwegians began to take hold. The Palestinian team
insisted on a number of minor modifications to the final document in line with Arafat's recommendation—but they were
face-saving changes in wording. The major points of the declaration were left intact. Savir and Zinger, meanwhile, consulted
with Rabin by telephone from another room. They read the
Palestinian changes in the declaration of principles in pieces, as
it was made available by Abu Alaa. After many tense moments,
Savir and Zinger returned from their consultation with a look
of relief, and gave Abu Alaa a thumbs-up.

In retrospect, it is apparent that the credibility of Holst was
the key to keeping the talks on track. He had had a substantive
and cordial meeting with Arafat in Tunis earlier in July, and
the PLO chairman had even bounced his little boy, Edvard, on
his knee. The PLO leader and Holst got along well. Arafat
made it clear that he trusted the Norwegian's ability to deliver
useful proposals that would make an agreement on a declaration of principles possible. Holst then visited Israel to reassure
the Rabin government that the negotiations were on track.
Holst's meetings in Jerusalem made the last hurdle that the

Oslo negotiators had to overcome—Israel's recognition of the PLO—that much easier.

In Oslo, the last *i*'s were dotted and the last *t*'s were crossed. With Hirschfeld, Savir, Zinger, Abu Alaa, Asfour, and Taher Shash looking on, Holst's Norwegian facilitator produced clean copies of the agreement for one last go-round. After hours of review, no new problems were found and there was a palpable sense of relief among all the participants. But there were still a number of steps that had to be taken before the agreements could be finalized. Savir and Zinger returned to Jerusalem, while Abu Alaa, Asfour, and Shash caught their flight for Tunis.

In Jerusalem, Uri Savir met with Peres to outline the final agreement. There were four explicit stipulations that had been finally agreed to by the Palestinians, he said. First, negotiations on the status of Jerusalem had been postponed; second, there would initially be no corridor between Gaza and Jericho; third, Israel would control access to the West Bank via the Allenby Bridge; and, fourth, the PLO said that it would explicitly renounce the use of terrorism. Peres was pleased.

Rabin was also satisfied with the final draft of the declaration of principles, but he insisted that he and Arafat exchange public letters of mutual recognition, and that the PLO's renunciation of terrorism be contained in Arafat's letter to him. The PLO must change its covenant, Rabin said, which called for the destruction of Israel. With these instructions in hand, Savir returned yet again to Oslo for one round of last-minute talks. Peres waited two days for Savir to report the results. When he did, confirming that an exchange of letters had been agreed to by the PLO, Peres boarded a flight for Stockholm, where he was scheduled to begin an official visit.

Peres's visit to Stockholm occasioned a number of press reports that he was secretly meeting with PLO officials. But despite the best efforts of the press, Peres never even came close to meeting with a Palestinian—in public or in private. "I cannot give you my entire life story but I can tell you that I met no PLO officials in Stockholm; I only met Swedes," Peres said to the press. At the end of his first day of meetings, Peres returned to the guest home of the Swedish government, picked up the telephone, and placed a direct call to Tunis. For the next eight hours, he spoke directly with Abu Alaa and Yasser Arafat. They reviewed the agreement word by word and line by line and opened negotiations on the PLO's renunciation of terror and Israel's recognition of the organization.

Peres and Arafat's discussion, the first ever between the two former antagonists, was extensive, detailed, and tense. Arafat was told that his organization must now conform to the commitments set out in the declaration of principles. It had to recognize the right of the State of Israel to exist in peace and security, reaffirm its support of UN Resolutions 242 and 338, renounce terrorism and other acts of violence, and negate those parts of its own national covenant that were inconsistent with the Oslo agreement. In return, Israel would recognize the PLO as the "sole, legitimate representative of the Palestinian people." These requirements would be set out in an exchange of letters between Arafat and Rabin. The discussion lasted from late on the night of August 17 to early in the morning of the eighteenth. After another round of meetings in Sweden, Peres boarded a plane for Oslo.

Johan Jorgen Holst, who could take so much credit for the final agreement, clearly understood the drama of the events that were about to unfold in Oslo. "Peace has not arrived yet in the Middle East. [But] it is now in the making. A new road has been opened. It is not a paved highway, nor is it a road safe from robbers and spoilers. Complex negotiations lie ahead. . . . The future has not been won, but the prospects for victory now seem brighter than before the historical breakthrough."

On the evening of August 19, Shimon Peres was an official guest of the Norwegian government at a state dinner, after which he was driven to the guest house of the Norwegian government. After a moment's hesitation, Foreign Minister Holst motioned to a nearby stairway and Peres began the short ascent to an upstairs meeting room. Waiting behind a closed door was Abu Alaa, who greeted him formally. They talked for a few moments. Peres found Abu Alaa to be a self-effacing and proud Palestinian. He was a man of few words and very dedicated to his cause. A serious man. Peres could understand that. After a few moments, Uri Savir and Abu Alaa's assistant, along with a group of Norwegian diplomats and the small coterie of hard-working assistants from FAFO, greeted Peres and Abu Alaa. Then, in a hushed atmosphere, all watched as Abu Alaa and Savir initialed the "Declaration of Principles on Interim Self-Government Arrangements" between the PLO and Israel. There were tears in the eyes of the onlooking Norwegians, but everyone was silenced by the somber scene. Abu Alaa and Shimon Peres shook hands. Somewhere in the background came the sound of a champagne bottle being uncorked.

CHAPTER TEN
JERICHO

On Wednesday, August 25, Shimon Peres returned to Israel from Oslo and immediately closeted himself with the prime minister during an intense early-morning meeting. They held a long discussion on the negotiations that would lead to the PLO's recognition of Israel, and Peres briefed the prime minister on what had happened in Oslo. Peres then went on to the next topic. It was time to discuss how best to tell the Americans about the successful conclusion of the Oslo negotiations, he said. It was a delicate problem. "For years we told the Americans, work against the PLO, and suddenly we are recognizing it," Peres said. "How did the Indian poet put it—'You are alone, I'm alone, so let's both be alone.'"

Peres said there was only one way to do it. "I told Rabin, 'Either you go to Clinton, or I go to Christopher.'" Rabin thought for a moment about the problem, turning it over in his mind, then nodded at Peres. "You go to Christopher," he said. Peres was pleased. Christopher would be surprised by the Oslo agreement, but the foreign minister had no doubt that he would support it. "For us, the report to Christopher was very important," Peres said. "We can't cut relations with America." Peres returned to his office to make the arrangements.

Later that morning, Peres received Lester Pollack and Malcolm Hoenlein of the Conference of Presidents of Major Jewish-American Organizations, who had come to pay a courtesy call and to be briefed about the Arab-Israeli peace talks. They wanted to know whether Israel had a strategy to break the impasse in Washington. Peres could not contain himself. After a moment's hesitation, he told his visitors that he had a little surprise. We have been negotiating secretly with the PLO, he said, and we have come to an agreement. The two men were stunned. Then Peres went into the details of the Oslo breakthrough.

"They [Rabin and Peres] were showing they had the confidence in us to give us a briefing like this in advance," Hoenlein later told *Jerusalem Post* reporter Hillel Kuttler. "They recognized the Conference is a vehicle to educate and brief the Jewish community." But both Peres and Rabin were walking a fine line. They knew that some segments of the American Jewish community would strongly oppose the agreement and they had to take steps to defuse that opposition. They wanted to be able to count on the support of their allies in the United States. In the coming months, Israel would need all the help it could get in its opening to the Arab world.

Over the previous two months, Rabin—whose own relations with the American Jewish community were strained at best— had taken a number of clear-cut steps to improve communications with Israel's American supporters. He had tried diligently to keep them informed of what was going on in Jerusalem, and had toned down his criticism of organizations he thought were aligned with Israel's Likud party. But Rabin had never told anyone in the American Jewish community that he was willing to open negotiations with Yasser Arafat. Just the opposite. In his trips to Washington, he had detailed his own outspoken views of the PLO leader. They had seemed set in stone.

In a series of background discussions with American journalists and leaders of the American Jewish community over a period of the past twelve months, Rabin had made it clear that he had a personal distaste for Yasser Arafat and the PLO. At times he could hardly contain his disdain for the men in Tunis. "Arafat is unreliable, untrusted, corrupt, and a man who is losing support among his own people," he told a group of Washington reporters the previous March 17. During that same visit to the United States, he told American Jewish leaders the same thing: He had no kind words for Arafat and he left no doubt that he would ever deal with him.

Rabin maintained this position even after the discussions in Oslo became serious. He never told anyone in the United States that Israel was negotiating with the PLO—except for President Clinton himself, who was informed in the most general terms. In May, Rabin told Clinton about the Oslo opening and he said that the talks were serious. The President, he advised, should tell no one. Rabin's language was precise: The information that he passed on about the Oslo discussions was highly sensitive. Clinton agreed to keep the information to himself.

It is apparent now that Rabin's personal request to Clinton was somewhat out of the ordinary. This was more than a general warning: His words seemed to express the fear that some of Clinton's most pro-Israel aides might actually spike the talks. Rabin did not say so explicitly, but his talk with Clinton about the Oslo opening was a courtesy. He was not asking for any help in any way. Instead, he was taking the President's admonition that Israel and its neighbors should negotiate peace by themselves—without American intervention—seriously.

When the Clinton administration knew about the Oslo channel, and *who* knew about it, have been hot topics of speculation ever since. The reason for the speculation is clear. It was general knowledge in Washington, even before Clinton's inauguration, that a number of new officials in his administration had closer ties with the Likud party than with Rabin. Some of these officials had very strong opinions about the conduct of Israeli foreign policy and how the Rabin government ought to conduct its negotiations with its neighbors. Those opinions definitely did not include negotiating with the PLO. Whether Rabin told

Clinton to keep the information secret in order to keep it out of the hands of these officials, however, will never be known. But there are hints.

"I think that we have to be very precise on this point," an Israeli official said after the PLO-Israeli agreement was made public. "It is not that the Israeli government was worried about a *specific* leak in Washington, or worried that a *specific* American official might purposely give out the information. Our concern was more general. We knew that any report, no matter how unsubstantiated, could ruin the discussions we were having in Oslo. We did not want that to happen. That meant that only a small circle of officials could be told."

But that is not the entire story. In the summer of 1993, as Israeli and PLO officials were meeting in Oslo, the President's closest foreign policy advisers sensed that they were being, as one of them claimed, "cut out" of the peace process. The complaints came primarily from the President's assistants on his national security staff, but they reflected the feelings of a large number of foreign policy officials. By August, however, this view had changed. It was not that the President was not communicating, it was that he was simply not engaged in the process; he was keeping silent about the peace negotiations because he did not have much interest in them.

But that information does not clear up the ambiguity. "I think that I have answered your question, but let me put it another way, so you will understand what I mean," the Israeli official said. "There were obviously people in Jerusalem and in Tunis who would not want this to happen. And frankly, there were people like that in Washington, who said that they were friends of Israel, but who might have had another agenda. They had the best of intentions, they wanted to protect Israel from its enemies. But we were negotiating with those enemies. I think it is safe to say that we wanted to keep the information out of the hands of those people."

The State Department's official in charge of monitoring the Israeli-Arab negotiations, Dennis Ross, clearly disagrees with that view. "We knew that there was a channel from the very beginning, which was more or less an academic channel," he says. "But even when it began to acquire a greater degree of authority we did not know the full depth of the talks. There were many channels. We did not know for sure which of these [were serious] although we had a sense that there was some movement. But there is no doubt, we did not get the full picture of what was achieved until late August."

Keeping the talks secret from even the upper levels of their opponents inside Israel itself was one of the primary goals of the Rabin government. That was also true when it came to officials in the United States. That group included National Security Adviser Anthony Lake, his assistant Martin Indyk, Secretary of State Warren Christopher, Assistant Secretary of State Edward Djerejian, and the official monitor of the bilateral negotiations, Dennis Ross. Like Arafat, Rabin took no chances. He decided to tell Clinton, and that was all.

After meeting with Hoenlein and Pollack, Peres made arrangements to meet with Warren Christopher in the United States. He telephoned the American secretary of state, who was in Santa Barbara, California, to request an important meeting on the peace process, and then boarded a flight for America. In California, meanwhile, Christopher telephoned Dennis Ross and told him that Peres was on the way. Ross was on vacation, and wanted to know whether the meeting was important. Christopher told him that it was. On the next day, Peres met Holst in Europe and they flew together to the U.S. Naval Air Station at Point Magu, California, where they met the two American officials.

After the preliminary welcome, Peres came right to the point. Israel and the PLO had successfully concluded discussions on a declaration of principles, he told Ross and Christopher. Peres then took out a copy of the agreement and passed it across the table to the two Americans. With Christopher and Ross listening closely, he went through the document point by point. Christopher was shocked and, while he tried to hide his surprise, he failed. After the document was presented, Christopher listened closely as Peres briefed him on the PLO links and how the final declaration had been written. "I came there with a completed agreement," Peres later said. "They didn't believe it possible. I told them we are about to finish the issue of mutual recognition."

After Peres was finished, Christopher rose to telephone President Clinton. When he returned, he reported that the President fully supported the agreement and he extended his congratulations to the Israeli government. Christopher added that the United States would be willing to hold a signing ceremony on the final document, in Washington, in mid-September. Peres was noncommittal. Late that afternoon, Peres boarded a plane for Israel, while Holst took a flight for Paris. By now, the details of the secret meetings in Oslo were becoming public. Journalists began to follow up on reports of the Oslo channel. This factor was predicted by Peres, who used it in the days ahead to keep the pressure on the PLO to sign an agreement on mutual recognition.

News of a possible Israeli-PLO agreement shook White House and State Department officials, who expressed disbelief that the Rabin government would ever negotiate with Yasser Arafat. The surprise was soon replaced by the reality that the PLO and Israel had conducted the negotiations without American help. Clinton's top foreign policy aides were skeptical. They felt blindsided: Israel was on the verge of recognizing the PLO, well ahead of the United States. The skepticism of the foreign policy establishment was reflected in Clinton's initial reaction to the agreement. "I am very much encouraged by what has happened there and very hopeful," he hesitantly told the press at the White House, but he did not want to add anything else. "If there is a new and different landscape in the Middle East, then I might be willing to entertain some questions."

By now, of course, it was clear to everyone that American officials were not the only ones cut out of the back channel. As Peres left California for the return trip to Israel, the Israeli opposition was beginning to form in the Knesset, where Likud party members expressed disbelief at the news of Rabin's agreement with the PLO. The Knesset sessions soon degenerated into raucous shouting matches between Labor party members and Likud stalwarts. The normally courteous Benny Begin was told to take his seat twice by the Knesset chairman. "This will lead to a Palestinian state," he shouted.

When Peres returned to Jerusalem from his meeting in California, he went immediately to Jerusalem, where Yitzhak Rabin was briefing Malcolm Hoenlein and Steve Grossman, the president of the American-Israel Public Affairs Committee, on the Oslo breakthrough. It was a very important meeting and Peres wanted to be in attendance to help Rabin in his plea for American support. After learning more details about the Oslo meetings, Hoenlein made a suggestion: He said that the American people had to be prepared on the issue. They needed to be educated about what the Israeli government was trying to do. Grossman agreed. "That this vocabulary can change overnight is profoundly disorienting," he said. But both men listened intently to Rabin's response and then told him that he could count on their support.

After Hoenlein and Grossman left, Peres and Rabin began to make plans on how to respond to the opposition to the breakthrough that was forming in the Knesset. Already the Israeli police were beginning to remove protesters from in front of the prime minister's residence and demonstrations were being planned for Israel's major cities. Despite the mounting protests, both men believed that they could win a vote on the agreement in the parliament, but they needed to maintain the fragile government coalition to do so. If need be, they knew that they could count on the votes from the Arab parties in the Knesset, though Rabin himself wanted to win a majority of votes without having to count on the Arab members.

On August 30, Rabin, Peres, and Beilin presented the draft declaration of principles to the Israeli cabinet. The cabinet approved it, with two abstentions. The next stop was the Knesset. In one of the most controversial parliamentary sessions in Israeli history, Rabin and Peres defended the agreement before the concerted attack of their Likud party opponents. The debate rivaled the face-off between David Ben-Gurion and Menachem Begin over German reparations payments in the mid-1950s. If anything, these sessions were even more tumultuous.

The attack on the government was led by Likud party chief Benyamin Netanyahu, who said that the agreement would lead to a Palestinian state "right next to Tel Aviv and Jerusalem." Netanyahu pressed his attack as Rabin and Peres presented the plan. The two leaders were heckled by the opposition and their defense could hardly be heard above the din. "Gaza first means Israel the end," Tsomet party leader Rafael Eitan shouted at Peres. Peres shouted back, turning to face his critics from the front bench of the government. "You are men of yesterday," he said. "The world has changed. . . . We bring news to the younger generation that after 100 years of terror, there is no return to the same situation. Rather, we will start 100 years of understanding and living together, each people with its flag, each people with its book of prayer."

The critics were not satisfied. Netanyahu and Begin vowed that they would win a vote of confidence and defeat the agreement in a Knesset vote. Netanyahu announced that the declaration would be opposed all across Israel. The protests would be taken to the center of Tel Aviv and Jerusalem. The Palestinians could not be trusted. Peres, exasperated, pleaded for understanding. He defended the Palestinians, saying that they too had rights. "They are not animals," he said, in the debate's most emotional moment. "They are people like us and we will live with them in peace."

The plea was the highlight of the Knesset session, but it did not convince the opposition. Benny Begin, for one, was more outspoken that he had ever been against the peace process. He even reverted to his father's habit of name-calling. For him, the central issue was Jerusalem. In an open letter to Rabin published in the *Jerusalem Post*, Begin excoriated the prime minister for spending a lifetime of criticizing Arafat and then concluding an agreement with him. "Over the past few years, you have repeatedly warned against capitulation to PLO demands. You stated that granting Arab residents of Jerusalem the right to be elected to the Arab Autonomy Administrative Council would severely damage Israel's sovereignty over the city. Now you have given in." Begin said that the declaration of principles was negotiated by Rabin's "government of fools." He said that the prime minister "wanted an agreement at any price . . . and we'll pay for it."

Begin's heated statement was only one among many. While polls showed that the Israeli public agreed with Rabin's negotiations with the Palestinians, the outpouring of worry over Israel's future was hard to miss. There was genuine concern, even among those who approved of the accord, that the uncharted days ahead could bring new surprises. There were no assurances that Arafat would be able to enforce the agreement. And there was also the certain knowledge that, while "you negotiate peace with your enemies, not your friends"—as Rabin was to say over and over again in the days ahead—you also negotiate peace with the weakest partner. And the PLO was the weakest that it had ever been.

The Palestinian delegation to the Washington talks was in an uproar. When news of the Oslo breakthrough was publicized during the last week of August, Faisal Husseini, Hanan Ashrawi, and other Palestinian leaders confronted Arafat. "I don't think that I have ever seen Faisal and Hanan that mad," one PLO official said. "Faisal could hardly bring himself to talk. Hanan was absolutely blue with rage. She felt betrayed, used." Husseini led the attack, telling the PLO chairman that he had given away too much. They would have a difficult time selling the agreement to the Palestinian people. Ashrawi was even more outspoken: The Palestinian delegation looked like fools, she said. She added that Arafat had no right to negotiate for the entire Palestinian people.

Before, in such confrontations, Arafat had always taken the "Who, me?" posture, especially when it came to explaining his controversial decisions to the PLO leadership. He had been on the defensive since the moment that he embraced Saddam Hussein in Baghdad before the American deployment to Saudi Arabia and again in July when he faced off against Hani Hassan. But now he was sure of himself. He attacked. "What should I have done?" Arafat asked. "What would you have done? Negotiate forever? This is our one chance, our only chance." Arafat made his argument stick. The agreement was already concluded. Now, he said, they had to come together to sell it to the Palestinian people. He expected Husseini and Ashrawi to help him.

PLO officials began to arrive in Tunis for high-level meetings during the last week in August. Some of the meetings went on for hours, as Arafat meticulously explained the declaration of principles article by article. An emergency meeting of the executive committee of Fatah was followed by a high-level meeting of PLO officials. Arafat was exhausted. He had been arguing for hours, and still PLO officials were arriving in Tunis. They were coming from all over the world. With Abu Alaa and his team still in Europe, Arafat was helped by a close group of allies: Yassir Abed-Rabbo, Bassam Abu-Sharif, and Abu Mazin, all of whom took turns supporting Arafat's decision. But the opposition to the agreement ran deep and affected even the most loyal of Arafat's supporters.

On August 26, as Shimon Peres was flying back to Jerusalem from Washington, poet Mahmoud Darwish, one of the best-known voices of the Palestinian community, told Arafat that he had no choice but to resign from the executive committee of the PLO. Standing before his colleagues in a meeting in Tunis, Darwish issued an impassioned plea. "What are we doing here?" he asked. "We are bidding a chaotic farewell to an historic stage and entering another stage for which we have not prepared ourselves. This is the question that haunts me. What are the features of this picture, its parameters, and the appropriate structural form for it?" He stopped for a dramatic moment, gathering his thoughts. "I will shock you," he said. "This organization, complete with its hierarchy and structure and figures and perhaps its content—this organization is finished."

After the meeting, Arafat attempted to calm Darwish and

convince him of the necessity of the Gaza-Jericho accord. Darwish said that his remarks had explained his position, and that he could not continue with the argument. The organization must be transformed now into something new, he argued. "Forgive me if I say that I am under no obligation to take part in this gamble," he told Arafat and others. When he was approached by Faisal Husseini, however, Darwish had just about had enough. The pent-up rage of a Palestinian who had spent his life in the territories came pouring out. "I know all about you Faisal and I know all about your family," he said and he leaned into him, his mouth set tightly. "Your family produces heirs, but my family produces martyrs."

When Peres flew on to Jerusalem, Johan Jorgen Holst flew to Paris, where he was scheduled to meet with Abu Alaa to work on a final exchange of letters between Arafat and Rabin. The letters would contain an exchange between the PLO and Israel on mutual recognition. Holst believed that he was now engaged in some of the most sensitive discussions between the two parties. The declaration of principles had been initialed, but it was still possible that the agreement could somehow fall apart. Holst knew he had to work quickly. Opposition was mounting in both Israel and Tunis. "There is no going back," he had announced to a group of reporters; but he wanted to make sure.

The exchange of letters was key: Holst believed that the PLO had yet to take the final step that would transform it from a national liberation movement to a national government; it had to renounce the use of terror, agree to abide by international covenants, and recognize the right of Israel to exist inside of secure borders. Holst negotiated these points with Abu Alaa in a series of meetings that were punctuated by telephone conversations with Tunis. The discussions were long and intense. Some of the negotiations took place in the apartment of Holst's daughter, so as to avoid the prying eyes of journalists.

The formula for mutual recognition was complex. Israel had explicitly insisted that the letter from Arafat to Rabin include specific wording of a pledge to overturn key provisions of the

PLO covenant. The Israelis wanted change in the covenant to be debated and voted on by the Palestine National Council. The vote would give the declaration of principles the imprimatur that it needed to succeed among the Palestinian people. Israel was debating the accord in their parliament; the PLO could now do the same. But Yasser Arafat was just as insistent. He argued that he could not get a vote on the covenant on such short notice. If Israel wanted such a vote, it would have to wait. Meanwhile, he said, he would agree to include wording in his letter saying that portions of the covenant had been "superseded." Holst attempted to mediate the dispute by talking to Arafat by telephone and drafting new language for the letter to Rabin. But there were still snags.

Peres traveled to Paris to confer with Holst on the evening of September 3 in an attempt to resolve the differences over the exchange of letters. After his meeting, Peres put public pressure on the Palestinians. When asked whether Yasser Arafat would be allowed to come to Jericho after the transfer of authority from Israel to the PLO, Peres gave a brief, but pointed, answer. "If there is mutual recognition, yes. Otherwise, no," he said. After two more meetings with Holst, Peres left to visit with other European officials to drum up support (and economic aid) for the PLO-Israeli agreement. When he left Paris, there was still no agreement on a letter of mutual recognition.

After Peres's departure, Holst presented the PLO with a formula that he believed could resolve the impasse over mutual recognition. The letter from Arafat to Rabin would confirm that parts of the covenant were "inoperative and no longer valid," but in the next sentence, Arafat promised to submit the changes in the covenant to the PNC for their approval. Since it was not known if the vote would result in a victory (two thirds of the 630-plus members was needed), Holst purposely left open what would happen if the PNC voted against the necessary amendments. Holst's amendments essentially grafted the Israeli and PLO positions together. Abu Alaa was not satisfied and Holst called Arafat one more time.

"The tensions associated with the historical leap, difficulties

of logistics and communication, and the impact of mutual physical exhaustion, threatened the historical achievement until the
very last moment," Holst later explained. "In many ways, pav-
ing the way for mutual recognition was the most difficult part
of the journey. It involved removing so much of the emotional
baggage accumulated during the prolonged conflict." Finally,
with Arafat on the telephone from Tunis, Holst maneuvered
the two sides past their mutual exhaustion.

The end was now clearly in sight. He read the letter to Arafat
and then patiently explained how he had resolved the question
of the PLO covenant. Holst allowed the silence to fill the line
between them. "I agree," Arafat finally said.

On September 8, Holst left Paris for Tunis. There, in a private ceremony on the evening of September 9, Arafat put his
signature on a letter recognizing Israel. It was a solemn moment, but it was a breakthrough for the PLO leader. Holst then
boarded a flight for Tel Aviv. He met early the next morning
with Yitzhak Rabin in Jerusalem and handed him the letter
from Arafat. At 9:00 A.M., they emerged before a bank of cameras, where Rabin signed a letter he had written to Arafat.
Reporters later noted that it was at precisely 9:14 A.M. on Friday, September 10, 1993, that Israel recognized the PLO. The
formal signing of the declaration of principles was scheduled to
take place in Washington, on the morning of September 13.
That was just three days away. Already, Arafat was on his way
to Washington.

Bill Clinton took the lead in organizing the Washington signing. At first, the Israelis hesitated at such a public ceremony,
but Clinton insisted. Such public events tended to solidify agreements in the public mind. This ceremony would draw down the
curtain on one of the most intransigent problems in modern
history. Rabin agreed that he would attend the White House
ceremony, but he did not want to sign the document himself.
That task should be left to Shimon Peres and his counterpart,
Abu Mazin, of the PLO. Clinton told Rabin that he could make
any kind of arrangement that he wanted, but that the Israeli

prime minister should plan to be in Washington. He wanted him there. But when Clinton said that he should also be prepared to shake Arafat's hand to seal the agreement, the Israeli prime minister hesitated before agreeing. But, he added, he did not want any other outward signs of agreement. He did not want to be hugged by Arafat, he said, as Sadat and Begin had hugged during the Camp David Accords. This agreement was different. He wanted a solemn ceremony.

American officials had already been in touch with Arafat, who was more eager to come to Washington than Rabin. He would bring along a small number of top officials. Abu Mazin would sign the agreement with Peres. When Arafat left Tunis, he shook the hands of his top assistants and boarded the plane with members of the Washington delegation. For Arafat and the rest of the Palestinian delegation, the trip to Washington seemed like the beginning of an impossible journey. The Palestinians could not believe that the chairman of the PLO would be meeting the prime minister of Israel and the President of the United States at the White House. By the time that Arafat's plane landed, its occupants—many of whom had opposed the accord just days before—were celebrating.

Arafat's arrival at Andrews Air Force Base outside of Washington, D.C., on the afternoon of September 11 was billed as a triumph. On the tarmac waiting for him was a group of Palestinian and Arab Americans who had been waiting for his arrival for nearly twenty years. Like their counterparts in Arafat's official delegation, they could hardly bring themselves to believe what was happening. One of the officials who waited for Arafat was Khalil Jahshan, the head of the National Association of Arab Americans. He brought along his family. When Arafat stepped off the plane, he hugged Jahshan and kissed his little girl, who looked up, squinting, at the PLO chairman.

Arafat arrived at his hotel in downtown Washington late on Saturday afternoon. The scene was chaotic. The hotel had slowly filled with journalists and Palestinian-Americans throughout the day. Ironically, a Jewish wedding was planned in the afternoon in the large garden in the center of the hotel, which was to be followed by a pharmaceutical conference. The wedding guests were surprised by the crowds that began to gather. After the wedding, there was a reception, where the groups of Palestinians mingled with the wedding party. "What's going on?" a wedding guest asked. Arafat is coming, a friend told him. He was dumbfounded. "Here?"

Outside on the street, State Department security officers sealed off parking areas while uniformed policemen closed off the street in front of the hotel to all traffic. The press clamored for a spot in the receiving line, waiting for Arafat's limousine. Young Palestinians lined the street holding the black, green, white, and red Palestinian colors, hoping to get a glimpse of the PLO chairman. When Arafat's motorcade roared up, however, the PLO chief was brought into the hotel by a side entrance, while Hanan Ashrawi and other Palestinian delegates came in the front. "This is a great day," Ashrawi said. She waved to the crowd. The other members of the delegation followed. When asked about opposition among the delegation to the accord, Saeb Erakat gave a sharp, angry look at the questioner. "There are bound to be disagreements," he said. "But they are resolved now."

Arafat immediately drew his top aides around him, adding Khalil Jahshan and Salah Ta'mari to their numbers. Over the next three days, in meeting after meeting until the signing, Jahshan and Ta'mari became his closest advisers. "I think it is a reflection of the isolation that Arafat feels in Tunis, but it was a wise move," a Palestinian official said of Arafat's sudden reliance on the Washington group. "This is a different world for him. Things have definitely changed. He needs people who know Washington, where the shoals and sandbars are, people in the community who know people here. The Washington Palestinians will now become more and more important while the diaspora groupings, which formed most of his support over the past years, will slowly fade away."

Arafat greeted his supporters two hours later during a press conference in a bare hotel banquet hall. Speaking in Arabic, he summarized the PLO-Israel declaration of principles. Then he translated his own words into English, turning his twenty-minute discourse into a two-minute summary. "We are here to sign a declaration of principles with the State of Israel and to begin a new era of peace," he said. "I am very confident that this event will mark a new beginning. We can now work to bring the Palestinian people their own government."

On the elevator back upstairs to his room, Arafat looked and sounded tired. "It has been a long trip from Tunis," he said. "We have much to do here. But this is a great day, a great day." He was asked bluntly about the accord and the mounting opposition to it from the Palestinian community. "Now we only talk of positive things," he cautioned. "You will see, this is a good thing." Arafat got off and went into his room to begin a briefing about a meeting he would have with Warren Christopher the next day at the State Department.

Over the next thirty-six hours, Arafat met with a host of officials: Former President Bush came to visit him, accompanied by Bush's former national security adviser, Brent Scowcroft. Jimmy Carter, who was much in demand by the news media, conferred with the PLO chairman and then issued a short statement to the press. He called the declaration of principles a "good beginning." Russian Foreign Minister Andrei Kozyrev met with Arafat, as did a group of United States congressmen. A variety of senators came to talk with the PLO chairman, as did the ambassadors of Saudi Arabia, Egypt, and Syria. Arafat gave interviews to almost all the major American television networks and he spoke with Arab-American leaders.

On the Sunday night before the signing of the declaration of principles, Arafat came into the lobby of the hotel and stood on a balcony waving to the throng of Palestinians below. He gave a short speech, but was interrupted by a heckler. "You don't even sound like a Palestinian," the man shouted up to him. "You sound like a traitor." Arafat responded. "This is the realization of our long struggle," he said. There was a short scuffle on the floor below the PLO chairman, and then Arafat disappeared back upstairs.

Yitzhak Rabin and Shimon Peres were across town at the

Mayflower Hotel, meeting with American officials and with leaders of the American Jewish community. The gathering was much more subdued. Both men were tired; they had arrived in Washington in the middle of the night. The Israeli leaders had already announced that they would be returning to Jerusalem right after the ceremony to observe Rosh Hashanah, the Jewish New Year. But American officials were already trying to capitalize on the coming event by arranging a visit by Rabin to Morocco, where the prime minister would be meeting with King Hassan. With the exception of Egypt, the Morocco visit would be Rabin's first official visit to an Arab country and was meant to symbolize the end of Israel's isolation.

At the White House, Clinton's aides were struggling with the details of the ceremony. It was a last-minute arrangement. While White House staff members called anyone they could think of who had anything to do with the Israel-PLO problem to invite them to the ceremony, protocol experts were wrestling with the correct procedure for welcoming Arafat. He was not a head of state; he was the head of the PLO. Outside, government workers were putting the last touches on the stand that would serve as a podium for the signing. None of this seemed to affect the new President, however, who seemed buoyed by the rush of activity. He was looking forward to the signing and to the White House dinner that was being held for visiting former Presidents.

A small crowd was on hand when Arafat left the hotel for the White House the next morning. He waved to the well-wishers. At about 9:30, Shimon Peres came out the side entrance of the Mayflower Hotel and walked down the street to a waiting limousine. He waved to a small group of supporters who were on hand. Behind him, Yitzhak Rabin, his wife, and Itamar Rabinovich came out of the hotel, waved to onlookers, and then departed for the White House.

Compared with all that had gone before, the White House ceremony must have seemed like an anticlimax. The negotiations in Oslo were far more dramatic than anything that happened in Washington. It was not like the Camp David Accords, where Begin and Sadat had brought an end to years of enmity between Israel and Egypt. It was not an end at all; it was a beginning. The fight for the land of Palestine would continue, but without weapons. Thrown together on the same land by circumstance or design, the two peoples now had to try to get along. Whether they could succeed was very much an open question.

This uncertainty marked the events at the White House, including the first meeting between the heads of the PLO and the leading officials of the Israeli government. While many in the crowd of onlookers later described the signing as an overwhelming emotional event, Peres, Rabin, and Arafat were subdued. Gone too was the usual talk of how everyone got along once they got to know each other. Instead, Rabin later said that he still did not like Arafat, but that one did not make peace with one's friends. Arafat, meanwhile, did something very unusual: He said almost nothing at all. It was almost as if Rabin did not exist.

The usual Washington cynicism was very much in evidence both during and after the ceremony. When Arafat went to shake Rabin's hands, the Israeli prime minister hesitated. Clinton brought his arms up behind both men, nudged Rabin closer to the PLO chairman, then nodded in satisfaction when the Israeli prime minister responded. "The handshake," as it was forever after dubbed, sealed the question that had been on almost every reporter's lips for the last forty-eight hours: Would it take place? What would Rabin do? Would it be limp? Firm? Would Rabin smile? Would the two hug? What if Arafat tried to hug him and Rabin refused?

In actuality, reporters later said, the two leaders had shaken hands before the ceremony, when they met each other in the White House. But that was not true. The meeting between the two in the Blue Room of the White House, just off the south lawn, was formal and stiff. Arafat and Rabin stared at each other and nodded. Clinton tried to bring the two together, but then decided against it. The same held true for the other Israeli and PLO officials, who stood at opposite ends of the room talking with each other.

There was the usual last-minute snag, even now. Arafat's aides insisted that the wording of the preamble of the declaration of principles be changed, so that it read "PLO" instead of "Palestinian people." Arafat wanted to make it clear that the organization he had built was responsible for the agreement. The Israeli team disagreed with the change but relented. With that done, President Clinton warily eyed Arafat and Rabin and the two groups of antagonists. Finally, wanting to end the awkward scene and begin the ceremony, Clinton walked over to the two, who were lining up to walk out onto the White House lawn. But he did not need to arrange a discussion. As the two moved together, they began to talk.

According to an account given to reporters by Clinton, Rabin turned to Arafat during the discussion. "We need to work very hard to make this work," he told the PLO leader. "I know and I'm prepared to do my part," Arafat responded. After that, the two lined up in their assigned spots and marched out onto the White House lawn.

Half a world away, in Jericho, Palestinians surged into the streets to celebrate the signing. Palestinian flags were everywhere, including atop the Hisham Hotel where, it was said, Yasser Arafat would soon be staying. The crowds were jubilant. According to the declaration of principles, Jericho would be liberated in exactly ninety days. Palestinians listened to the ceremony in Washington by radio and were interviewed by American television correspondents.

Back in the United States, Clinton welcomed his guests to the ceremony and then thanked those who had made the signing possible: Jimmy Carter, George Bush, the government of Norway, and the participants, Yasser Arafat and Yitzhak Rabin themselves. Foreign Minister Peres followed. "Deep gaps call for lofty bridges," he said. He ended his speech in Hebrew: "From the eternal city of Jerusalem, from this green, promising lawn of the White House, let's say together in the language of our Bible: 'Peace, peace to him that is far off and to him that is near, sayeth the Lord, and I will hear.' "

Abu Mazin spoke next and then Warren Christopher, who was followed by Russian Foreign Minister Kozyrev. But the most eloquent speech of the day, by far, was given by Yitzhak Rabin who had decided, just days before, that he must speak directly to the Palestinian people. "Let me say to you, the Palestinians, we are destined to live together on the same soil in the same land," he said. "We, the soldiers who have returned from battle stained with blood; we who have seen our relatives and friends killed before our eyes; we who have attended their funerals and cannot look into their eyes; we who have come from a land where parents bury their children; we who have fought against you, the Palestinians; we say to you today in a loud and clear voice, enough of tears and blood. Enough!"

Arafat followed; giving his speech in Arabic, he addressed his remarks to the American people. "Mr. President," he said, "I am taking this opportunity to assure you and to assure the great American people that we share your values for freedom, justice and human rights, values for which my people have been striving." Later, he turned to the task that awaited him in the occupied territories. "The battle for peace is the most difficult battle of our lives. It deserves our utmost efforts because the land of peace, the land of peace yearns for a just and comprehensive peace."

Abu Mazin and Shimon Peres then signed the "Declaration of Principles on Interim Self-Government Arrangements." Yoel Zinger held the agreement that he had helped to draft for each of the officials, turning first one page and then another. At the end of the signing, Arafat extended his hand. Clinton moved slightly forward and brought up his arms. Rabin turned and, clearly hesitating, reached out to Arafat.

The two then moved toward the row of dignitaries, who were sitting closest to the stage. Arafat started down the line, shaking hands. There were some grimaces and some obviously uncomfortable people. More often, though, there were quizzical looks, and a deep curiosity to get to speak to someone who, over the course of two decades, had had a profound effect on the Middle East. For some, he was still a villain. Itamar Rabinovich shook his hand and then looked away, almost in physical recoil. James Baker also shook Arafat's hand, bending forward from the waist, and looking at him. It was the first time that the two had met.

Arafat understood this part of the program and the value of unrehearsed acting. "He has always been an actor," an associate says. "This is what attracts so many people to him." It was true; many of those in Washington who met him for the first time began to understand what attracted so many people to him. "My God, he has charisma," a high-level White House aide said in surprise. "I would have never guessed it."

Rabin moved along the line, shaking hands with many officials whom he knew very well. He smiled when he reached James Baker. Baker was the forgotten man of the ceremonies and had actually been snubbed by George Bush the night before, when the former President met with Arafat. Bush was upset with Baker and had started blaming him for his election loss. He brought Scowcroft instead. Seated as an onlooker during the ceremony, Bush seemed out of place and very uncomfortable. But Baker seemed right at home. More than any other single person that day—with the exception of Arafat and Rabin themselves, of course—Baker had made the signing of the declaration of principles possible. It was through his foresight and patience that this had happened, when no one else thought that it really would. No one had said that during the ceremony, but many people in the crowd knew it was true.

Arafat greeted a group of Palestinian and Israeli children at the end of the line of well-wishers, boys and girls who had gone to camp together. They had shared the usual childhood experiences of attending camp, and had begun to talk with each other about their mutual nightmares and catastrophes. Arafat beamed. Rabin smiled broadly. Two politicians, suddenly in their element.

Afterward, in the White House, Arafat and Rabin stood uncomfortably close to each other again, with Clinton between. Not a word was exchanged.

The rest of Arafat and Rabin's stay in Washington seemed like an anticlimax. The Israeli delegation was eager to return home. But they were also enthusiastic about their stop-off in Morocco, a visit that had been arranged at the last minute in an attempt to break through the circle of Arab enemies that surrounded them. Now, with the PLO declaration signed, they expected relations with the Arab world to improve.

Before they left, however, Rabin and Peres hosted a reception at the Israeli embassy. Under a large tent, the two greeted Jewish notables from across the country who had made the trip to Washington to watch the signing. In the middle of the reception, Rabin moved to a makeshift stage to address the crowd. He was accompanied by Peres, Rabinovich, and Lester Pollack. "You may ask, 'Is it a day to celebrate?' Again, the answer is not so simple." Rabin then attacked the extremism of Arab fundamentalists. But the crowd was in a festive mood, so he quickly changed the subject. "People can ask, 'Do you trust Arafat?' We'll see." The statement brought a ringing applause.

Elsewhere in Washington, a joint reception was being held by the American Jewish Congress and the National Association of Arab Americans. It was an unprecedented reception. Faisal Husseini came in, smiling broadly, and immediately walked over to Steve Grossman, the head of AIPAC. Photographers stumbled over themselves to get a picture of them together. It seemed a coda for an otherwise monumental day.

Across town, Project Nishma, a group that had been pushing for reconciliation in the Middle East, was having its own celebration. In many ways, it was the hottest ticket in town. "Project Nishma is now the place to be," one of its organizers said. "We have everyone coming here. Palestinians, Israelis, Americans, even AIPAC officials. Everyone." On one side of the room, Arafat biographer John Wallach escorted the group of Palestinian and Israeli children who had attended the signing ceremony. When Rabin and Arafat shook hands with attendees at the end of the White House ceremony, they paid special attention to the group of children.

Yasser Arafat was supposed to attend the Project Nishma reception, but his limousine circled the block where it was being held and turned away, back to the hotel. His security detail decided that the building was not secure. Arafat had enough to do anyway, including reviewing the remarks for his speech before the National Press Club, which was scheduled for the next day. He wanted to make sure that his address was warmly welcomed.

Arafat had already been told that his White House address had fallen flat. Not only was it in Arabic, it did not contain the kind of emotional ammunition that was embraced by Rabin. A number of Arafat's advisers mentioned this to him and one of them had passed a joke around the Palestinian delegation. "If anyone asks," he said, "just tell them that the chairman's speech was stolen at the last minute by the Mossad. They substituted the one he gave today for it. We had no idea what was going on."

Arafat knew the critics were right and he wanted to make sure that the same thing did not happen when he talked to the press the next day. He reviewed the speech he would give and then attended his last meeting of the evening—with the leaders of the American Jewish community. The gathering had been arranged secretly by his top advisers. When the American Jewish leaders, some of whom represented the most powerful voices of the Jewish community in the United States, entered the meeting room at his suite in the PLO headquarters hotel, Arafat was standing, waiting. He shook their hands one by one, just as he had shaken Rabin's.

In Jericho, New York, Rabbi Stanley Steinhart watched the momentous events in Washington on television. He was overcome by what he saw. After years of supporting Israel, he had difficulty accepting that Yitzhak Rabin, the warrior, would sign an agreement with Yasser Arafat, the terrorist. With the Jewish New Year coming up, Steinhart considered speaking about the accord to his congregation. But he put the thought out of his mind. Others, perhaps the local congressman, he thought, would be better suited to that task.

Steinhart had been at the Jericho Jewish Community Center, in Jericho, New York, almost his entire adult life. He applied to be the rabbi at Jericho in 1960, and interviewed for the job with a committee of men for the synagogue. They were impressed by the young rabbi's modesty, erudition, and sincerity. They thought that he could grow as the congregation grew, and they gave him the job. A native-born American, Steinhart was educated at Queens College ("I grew up in Queens," he says, proudly) and at the Jewish Theological Seminary. He was the perfect choice for the job.

The synagogue's committee of men were right: As Long Island, and Jericho's already burgeoning Jewish population, grew, so did Steinhart. He seemed to be everywhere at once. Jericho's Jewish congregation eventually became very large, but Steinhart seemed to enjoy the extra work. He formed youth groups and adult organizations and he helped to raise money for Jewish and Israeli causes. He was proud of the work that he did, and he tried mightily to keep up the interest of his adolescent congregants in their Jewish heritage. In the meantime, he became the father of three children.

Steinhart is one of the most respected rabbis on Long Island. He is well known for giving rousing orations and is especially adept at speaking from the heart when it comes to the subject of Israel. Like most Jewish residents of Long Island, Steinhart has deep feelings about Israel and visits there nearly every year—or more often. Still, he did not seem comfortable with a sermon on Israel, especially now.

"I think that I will leave the topic to someone else," Steinhart said after viewing the handshake. "It is not that I am not qualified; it's just that everyone is talking about it. So maybe I should talk about something else." Instead, Steinhart decided, he would give an address on the hopes for the New Year. When Congressman Peter King of Jericho said that he would talk about the Washington signing, Steinhart was certain that he had made the right choice.

But Steinhart had not bargained on the telephone calls and personal visits of his congregants, almost all of whom told him they wanted to hear what he thought about the PLO accord. They wanted to hear what he had to say, they said. He was their rabbi. And so he relented. "I simply had no choice," he later admitted, "and even though I did not want to really deal with the signing, I thought that I had to follow what the congregation wanted. Everyone was talking about it. I just couldn't remain silent."

The night before his sermon, Steinhart sat down to write an outline. "That's what I normally do," he said. "Even for the important sermons, and this is as important as any that I have given." He titled his first page, "Rosh Hashanah—First Day—5754—JJC," and then below it wrote, "Israel—PLO—Peace." He sat for many minutes thinking about what he would say. He wanted the message to be simple and evenhanded. But he also wanted it to be from the heart. Finally, he decided that he would give a straightforward sermon on the signing and then talk about Israel. He reviewed his own thoughts as he typed the outline.

"I want to talk extemporaneously," he told the packed synagogue on the Sabbath Friday, and he went ahead to issue a disclaimer. "Some of you may disagree with what I say [about the accord] and you may be right. First of all, though, I want to say, *Kol Hakavod Lamishtatfi*—congratulations to all the participants." He took a breath and continued. "This is not easy [for me] to say; I have spoken out often against the PLO, and I cannot look at Arafat. But I ask, 'What choices do I have?' I can condemn the treaty and we can go on as before, or we can accept the treaty and try to start something new." The congregation was hushed. Steinhart was obviously speaking from the heart, as he had often in the past on the subject of Israel.

"Prime Minister Rabin said it best: 'One concludes a peace agreement with a former enemy, not a friend.' " Steinhart paused, choosing his words. "No one is forgetting the past," he said, "for if we forget it, we will relive it, and live to regret it." Steinhart continued by outlining the reasons why Israel would want to conclude an agreement with the PLO. There was the end of the cold war, and the acceptance of realism on the part of the Palestinians. "Israel is here to stay," he said. Israel was strong and vibrant, thanks to America's continued military support. All of these were factors in the final agreement, he said.

He then continued by trying to look at the situation from the PLO's point of view. It was clear to them that Rabin would strike a better deal than the Likud party and that recognition meant status for their organization. The PLO must have concluded, he said, that this was, finally, the only way that the Palestinian people could ever hope to gain statehood. The "all or nothing" rhetoric of the PLO leadership and the belief that the Arabs could "drive the Israelis into the sea" had passed, Steinhart maintained.

Steinhart then dabbled briefly in diplomacy, explaining why the Norwegians had become the brokers between the PLO and the Rabin government. Both sides, he said, believed that the Norwegians were "always fair" and they had proved to be so during the Oslo talks. "It was quite clear then," Steinhart told his congregation, "face to face talks were a must and the negotiations had to be conducted in absolute secrecy." He added that "it was miraculous that in this day of rapid and mass communication not one word of the talks leaked to the press. The highest levels of the PLO and the highest levels of the Israeli government became involved and an understanding was reached."

Steinhart said that he believed that the PLO-Israeli agreement would work. Everyone was behind it—the United States, the world community—and it left the most controversial questions for later negotiations, including refugees and the status of Jerusalem. The signing of the treaty at the White House on September 13, Steinhart added, was a good way to start the Jewish New Year. "All the parties conducted themselves correctly," Steinhart said, "and everyone spoke well." Steinhart then quoted Yitzhak Rabin's exhortation: "Enough of blood and tears, enough." Rabin was very "ill at ease," Steinhart noted, ending this first section of his sermon, "but the step had to be taken."

Steinhart then turned to the topic that his congregation had waited for. He had often issued blistering attacks on the PLO and Arafat, and he took note of this now. "I don't like Arafat any more now than I did last week," he admitted, "but he may offer the best hope for peace in the Middle East. Do I trust him? Time will tell. And perhaps time will heal, if not in our generation, then hopefully, in the next."

For all intents and purposes Steinhart's sermon was over. But after a short pause, the rabbi continued to speak, barely looking at his notes. This was the part of the sermon that he had worked on longest, and it was the most important thing that he would say. "Until this week," he said, "I would tell my children, 'I will not live to see peace in the Middle East, I hope that you will, but I will not.'"

He looked out at his congregation. "But to my daughter in Israel, I say now, 'I would rather have my grandchildren die for peace than die for war.' This is my hope. That there will be peace and security for all, living side by side. This is the reason why I support this process." But Steinhart was still not done. He said that he understood why some Israelis would oppose the peace agreement. "I have a great deal of respect for Ariel Sharon and Benyamin Netanyahu," he announced. Those in Israel who did not agree with the declaration, he added, had a right to do so—more so than anyone else. "They live in Israel, they fight, they die, they have a right to oppose it.

"But I hold in utter disdain those who live here and tell Israel, 'Don't give up territory, don't trust and don't believe,' and want to drive the others out." He described the rhetoric of American Jews who say that "G-d is on our side" as "puerile." He continued: "Isaac and Ishmael, both sons of Abraham, are at last talking together, working together, walking together . . . and shaking hands. Maybe it is a dream, but who says that dreams don't come true." He concluded the sermon by talking about the New Year, which was the topic that he had originally chosen for this Sabbath. Like many rabbis in synagogues across the country that Rosh Hashanah, he spoke directly, plainly, almost personally.

"We have come to ask for another year for ourselves and our loved ones," he said. "We now stand on the threshold of a real peace in the land You promised us. You almost owe us another year. Give it to us, so that we may enjoy the fruits of peace in our homeland."

EPILOGUE

In looking back at the Oslo channel and the Washington handshake from a distance of only a few months, American, Israeli, and Palestinian commentators were nearly unanimous in pointing out that a number of incontrovertible facts made the signing of the Israel-PLO declaration of principles inevitable. The most important of these was the fact of Israel itself. Israel had been in existence for over forty years and the nation's leadership had successfully created a stable, democratic, and economically viable nation where none had existed before. Israel was well armed and supported by the last remaining superpower.

But there were other facts.

Israel was alone. After forty years, it was not even close to becoming accepted in the Middle East, and its neighbors seemed more distant than ever. The Israeli economy was booming, but it was not part of a regional economic and trading system. And for all the talk of Israel's importance as a cog in the Western economic and strategic system, a look at the map showed otherwise. In addition to this, Israel's population was slowly being transformed. The great mass of European Jews were now being supplemented by Jews from the Middle East. Like Rabin, they had lived and worked with Arabs.

Israel's alliance with the United States meant that it could maintain a strong military; but the ties between Israel and the United States placed enormous pressures on Israeli leaders. Rabin and his top Labor strategists uniformly resented the relationship that Shamir had struck up with American Jewish groups. The friendship was starting to wear thin, and Rabin was committed to doing what was best for Israel, regardless of the views held by the diaspora. He wanted to strengthen the relationship, but on his terms.

Israel's forty-year existence was a cause for celebration, but Yitzhak Rabin knew that the fact of the state was no guarantee of its continued existence. For Israel to prosper, it had to reaffirm its central belief—that it would remain Jewish. The greatest threat to Israel in the aftermath of the Gulf War was not an attack by its enemies, but the slow absorption of some 1.7 million Palestinians in its midst. Any traveler to Tel Aviv, Haifa, or Ashkelon could have seen this in any restaurant or office building.

Already in 1993, it was painfully clear that the Jewish state was on the road to becoming a bilingual society, where Arabic was heard as often as Hebrew—even in the heart of the business district of Tel Aviv. It took only a marginal leap of the imagination to believe that forty, fifty, or one hundred years hence, but inevitably, Israel would have become a nation of Jews and Arabs living together, with a burgeoning and possibly majority Arab population. At that point, Israel would no longer be a Jewish state, but something else entirely.

Rabin believed that Israel was facing a major domestic catastrophe of its own. Successive aliyahs, the taking in (or, literally, "going up" to Israel) had built the Jewish state, but the constant, historical taking in of the world's diaspora Jews had ended. Rabin must have realized that the last aliyah, of Russian Jews, was the final aliyah. Israel could no longer count on other regimes to inadvertently build its population. The fear now was that there would be a massive movement of Israeli citizens leaving the country—a *yerida.*

"How much can you sacrifice before you become tired?" the Israeli woman Alya asked on her return trip to the adopted land that she loved, but was leaving. "How many years can you go on and on before you need some peace?"

No country—let alone Israel—can afford to allow such questions to remain unanswered.

While Palestinians and Israelis alike focused on Rabin's dramatic call for peace in his first speech to the Knesset on becoming prime minister in July 1992, Rabin himself returned to the theme of building a nation where people would want to live. "We want the new immigrants and our sons and daughters to find work, a livelihood, and a future in this country. We don't want Israel's main export to be our children," he said, then, later, repeated his special plea. "The homeless, families living in overcrowded conditions, and others overburdened by their mortgages will come first in our order of priorities. Israel will be not just a state; it will also be a home."

Few realized what Rabin was saying in July 1992, but in September of 1993, his vision for Israel became a reality; he wanted a Jewish state that was more than a refuge for the world's dispossessed and hunted Jewish population. He settled Israel's future course, finally, when he ordered the closing of the West Bank and Gaza. "Let them stay there," he said of the Palestinians. On September 13, he confirmed his belief by returning Israel, not just to its borders, but also to the ideals that had founded it.

Yitzhak Rabin's actions set aright the words of the prophet Jeremiah, the reputed author of the Book of Lamentations, a series of dirges in the Hebrew Bible that tells of the destruction of Jerusalem by its enemies. The elegy is for a people in agony who, the author implies, had lost their land through the "iniquities" of its leaders. Seeing this, "the Lord gave full vent to his wrath, he poured out his hot anger; and he kindled a fire in Zion, which consumed its foundations."

Yitzhak Rabin would surely agree with Benny Begin's cry: "We are not a nation of victims." But he would also expand the thought: "We are not a nation of victims—nor are we a nation of oppressors."

The Palestinians were facing their own set of facts. The PLO was bankrupt and divided. Yasser Arafat was under fire from his top aides, and criticism of his leadership was mounting in every part of the Palestinian community. Hamas was gaining strength and, while it was evident that it could never totally control the political environment of the occupied territories, its growing credibility provided a daunting challenge to Palestinian moderates.

Arafat needed to maintain PLO dominance in an uncertain political environment, but he couldn't. The PLO was failing. Knowing that the leadership of the territories was incapable of reaching an agreement with Israel and that Hamas was unwilling, Arafat acted on their behalf. He was convinced that if he didn't, the PLO would die. With it would go the dream of a Palestinian state. He had no choice but to negotiate with Israel.

Arafat, like Rabin, was being pushed to extremes by his own diaspora community. When the PLO chairman journeyed to Washington, Palestinian leaders in Syria and Lebanon condemned the agreement and vowed to overturn it. Just as a small group of conservatives in pro-Israel organizations in America condemned Rabin for being naive, so Arafat's opposition denounced him for selling out to "the Zionists." There was a curious dynamic at work in both cases, a kind of "diaspora mentality" that placed Jews and Palestinians not living in the lands of the former Mandate in an uncomfortable association.

Jews and Palestinians who oppose the agreement indignantly resent the notion that they have anything in common with each other. But a look at the position they share shows otherwise. The salient feature of the "diaspora mentality" is that it rejects compromise in favor of continued confrontation, and advocates the realization of maximalist dreams: a fight to the death for Eretz Yisra'el; all of Palestine or nothing for the Palestinians. The only requirement is that someone else do the fighting.

Neither Rabin nor Arafat was so removed from the harsh realities of war that he could afford to choose this extreme position. Rabin had seen men die in battle and he was thoroughly sick of it, while Arafat had had more than twenty years of "nothing at all." Both realities led to Oslo, and then to Washington.

Will it work? Will the one-hundred-year war for the land of Palestine end? Will Israelis and Palestinians learn to live together? There is no certain answer to the question, and no way to predict the future. But there is a hint, and a clue on how the two sides might cast their lot together.

Not so long ago the Soviet empire crumbled and washed away. The collapse set loose the stored creative energies of millions of people in the former lands of the USSR and in Eastern Europe. One of them, the writer Milan Kundera, reflected on a generation of men and women who had lost their past. The simple act of remembering the past, investigating and researching it, and writing its true history, he suggested, is a political act of liberation. "The struggle of man against power," he wrote, "is the struggle of memory against forgetting."

The Palestinians and Israelis have a different problem. If they are to get along in the future, they have to go on without looking back. Ideas must triumph over beliefs. The struggle of man against hatred is the struggle for the future against remembering. The Eastern Europeans have to retrieve the past, but the Palestinians and the Israelis have to forget it.

A NOTE ON SOURCES

Material for *A Fire in Zion* was taken primarily from interviews conducted with the key officials involved in the Israeli-Palestinian bilateral negotiations in Washington, D.C., supplemented by interviews with officials in the Israeli government in Jerusalem, the PLO leadership in Tunis, and officials of the United States government involved in monitoring the negotiations. Interviews of people living in the Gaza Strip, West Bank, and Israel were conducted by the author during trips to the region over a period of five years.

Materials on background to each of the rounds of negotiations was disseminated by each of the delegations and are used herein to provide necessary facts on positions, policies, and personalities engaged in the Washington talks. Transcripts of press conferences were used to detail the background of the negotiating positions of the delegations.

Key works on both Israeli and PLO leaders and on the Middle East in general provide the necessary background to the Washington breakthrough: Janet Wallach and John Wallach, *Arafat: In the Eyes of the Beholder* (New York: Lyle Stuart, 1990); Janet Wallach and John Wallach, *The New Palestinians: The*

Emerging Generation of Leaders (Rocklin, Calif.: Prima, 1992), Matti Golan, *Shimon Peres: A Biography* (London: Weidenfeld and Nicolson, 1982); Robert Slater, *Rabin of Israel* (New York: St. Martins Press, 1993); Tom Segev, *The Seventh Million: The Israelis and the Holocaust* (New York: Hill and Wang, 1993); William B. Quandt, *Peace Process* (Washington, D.C.: Brookings Institution, 1993); Stanley Fischer et al., eds., *The Economics of Middle East Peace* (Boston: MIT Press, 1993); Ze'ev Schiff and Ehud Ya'ari, *Intifada, The Palestinian Uprising—Israel's Third Front* (New York: Simon and Schuster, 1989); Eric Silver, *Begin, The Haunted Prophet* (New York: Random House, 1984); Edward W. Said, *The Question of Palestine* (New York: Times Books, 1979); Thomas Freidman, *From Beirut to Jerusalem* (New York: Farrar, Straus, Giroux, 1989) are indispensable guides to this period and the processes that led to the PLO-Israeli negotiations.

PROLOGUE

Remarks by Salah Ta'mari are from interviews with the author conducted over a period of one year in Washington, D.C. The remarks by Itamar Rabinovich are from a presentation that he gave before a group who attended a talk at the Institute for Near East Policy, Washington, D.C., on May 25, 1993. For a concise history of early Zionism, see Tom Segev, *The Seventh Million: The Israelis and the Holocaust* (New York: Hill and Wang, 1993); Shlomo Avineri, *The Making of Modern Zionism: The Intellectual Origin of the Jewish State* (London: 1981); and Walter Laqueur, *A History of Zionism* (London: 1972).

CHAPTER ONE:
JEBALYA

The interview with Haidar Abdul Shafi was conducted by the author at the end of May 1988. Material on Abdul Shafi's life was obtained from his aides and assistants and from members of the Palestinian delegation to the Washington talks in 1992. There is no standard reference work on Dr. Abdul Shafi in existence. Dr. Abdul Shafi was interviewed a second time by the author at his home in January 1993, and then again for short sessions during the third round of talks held in Washington. (The scene in the cab is from the ride into Jebalya by the author with other researchers at the height of the intifada, in May 1988.)

For information on the intifada, see Ze'ev Schiff and Ehud Ya'ari, *Intifada* (New York: Simon and Schuster, 1989) and Gloria Emerson, *Gaza* (New York: Atlantic Monthly Press, 1991). Other information is derived from participants on the ground or from Israeli soldiers or Palestinians who remembered the events of late 1987 and recounted them during subsequent trips to the West Bank and Gaza. Schiff and Ya'ari's account is still considered the standard work on this movement and on Israel's belated reaction to it.

Information on Rabin's views on the intifada are from interviews with Israeli officials and from Robert Slater, *Rabin of Israel* (New York: St. Martins Press, 1993). Less valuable is Yitzhak Rabin, *The Rabin Memoirs* (Boston: Little, Brown, 1979), in which Rabin refuses to make a unilateral statement about the status of the occupied territories.

CHAPTER TWO:
LA MARSA

Information on the internal debate over the PLO's alliance with Saddam Hussein is from a series of discussions with PLO officials Yassir Abed-Rabbo, Bassam Abu Sharif, Khalid al-Hassan, Abu Iyad, and their assistants, secretaries, and deputies. Interviews were also conducted with their close aides, senior associates, and, in some cases, members of their families. Other Palestinian officials serving the PLO outside of Tunis were consulted on their information on Arafat's decision to side with Saddam Hussein.

Palestinians living in the United States provided details and anecdotes about Abu Iyad's life. Abu Iyad was interviewed in his home in Tunis on September 7, 1990, by the author and journalist Tom Martin. Information on Abu Iyad's disagreement with Arafat's opening to Saddam Hussein was provided by PLO officials in Tunis and in Washington, D.C. See also Youssef M. Ibrahim, "Arafat's Support of Iraq Creates Rift in PLO," *New York Times,* September 14, 1990; Murray J. Gart, "The Twilight of Yasser Arafat," *Washington Post,* August 9, 1992; David Ignatius, "History of U.S.-PLO Terror Talks," *Washington Post,* December 4, 1988.

Background information on the murder of Abu Iyad was provided by Palestinian officials during telephone interviews conducted with the author on Friday, January 18, 1991. Some of these officials requested anonymity. See also Abu Iyad with Eric Rouleau, *My Home, My Land* (New York: Times Books, 1981); Salah Khalaf (Abu Iyad), "Lowering the Sword," *For-*

eign Policy, Spring 1990; T.D. Allman, "Death in Tunis," *Vanity Fair,* April 1991. Allman's article is the most definitive account of the murder. Additional information is contained in Jim Hoagland, "The Assassin of Arab Hopes," *Washington Post,* January 17, 1991; Youssef M. Ibrahim, "Suspicion in Palestinian Slayings Now Focuses on Abu Nidal Group," *New York Times,* January 16, 1990.

Yasser Arafat's actions on the two days leading up to the Gulf War are from a detailed discussion with Bassam Abu Sharif and with American writer Thomas Martin. Martin shared his recollections with me during several hours of interviews in Washington, D.C., in the summer of 1991.

For further background material on the state of the PLO prior to the outbreak of the Gulf War, see Harry Anderson and John Barry, "A Slow Slide Toward War," *Newsweek,* July 2, 1990; Nora Boustany, "For Arab World, A Sea Change," *Washington Post,* August 19, 1990; Jack Anderson and Dale Van Atta, "Why Arafat Backed Saddam," *Washington Post,* August 26, 1990.

For postwar views of Arafat and the PLO, see Youssef M. Ibrahim, "Arafat, the Survivor, Now Finds Support Vanishing," *New York Times,* February 13, 1991; Caryle Murphy, "Palestinians Look Beyond Wily Bookkeeper Arafat," *Washington Post,* June 5, 1992; Murray J. Gart, "The Twilight of Yasser Arafat," *Washington Post,* August 9, 1992.

Other background material, including biographical information on PLO leaders and the internal workings of the organization are from Helena Cobban, *The Palestinian Liberation Organization* (Cambridge, U.K.: Cambridge University Press, 1984); Sami Mussalam, *The PLO* (Brattleboro, Vt.: Amana Books, 1988); Janet Wallach and John Wallach, *Arafat, in the Eyes of the Beholder* (New York: Lyle Stuart, 1990); Andrew Gowers and Tony Walker, *Behind the Myth: Yasser Arafat and the Palestinian Revolution* (New York: Olive Branch Press, 1991); Ze'ev Schiff and Ehud Ya'ari, *Israel's Lebanon War* (New York: Simon and Schuster, 1984).

CHAPTER THREE:
WASHINGTON

Information on Baker's views on Arafat was derived primarily from officials in Israel, not in Washington. A number of reporters who escorted Baker on his trips and then sat with him during background briefings provided their views on him for this portrait. For a detailed analysis of the period leading up to the peace process, see William B. Quandt, *Peace Process* (Washington, D.C.: Brookings Institution, 1993). I have relied heavily here on eyewitness testimony given by the participants and aides of Palestinian leaders in the West Bank, and by an Israeli official who requests anonymity.

The perspective of the Arabs and Palestinians is given for the period in a series of articles written from the region in *Middle East International* magazine. See especially Donald Neff, "The Window That Isn't There," *Middle East International,* May 3, 1991; Donald Neff, "Settlements and Guarantees: The U.S. Threatens Linkage," *Middle East International,* September 27, 1991; Peretz Kidron, "Shrouds over the Baker Visit," *Middle East International,* March 22, 1991; John M. Goshko, "Baker Tour: A Two-Edged Mission," *Washington Post,* July 25, 1992.

Information on James A. Baker III is contained in "Playing for the Edge," *Time,* February 13, 1989; Sidney Blumenthal, "I, Baker," *The New Republic,* November 2, 1992; and Ina Ginsburg, "Baker on Baker," *Town and Country,* October 1992.

For background information on the Palestinians in the West Bank, John Wallach and Janet Wallach, *The New Palestinians,* (Rocklin, Calif.: Prima Publishing, 1992) is invaluable. Information on Faisal Husseini is the result of two in-depth interviews with him. For further information, see also Mark Perry, "A Castle with Forty Doors: An Interview with Faisal Husseini," *Middle East Insight,* May–June 1993, and "Faisal Husseini's Legacy," *Middle East Insight,* May–June 1993.

CHAPTER FOUR:
MADRID

Material for this chapter was primarily derived from press releases, transcripts, and videotapes of the Madrid Conference; from discussions with Israeli, Palestinian, and Syrian officials after the event; and from interviews with members of each of the delegations. Information on Secretary Baker's strategy for the conference was set out by one of his assistants who was with the secretary in Madrid. The incident involving David Kimche was related to the author by two Palestinians who viewed the event.

A complete and detailed understanding on the conference and the strategies of its differing sides is not possible, but one of the better treatments is in *Peacewatch Anthology* published by the Washington Institute for Near East Policy in 1993. The anthology includes a number of papers from officials who had played, were playing, or would later play leading roles in the peace process; and biographies of members of the Palestinian and Israeli delegations.

Quotes are from the transcripts of addresses given by James A. Baker III, Syrian Foreign Minister Farouk Sharaa, Shamir aide Yossi Ben-Aharon, and Haidar Abdul Shafi. The "terms of reference" and the stipulations contained in the Camp David Accords come from documents published at the time, and reprinted in the *Peacewatch Anthology;* and from Yehuda Lukacs, ed., *The Israeli-Palestinian Conflict* (Cambridge, U.K.: Cambridge University Press, 1992). Interviews for this chapter included discussions with Palestinian delegates Saeb Erakat, Elias Freij,

Ghassan al-Khattib, Sameh Kanaan, Mamdouh al-Aker, Haidar Abdul Shafi, Nabil Kassis, and Zajarua al-Agha. See also Khaled Abu Toameh, "Riding the Tiger," *Jerusalem Report,* November 28, 1991.

A review of the first rounds of the bilateral talks is from material collected by researcher Daniel Shapiro, and is contained in Daniel A. Shapiro, "A Chronology of the Middle East Peace Talks," *Middle East Insight,* July–August 1993. See also Jackson Diehl, "Palestinians Find Decision-making Unwieldy in Talks," *Washington Post,* September 21, 1992.

CHAPTER FIVE:
TEL AVIV

Information on the election campaign was obtained, in part, through newspaper and magazine reports issued at the time. See Jackson Diehl, "Likud's Emerging New Look," *Washington Post,* June 2, 1992; Clyde Haberman, "Israel Voter Surveys Show Lead for Labor," *New York Times,* June 23, 1992; David Hoffman, "Israel Names New Negotiator with Syria," *Washington Post,* August 4, 1992; Don Oberdorfer, "Improved U.S.-Israel Ties Seen," *Washington Post,* June 25, 1992; David Hoffman, "Shamir Plan Was to Stall Autonomy," *Washington Post,* June 27, 1992. For reports on the details of the Shamir-Rabin campaign, the author relied on press reports during the months of April, May, and June that appeared in *The Jerusalem Post.* Also see Yossi Klein Halevi, "No Holds Barred," *Jerusalem Report,* June 18, 1992. For information on diplomacy between the rounds and the attempt to break the deadlocks in the talks that occurred, see John M. Goshko, "Baker Tour: A Two-Edged Mission," *Washington Post,* July 26, 1992; Thomas L. Friedman, "Arab-Israeli Talks: Slow, but Not Lost," *New York Times,* September 27, 1992; John M. Goshko, "Israel and Syria Come Up Short on Mideast Talks Breakthrough," *Washington Post,* September 24, 1992; Jackson Diehl, "Mideast Negotiators Wrap Up 6th Round," *Washington Post,* September 25, 1992; John M. Goshko, "U.S. to Press Israeli, Arab Negotiators in Peace Talks," *Washington Post,* October 21, 1992.

For biographical information on the candidates, I relied on two brilliant articles published in *The New York Review of Books* in

May of 1992 by Avishai Margalit. Margalit's analysis of Zionism also provides helpful background information on the subject. See also Tom Segev, *The Seventh Million* (New York: Hill and Wang, 1993). Arguments on the structure and meaning of the Zionist dream and its contradictions can be found in Arthur Hertzberg, *Jewish Polemics* (New York: Columbia University Press, 1992).

For information on AIPAC, see Edward Tivnan, *Jewish Political Power and American Foreign Policy* (New York: Simon and Schuster, 1987); David Hoffman, "Rabin Criticizes Congressional Lobby for Israel," *Washington Post*, August 15, 1993; Robert I. Friedman, "The Wobbly Israel Lobby," *Washington Post*, November 1, 1992. Hoffman cites five AIPAC officials as present during the crucial standoff with Rabin: AIPAC executive director Thomas Dine, AIPAC president David Steiner, and three of its former presidents: Ed Levy, Abe Pollin, and Mayer Mitchell. For a more complete treatment of the crisis in the conservative wing of the American Jewish community see Jonathan Broder's excellent summary in "The Politics of Transformation in the American Jewish Community," *Middle East Insight,* March–April 1993. Matti Golan's arguments appear in *With Friends Like You* (New York: Free Press, 1992).

I have changed the woman's name at the end of this chapter to guard her privacy. The author met the woman "Alya" aboard an Air France flight from Paris to Ben-Gurion Airport in early 1993.

CHAPTER SIX:
JERUSALEM

Information for this chapter was obtained primarily through personal interviews by the author on the scene in the West Bank, Gaza, Tel Aviv, and Jerusalem. The author interviewed Knesset member Benny Begin for an extended period. The conversation in the beginning of the chapter is a verbatim exchange between the author and a member of Mr. Begin's staff. The author spent an extensive amount of time interviewing both Israelis and Palestinians during the crucial period of the deportations. Included among these interviews were Faisal Husseini, Bassam Abu-Sharif, Salah Ta'mari, Hana Ashrawi, Elyakim Rubinstein, Haidar Abdul Shafi, Sari Nusseibeh, Yossi Gal, and selected Israeli army officers.

See also John M. Goshko, "Israel Agrees to Let Deportees Return," *Washington Post,* February 2, 1993; John M. Goshko, "U.S. Hopes Israeli Concessions Will End U.N. Sanctions Drive," *Washington Post,* February 3, 1993; "10 Deported Palestinians Can Return, Israel Says" (Reuters), December 29, 1992; "Lebanon Denies Appeals to Let in Palestinian Deportees" (Reuters), December 27, 1992; David Hoffman, "New Errors Cited in Palestinians' Expulsion," *Washington Post,* December 30, 1992; David Hoffman, "Israelis Shift Tactics Against Palestinians," *Washington Post,* February 16, 1993.

Information on Clinton's selection of his top national security advisers and their influence on the peace process comes from Jonathan Broder, "Balancing Act at the NSC," *Jerusalem Report,* February 11, 1993. Broder's excellent report on Martin Indyk says, in part; "This is the first time that a figure so closely identified with pro-Israel advocacy groups has been given such a senior Middle East policy position." Other articles of interest include "The Flint Beneath the Suit," *The Economist,* February 13, 1993 (on Warren Christopher); Russell Watson et al., "Call Your Peace Broker," *Newsweek,* March 1, 1993; Robert Scheer, "Clinton's Globe Trotter," *Los Angeles Times Magazine,* February 21, 1993; "Goodwill and Hopes . . ." *Mideast Mirror,* September 25, 1992 (on Edward Djerejian); "The U.S. and the Middle East in a Changing World," an address by Edward P. Djerejian, (U.S. Department of State release), June 2, 1992. On reaction to Clinton's appointments, see "All the President's (New) Men," *Mideast Mirror,* November 12, 1993; "Rabin Said Working for Mid-March Meeting with Clinton," *Mideast Mirror,* November 5, 1992. This article includes an analysis of the American Jewish votes and extensively quotes from Israeli newspapers. Also see "Bush-Clinton Transition Seen Threatening the Peace Process," *Mideast Mirror,* November 12, 1992.

CHAPTER SEVEN:
BETHLEHEM

Information for this chapter was obtained by the author during trips to Israel, the West Bank, and the Gaza Strip. The conversation on the road to Bethlehem took place between Jawdat Maana, a Palestinian journalist, and an unnamed Palestinian sharecab driver. Information on Hamas was gained from a number of individuals on the West Bank and Gaza. The author conducted an extensive interview with the leading authority on fundamentalism in Palestinian society, Dr. Ali Jirbawi. Dr. Jirbawi was interviewed in his home in Ramallah. The author also interviewed Ibrahim Yazoorie in his store in Gaza during a trip to the Gaza Strip at the time of these events. The charter of Hamas is readily available, in English, in the occupied territories.

See also Milton Viorst, "Learning to Live with the PLO," *Washington Post,* April 11, 1992; David Hoffman, "Six Palestinians Slain by Troops During Riots," *Washington Post,* December 20, 1992; David Hoffman, "Rival Palestinian Factions Step Up Struggle in Gaza," *Washington Post,* July 10, 1992.

Interviews with Hosein Shaheen and Jad Isaac were conducted by the author.

For information on PLO-Hamas rivalry, see "PLO-Hamas Rivalry May Be Heading for Choppier Waters," *Mideast Mirror,* November 17, 1993. For information on Hamas and the events that followed the deportations, see "Fatal Stabbing . . ." *Mideast Mirror,* February 15, 1993.

CHAPTER EIGHT:
TUNIS

Information from this chapter was obtained largely from Israeli officials who witnessed the events and understood the thinking of Prime Minister Rabin. Information on Clinton's views can be found in Rowland Evans and Robert Novak, "Clinton's Israel Stretch," *Washington Post,* August 15, 1992; Rowland Evans and Robert Novak, "Staying the Mideast Course," *Washington Post,* December 2, 1992; James Zogby, "Clinton's Tilt on the Mideast," *Washington Post,* July 2, 1992.

The author relied on firsthand accounts for information on the sealing of the territories. See also Jon Immanuel, Sasha Sadan, and Asher Wallfish, "3,000 Workers Allowed from Territories," *Jerusalem Post,* April 17, 1993; Bill Hutman, "Security Tightened as Terrorists Claim Three More Victims," *Jerusalem Post,* March 20, 1993; "Security Forces Broaden Measures Against Terror," *Jerusalem Post,* April 10, 1993; "Rabin Says Closure of Areas Has Achieved Objectives," *Jerusalem Post,* April 24, 1993; David Makovsky, "Now Is the Moment for Peace, Says Premier," *Jerusalem Post,* March 27, 1993; "Rabin Returns Early from U.S. to Angry Protests over Security," *Jerusalem Post,* March 27, 1993.

The information on the Harvard Group, its reports, and plans was obtained through direct interviews with the participants themselves, including Leonard Hausman, Stanley Fischer, Anna Karasik, Ghassan al-Khattib, a high-level official at the IMF who was privy to their deliberations, and a Palestinian economist. The meetings and information were confirmed independently by Israeli officials in the foreign ministry. Information about the ties among the delegations, the Oslo back channel, and the World Bank was obtained in an interview with Stanley Fischer and with an official of the Israeli foreign ministry. See also "Developing the Occupied Territories: An Investment in Peace," *The World Bank*, Vol. 1 (September 1993), Washington, D.C.; Mary Curtius, "Mideast Focus May Shift to Economy in Territories," *Boston Globe*, September 9, 1993; Leonard Hausman, Anna D. Karasik, et al., "Securing Peace in the Middle East: Project on Economic Transition," Cambridge, Mass.: Harvard University, June 1993.

Information on the substance of the Oslo channel discussions was derived from research conducted by the author, working in association with researcher Daniel Shapiro. An initial article on this topic appeared as "Navigating the Oslo Channel," Mark Perry and Daniel Shapiro, *Middle East Insight*, September–October 1993. A primary account was received on a background, for-the-record briefing by an Israeli official who took part in the initial and all subsequent meetings in Oslo. Interviews on the Palestinian part of the Oslo breakthrough were conducted with PLO officials in Tunis, who had direct knowledge of the events and Abu Alaa's part in them.

CHAPTER NINE:
OSLO

Arab and Israeli papers provided the accounts of the events leading up to the Washington signing. I have used summaries and verbatim reprints of those articles as they appeared in *Mideast Mirror*. Included among those articles are "How We Found the Reliable Channel to the PLO in Tunis," *Mideast Mirror*, September 16, 1993; "Economic Aspects of the Gaza-Jericho Deal as Envisaged by the Bank of Israel," *Mideast Mirror*, September 16, 1993; "PLO Official Allowed to Visit and Rabin Confirms He Authorized Sarid's Meeting with Shaath," *Mideast Mirror*, August 11, 1993; "Debate on Agreements with PLO Gathers Steam, Turning Emotional," *Mideast Mirror*, September 6, 1993; "Abu Mazen: 'The Pact I Signed with Israel,'" *Mideast Mirror*, September 17, 1993; "Peres's Follow-up Talks on Mutual Recognition Focus on Timing and Procedures to Amend PLO Charter," *Mideast Mirror*, September 3, 1993; "Kurtzer: Four Key Challenges to the Declaration of Principles," *Mideast Mirror*, November 10, 1993; "Norway Says It Hosted Secret Israel-PLO Talks," *Mideast Mirror*, August 31, 1993.

Johan Jorgen Holst's summary of the back channel was obtained in a transcript of an address he gave at Columbia University, "Reflections on the Makings of a Tenuous Peace." The article was reprinted as "Reflections on the Makings of a Tenuous Peace," Johan Jorgen Holst, *Middle East Insight*, September–October, 1993.

Information on divisions inside the PLO and between the

PLO and the delegation to the Washington talks was carried almost exclusively in Arab and Israeli papers. For one of the best and most detailed examples, see the August 10 edition of the Israeli newspaper *Yediot Aharanot.* Primary information on the fight inside the PLO was derived from sources inside the organization in Tunis, from Palestinian officials in the diaspora, and from a source inside the advisory team to the Palestinian delegation. An article on this appeared as Mark Perry, "Arafat-Hassan Conflict Bares Internal Divisions," *Middle East Insight,* May–June, 1993. See also Pinhas Inbari, "Fatah Military Wing Revolt . . ." *Al Hamishmar* (in Hebrew), Tel Aviv, June 25, 1993; Julian Ozanne, "Palestinians Face Leadership Split," *Financial Times,* August 9, 1993.

Articles on the breakthrough itself carried varying accounts. The most important were Kevin Fedarko, "Swimming the Oslo Channel," *Time,* September 13, 1993; David Hoffman, "Israel Floats New Option on Mideast," *Washington Post,* August 29, 1993; David Hoffman, "Israel's Evolution: From Besieged State to Yearning for Normalcy," *Washington Post,* September 11, 1993; Clyde Haberman, "How the Oslo Connection Led to the Mideast Pact," *New York Times,* September 5, 1993; Laura Blumenfeld, "The Absent-Minded Miracle Worker," *Washington Post,* September 22, 1993. The most valuable article on the back channel is William Drozdiak, "Arafat Kept Israeli Talks Secret from Most Top PLO Aides," *Washington Post,* September 6, 1993.

CHAPTER TEN:
JERICHO

Accounts of Israeli-PLO discussions on mutual recognition are taken from firsthand sources who were involved in the negotiations themselves. See also "Mideast's 'Berlin Wall' Falls," *Mideast Mirror,* September 10, 1993; "U.S. Resumes Dialogue with PLO," *Mideast Mirror,* September 10, 1993; "90% of U.S. Jews Call Israel-PLO Deal 'Positive' and 57% Favor Palestinian State," *Mideast Mirror,* September 28, 1993; "Simple Problems of Formulation Holding Up Mutual Recognition," *Mideast Mirror,* September 2, 1993; "Rabin's Self-Entrapment," Ze'ev Binyamin Begin, from *Jerusalem Post,* in *Mideast Mirror,* September 9, 1993; "Israel to Consider Palestinian Self-Rule," David Hoffman, *Washington Post,* August 30, 1993; "The 'Gaza-Jericho First' Deal," *Mideast Mirror,* September 1, 1993; "Palestinian Officials Say Pact with Israel Is Near," Roger Cohen, *The New York Times,* September 3, 1993; "Arafat Playing Political Game with Signing," William Drozdiak, *Washington Post,* September 12, 1993; "PLO Accepts Israel, Disavows Force," Clyde Haberman, *New York Times,* September 14, 1993; "Israel and PLO Sign Peace Pact," Ann Devroy and John M. Goshko, *Washington Post,* September 14, 1993.

The remarks of the signing ceremony can be found in *Mideast Mirror,* September 14, 1993. For further information on the last days of negotiations, see "What Next?" Leslie Susser, *Jerusalem Report,* October 7, 1993; "The Start of a Long Journey," Hanan Sher, *Jerusalem Report,* October 21, 1993; "Peace at Last?" *Newsweek,* September 13, 1993.

Information on postsigning events can be obtained from "History in the Making," *Jerusalem Report,* September 23, 1993; "Peace Parties Break Out," Aviva Kempner, *Washington Jewish Week,* September 16, 1993; "Israel Was Worried About Arafat," Robert Epstein, *Washington Jewish Week,* September 16, 1993; "Rabin, 'This Was Not So Easy,' " Sam Skolnik, *Washington Jewish Week,* September 16, 1993.

EPILOGUE

The title quote is from "The Lamentations of Jeremiah," *The New Oxford Annotated Bible* (New York: Oxford University Press, 1977), p. 997.

INDEX